MARK. PLAN. TEACH. 2.0

Save time. Reduce workload. Impact learning.

Ross Morrison McGill

BLOOMSBURY EDUCATION

LONDON   OXFORD   NEW YORK   NEW DELHI   SYDNEY

Praise for *MARK. PLAN. TEACH.*

'Teachers go beyond the call of duty for our children. However, this book enables them to do even more in less time, which can support teachers in making a greater impact in the classroom. This is a must-read for all those who really want to tackle teacher workload to adopt classroom strategies that are easy to use, as well as grounded in research.'
Suella Fernandes, MP for Fareham, Attorney General and Former Chair of Governors, Michaela Community School

'Marking can have a massive impact on teacher workload. Worryingly, it often has very little impact on students' learning. Ross makes an important contribution by reminding us that marking is merely a type of feedback – and that there are other forms of feedback, verbal and in-lesson, for example. He emphasises that it is the quality, not the quantity, of marking and feedback that is important. Applied with care, these ideas can help build schools that work for pupils and for staff.'
Russell Hobby, CEO, Teach First

'There is a reason why Ross is the most followed British teacher on Twitter. He isn't didactic or patronising. He doesn't have a political agenda. He just wants to help educational professionals to be the very best they can be, using a combination of his personal experience and the wealth of expert voices at his disposal.'
Natasha Devon MBE, Writer, Campaigner and Educator on Mental Health

'*Mark. Plan. Teach.* is not only a very practical book for teachers but also a must-read for school leaders and teacher trainers. Its suggestions are grounded in educational practice and supported by education theories. The diagrams and straight-forward language make it so much easier to understand, demonstrate in teacher training or use as posters. I wish every school leader would read this book and make strategies accordingly to raise teaching quality while reducing teachers' workload.'
Dr Min Du, Teacher, Researcher and International Education Consultant

'What strikes me about this book is how practical and applicable it is […] Not only is it full of guidance teachers can apply no matter when and what they teach but the ideas are grounded in research and – best of all – even framed with pros and cons to help teachers decide when to use them and why.'
Doug Lemov, Managing Director at Uncommon Schools and author of *Teach Like a Champion* and *Reading Reconsidered*

'Ross has done it again! *Mark. Plan. Teach.* is packed full of practical, innovative and easy-to-follow examples of how teachers can be more effective in the classroom, without increasing their workload. I will certainly be recommending it as essential reading for my staff!'
Ben Solly, Principal, Uppingham Community College, Rutland

'Ross has been at the forefront of supporting teachers new to the profession. With this latest offering, he continues to clarify the essentials of excellence in the profession. It's a great mix of theory, current debate and practical advice for teachers new or seasoned.'
Bennie Kara, Deputy Headteacher

'There's a lot of pressure put on teachers to be exceptional educationalists but without all the tools. Ross Morrison McGill addresses a wide range of practical approaches such as celebrating mistakes and working smarter not harder, providing clarity, insight and plans into the areas we don't talk about. It's a wonderful book which non-educators will find equally useful.'
Zubeda Limbada, Director of ConnectFutures

'Ross McGill's *Mark. Plan. Teach.* goes straight to a teacher's conundrum, how to be a better teacher and keep workload at sustainable levels. As ever, it is informed by his ongoing teaching work and offers practical solutions for teachers. Effective feedback and good planning are at the core of great teaching, and ideas and tips in this book should help those struggling under the burdens of getting this done.'
Lord Jim Knight, Chief Education Adviser, Tes

'Nobody does it better: in terms of providing practical, accessible, do-able, evidence-informed tips to improve teaching and learning, Teacher Toolkit is simply the best.'
Lee Elliot Major OBE, Professor of Social Mobility

'*Mark. Plan. Teach.* is a book packed with evidence-informed practical ideas for the classroom that reduce rather than increase teacher workload. The thought-provoking contributions from Professor Tim O'Brien add challenging and exploratory psychological insights as well as theoretical underpinning for many of Ross McGill's ideas.'
Dr Dennis Guiney, Child and Adolescent Psychologist

'We have to be critical of our own impact to reflect on what works for the young people in our care and what steps we can take as professionals in our actions and values to make what we do matter and be meaningful, manageable and motivating. A good reminder of the importance of evaluation and moderation of our marking and its impact on our pupils.'
Rehana Shanks, Principal, English Schools Foundation

'*Mark. Plan. Teach.* is an honestly written and research-informed book. It offers numerous gems in an easily digestible and conversational tone. Ross makes an excellent case for feedback being the cornerstone for both pupil and teacher progress, while fully understanding the problems of teacher workload. This book will be invaluable to teachers in any stage of their career.'
Arushi Prabhakar, Teacher of Chemistry and M.P.Ed Candidate, Western University, Canada

BLOOMSBURY EDUCATION
Bloomsbury Publishing Plc
50 Bedford Square, London, WC1B 3DP, UK

BLOOMSBURY, BLOOMSBURY EDUCATION and the Diana logo are trademarks of Bloomsbury Publishing Plc

First published in Great Britain, 2017 by Bloomsbury Education

This edition published in Great Britain, 2021 by Bloomsbury Education

ISBN: PB: 978-1-4729-7862-2; ePDF: 978-1-4729-7853-0; ePub: 978-1-4729-7854-7

2 4 6 8 10 9 7 5 3 1 (paperback)

Text design by Marcus Duck Design

Printed and bound in the UK by CPI Group (UK) Ltd, Croydon, CR0 4YY

About the author

ROSS MORRISON McGILL works with pupils, teachers and school leaders across the world, supporting teaching and learning, workload and mental health. A former deputy headteacher, he has been teaching across three decades, working in some of the most challenging secondary schools in London. In 2015, he was nominated as one of the '500 Most Influential People in Britain' by *The Sunday Times* as a result of being most influential in the field of education. He remains the only classroom teacher to feature to this day.

Throughout his school leadership, he has been responsible for improving quality of teaching and learning and has an international profile as a leading contributor and organiser of professional development, research, workload and teacher wellbeing. As the most followed educator on social media in the UK, he offers unique social media insights and support for schools and organisations and is frequently asked to speak at national conferences with teachers all over the world.

Mark. Plan. Teach. 2.0 is his fifth book with Bloomsbury and when not working with teachers in schools, he is completing his doctoral research at the University of Cambridge. One of his foci is evaluating whether school inspection grading is a reliable indicator of quality and outcomes.

When I wrote **Mark. Plan. Teach. 1.0**, I dedicated the book to all teachers who have had their careers blighted by school inspections. I still hold this view today. We still seek a more reliable and intelligent inspection process that drives school improvement. For the last three years, I have been researching any sources of evidence that suggest school inspections improve teacher quality.
It is very rare to find...

I hope this book keeps more teachers in the profession for longer and, to those school leaders and inspectors reading, that we all work harder to create conditions where those people who choose to work in very challenging circumstances are not penalised. The result of this will be that we have all teachers working in whatever scenario they wish and contributing to the local community, which improves society for everyone.

Contents

. . . .

Section 1: Mark   **1**

Section 2: Plan 60

Section 3: Teach 118

And finally 174
Bibliography 180
Index 185

Acknowledgements

Firstly, to all teachers who have read the original copy of *Mark. Plan. Teach.* in schools all across the world, as well as the 30,000 teachers I have worked with physically, bringing the book content to life in schools, colleges and universities.

The original concept grew from a school community working in an incredibly challenging context, with increasing external pressures, in which teachers sought clarity and consistency across the corridors and classrooms. The beginning of the process involved discussions, meetings, training sessions with colleagues, reading countless books, journals and research papers, writing and tweaking content, and publishing excerpts on my website to gauge feedback.

Over the last three years, having lived the theory and practice of *Mark. Plan. Teach.* in a wide variety of educational settings, I have been reassured that what teachers truly need is a forum to take risks and discuss complex teaching ideas on a regular basis. Those school and college leaders who create these conditions for teachers to talk about teaching and learning on a regular basis are leading happier institutions, and my work to date confirms the original principles of *Mark. Plan. Teach.* Strip away much of the external accountability and increasing workload pressures on teachers, and we remove all of the distractions and help teachers focus on their core purpose: to assess, to create coherent curriculum sequences, and to impart this in the classroom using highly effective and research-informed teaching strategies.

I want to work in a school setting where teachers can bring their unmarked books to discuss how best to assess, rather than presenting 'shiny stamped and ticked' books and teachers being asked to 'mark this way'. I want to teach in a school where we can watch one of our teachers teach a lesson through video observation, teaching our challenging students in our school, and where we can learn from one another through 'car crash' moments, rather than polished lesson plans and classroom delivery. This is what teachers want too. This is what they need: the reality of the classroom shared in a climate of trust. Teachers do not need teaching and learning policies. They need time to practise, and this is where school leaders should focus their efforts.

Finally, thank you to Hannah Marston, who has seen *Mark. Plan. Teach.* evolve from difficult circumstances to a place where the book has reformed and supported many schools and college cultures around the world. Thank you to Professor Tim O'Brien for his psychological insights, to Polly Nur for her incredible graphics and to Marcus Duck for the text design. Finally, to my beautiful family for keeping me grounded, fed and watered!

Foreword

We've all been there. Whether our students are seven, 17, or 37, there's something about the end of the weekend that most of us would much prefer to avoid. It's the marking. The end of a hard week's teaching is celebrated on a Friday night, perhaps. For many teachers, Saturday's a time for getting jobs done, doing the week's shopping, perhaps going to a football match or other event, a bit of family time, and then a relaxing night at the end of it all. Sunday's a slower start to the day, possibly followed by a long walk with the kids, the dog, or each other, if you have someone. Then, in the midst of all this Hobbit-like happiness, as evening awaits, there it is, on the table, in the corner – that gathering shadow of Mordor that is the big pile of books or papers that have to be marked by Monday morning.

Suddenly, it's time to procrastinate. Look for your pens. Organise the piles. Make a cup of coffee. Check your emails. Read your horoscope. Make another cup of coffee. Start to behave like all the kids in your class when they want to avoid their work. Do anything except confront that dreaded mountain of marking.

Marking is often the last thing teachers think about. The actual teaching is what teachers live for – being in the moment, having the class spellbound, dealing with the unexpected, seeing the light bulbs turn on. And the planning's not bad either – imagining what a great lesson might look like, designing adjustments for kids with different backgrounds and levels of understanding, perhaps brainstorming innovative ideas and strategies with a few colleagues. But the marking! It's still there. It has to be done. You can change the colours of your pens. You can develop awesome rubrics. You can create group assignments as well as individual ones. You can do it digitally instead of physically. But in the end, there's no escaping it. Like death and taxes, marking never goes away.

So how refreshing it is to see a great book on teaching and learning that opens with marking rather than tacking it on at the end. How could anyone possibly write a bestselling book about marking? Well if anyone could, and has, it's Ross Morrison McGill. Ross is a highly accomplished teacher and leader. He's the world's most gigantic squirrel of practical strategies and resources for teachers. He's taught in some of the most challenging circumstances, and not only survived, but thrived.

Ross is a self-confessed maverick. He is proud to be a thorn-in-the-side of England's much criticised education inspection service – the overburdening bureaucracy he calls the *Grim Reaper*. He's an outspoken champion for and protector of teachers against insensitive governments and passing fads. He is a survivor of sexual abuse and of workplace bullying. Yet he doesn't use all this to wallow in self-pity. Rather, as a feature on him by Liz Lightfoot in the *Guardian* put it in 2019, he draws on everything he has to take 'the side of the underdog'.

Ross's book is deeply grounded, immensely practical, and full of simple, proven ideas that work. He is a teacher's teacher: salt of the earth. Lightfoot's impression is that his understated private persona communicates how 'what you see is what you get'. Having met Ross, I can vouch for that completely. But he is not averse to theory, ideas or research. He's been on the frontline but hasn't turned into an anti-intellectual curmudgeon who takes refuge in the so-called school of hard knocks. His work, like this book, is all about connecting great teaching ideas to evidence and to research about what works and what improves insight into the kids and the job.

Ross also connects teachers with each other. The final three ideas of his set of ten on great teaching are all about professional development and collaboration. Your kids can't be learning unless you are. And they can't be well if you're sick, excessively stressed, hyper-vigilant about punitive inspections, or just burnt out. But in the midst of all that, Ross begins this book on truly great teaching in his inimitably counterintuitive way – with the opening gambit you'd least expect, the one that seems to have the smallest potential for capturing teachers' interest and motivation: marking.

Like all great leaders, Ross knows how to go with a counterintuitive winning strategy. Great leaders turn weaknesses into strengths. This is Ross all over – starting rather than ending with marking, and making it important, practical and motivating so that his book is impossible to put down. Let's take just a couple of examples that resonated with me as a researcher and a teacher of mature students.

First, about 20 years ago, my colleague Lorna Earl and I invented the concept of assessment *as* learning. Our work on educational reforms in Ontario in Canada included evaluation of efforts to develop alternative assessments to standardised tests in the form of peer-assessments, self-assessments and performance-based assessments. It also highlighted how many students and their teachers didn't already know how to assess in this way. They had to learn it. Processes like self-assessment and peer-assessment had to be learnt for the first time. They were assessment skills of lifelong value that amounted to forms of learning in their own right. Ross's book takes fundamental ideas about assessment like these, spells them out in practical terms, connects them to the research, and slays a few popular and political misconceptions along the way. I am bearing this all in mind right now as I spend a couple of mornings a week with my 8-year-old grandchild to assist him with his mathematics during his virtual schooling experience.

Second, there's the issue of planning – yet another apparent kiss of death to inspired teaching and learning. Planning needn't be a cookie-cutter, one-size-fits-all template, Ross tells us. It is important to plan, of course, but it needn't be detailed, written down neatly in a way that passing observers or inspectors can review, or be standardised. This kind of compliance-based planning can suck the life out of teachers and teaching. But it *is* important to jot down what you plan to do and know why, he says, bearing in mind that classroom events can divert the best-laid plans at any moment. You might do it on your laptop, a sheet of paper, or a few sticky notes. It may not look pretty or perfect to someone else – but it's still planning. And you can even improvise and go with the flow from the moment you put your hand on the classroom doorknob. But if you think this is just a licence for pedagogical anarchy, Ross reminds all his readers that even when you go with the flow, it should all be based on and rooted in what he calls a secure foundation – a collaborative understanding and agreement across the school about the curriculum, learning goals, and a broad pedagogical approach that is most appropriate for kids.

A few years ago, some of my students successfully nominated me for Boston College's *Excellence in Teaching with Technology Award*, which I received in 2015. Yet, at the very same time of my nomination, I had one of my most difficult teaching moments ever. I regularly receive manuscripts like Ross's book to endorse or review. Could this be a resource for my students too, I wondered? How exciting it might be to review manuscripts before publication and then send them back to the actual authors for feedback! My students were not impressed, though. Instead of being excited, they were petrified. How could they possibly present criticisms to world-renowned writers who had given their lives to their scholarship? The students' reviews were bland in the extreme. They had no voice and very little critique. After reading their reviews, I entered the next class early. I struck up a sombre tone. All but one of their assignments had failed, I said. I left a long, dramatic pause. Then I continued. If one or two assignments failed, I reflected, that could be a problem with the students concerned. If most had failed it was impossible to avoid the fact that there was a problem with me!

What did I learn from this experience? For one thing, as innovation after innovation had landed successfully in my classes, I just wanted the rush of more of them. I was over-planning due to over-excitement. The classes were becoming expressions of *my* passions but ignoring theirs. Second, I was a victim (or beneficiary) of my own hubris. Just because I was *Teacher of the Year* with one bunch of classes didn't mean I could be *Teacher of the Year* in all of them. As Ross tells us, great teaching is partly about getting the context right. And this is a salutary lesson for everyone to remember who gets lucky with a *Teacher of the Year Award* at some point. Last, I needed to involve my mature students more in both the planning of as well as the assessment in my classes, especially the most innovative ones. So, as if I had already taken some leaves out of Ross's book, I got back to some good inclusive planning and assessment basics, dropping the next assignment to make space.

Whether you are an infant school teacher, a researcher and teacher in higher education, or a parent trying to help your child's learning in virtual school or after school with their homework, this book will have something to say to you. It's practical and clear but philosophical and inspirational too. This is not only a book I'll advise other educators to use. It's a book I will gladly use myself.

Andy Hargreaves

Director of CHENINE (Change, Engagement and Innovation in Education), University of Ottawa, Canada, October 2020

Introduction

In a landscape fuelled increasingly by data and lack of funding, teachers' workload is still at a very high level. Whether you believe it or not, workload has reduced over the past couple of years, at least in England, and I see this as a significant recognition by the government and school leaders in consciously looking to reduce the burden. Things are still far from perfect, however, and evidence suggests that teacher recruitment, retention and budget remain the top issues in education. Teachers and school leaders continue to be eager to discover evidence-informed ideas that work in the classroom on a shoestring (through no fault of their own).

As ever, I firmly believe that there are three things that teachers need to do well: mark work, plan coherent lessons and teach students. The original intention of **Mark. Plan. Teach.** was to encourage teachers to view the teaching process as a continuous cycle:

Each stage of the **Mark. Plan. Teach.** cycle informs the next; no stage exists in isolation and the above graphic represents a fluid motion between each aspect of what a teacher does and how one stage correlates to and influences the next. More importantly, **Mark. Plan. Teach. 1.0.** intended to strip back a lot of the nonsense that has emerged in the classroom, focus on the core components of the day job, without getting distracted by external administration, and enable teachers to take back control of pedagogy, albeit in line with the whole-school vision.

These intentions remain the same in **Mark. Plan. Teach. 2.0.** Three years on, I have updated the book to include new research, signpost what I have learnt from delivering training based on the book with 30,000 teachers in schools across 15 countries, and share stories of how schools are using the ideas. You will also find alongside this new edition a visual guide to the book, beautifully illustrated by Oliver Caviglioli, to translate the ideas through words and images. The visual guide is designed to help you access the content of the book in short, one-minute summaries. If you haven't already read **Mark. Plan. Teach.**, use the guide to spark your imagination and then open this book to dig deeper into the theory and strategies suggested. Alternatively, you can use the visual guide as a quick reminder of the key ideas when you're busy planning lessons or teaching.

This updated edition continues to offer a range of strategies for each stage of the *Mark. Plan. Teach.* cycle, backed up by countless pieces of educational research and psychological perspectives, which will help shed light on why some strategies work better than others. These ideas will enable teachers to develop their classroom repertoire over time, reduce their workload and leave them in no doubt that they're doing what's right for the students, their own workload and their mental health – as long as school leaders create the right conditions for this, of course.

In *Mark. Plan. Teach. 2.0*, I promise to offer:

1. Tried-and-tested classroom ideas, supported with a wide range of academic research and methods.

2. Teaching strategies based on cognitive processes, backed up by insights from leading psychologist Professor Tim O'Brien.

3. Ideas that are accessible for every teacher, regardless of government fad or whim.

Throughout this book, I will also pose many questions that all teachers must ask of themselves to help them to reflect, manage their own workload and begin to drive change within the education sector as a whole. I have lost count of the number of times I've heard the expression 'I'm just a teacher' when I explain this intention in training sessions. If you want to drive change in one particular area, make sure you are the most knowledgeable about it. Gather as much information as possible and use it to challenge those in positions of power and influence their decision-making.

We need to get in a position where all teachers are empowered to take back control of their classroom domains, where the government and external agencies support teachers to thrive, rather than control pedagogy from a distance. Every single person working in a school has something to offer and something to learn, regardless of their level of seniority. By working together to adapt classroom practice, we can maximise students' potential no matter what league tables or attainment and progress reports say. I would ask all teachers to empower yourselves by learning about educational research and cognitive science, particularly on the domains of memory. This will transform your classroom practice.

There is one final point I would like to make before we get started: these ideas are not mine. They are ideas I have learnt from others in my teaching career, from the schools I have visited and from the millions of teachers I interact with through my social media networks. *Mark. Plan. Teach. 1.0* was created when I was a deputy headteacher and I worked with the teachers in my school to develop the methodology on which the book was based. It was also built around some of the books and blogs I was reading at the time. This updated edition is no different. There are countless signposts in this book to other schools, educators and pieces of research, as well as curated ideas from other schools as well as my own. Teaching is a team sport and no individual, including myself, can solve complex classroom problems on their own. Good-quality teacher training must happen in the day-to-day rhythm of school life and school leaders must create the conditions for teachers to talk about teaching, so each school can develop its own teaching and learning methodology for its specific context.

What makes a good teacher?

There are still many unanswered questions within the world of education. First and foremost, what makes a good teacher is a never-ending question! It is my belief that teacher personality makes a difference in the classroom and this is often dependent on our own circumstances, the cards we have been dealt and how we respond to different situations. This, in turn, is of course influenced by the school we choose to work in and how we are supported. You will see that there is a lot of research in this book that appears to confirm the same messages about good-quality teaching, but context matters. A great teacher in a stable and affluent school will be working very differently to a great teacher working in a challenging school. And the rewards for both these teachers and what a school can do to support them will also vary significantly. I have used many of the ideas I present in this book throughout my career – in both stable and challenging institutions. I'm not pretending they will work in your school, but I am confident most will, if you are able to translate them for your own context.

The structure of the school building and all its internal operations haven't changed very much over the past century. In secondary schools, the school bell generally still rings on the hour, and every teacher and student must then close their books and move on to another lesson. However, how we learn as students – and as teachers – has shifted considerably over the past decade. We can now discover knowledge far beyond the walls of our own classroom, with information available to teachers from every angle: the news, social media and from our colleagues at the chalk face. Children are more informed than ever and our teachers are doing more in the same amount of time. Teachers know so much more about cognitive load theory, memory and how we learn. All this poses an interesting dilemma for the future of schools. It is therefore critical that schools develop a common-sense approach to helping their teachers keep abreast of research, and teachers must remain engaged and critically informed about their practice.

Teachers make a difference, but no one quite knows for sure what makes a good teacher. We are aware of certain strategies that work, for example retrieval practice and spaced practice, but many of us are still working on our assumptions and what we've learnt from other teachers before us. We should acknowledge there is no single answer to being a great classroom practitioner. There are many roads to greatness in the classroom. Yet, we should also recognise that whatever your teaching style, specialism or approach, 'what works' does actually work! So, keep doing what you're doing and have faith in your ability to change the lives of thousands of children, but equally make sure your practice comes from a range of sources, that it's evidence informed and that the strategies you're using have been given time to be properly introduced and road tested. Don't get me started on gimmicks!

Of all the things I've learnt in the education sector, the ability to self-reflect is probably the greatest tool all teachers should possess throughout their career. Reflection is a quality we all share and doing this reliably is fundamental. If this is lost for whatever reason, we know how it can hold back ourselves as professionals, as well as the students in our care. I've been there myself. I've also had to take action on others. I know that every teacher at some point wants to be better, while at some points, when things get a bit busy, we rely on our wisdom to carry us through. Questioning our practice is essential if we are to build an awareness of where we are in our teaching practice and which areas we need to develop further, collectively, as well as in our own professional journey, no matter how experienced we are. Nevertheless, questioning your own practice is one thing, but having it questioned by others, particularly school leaders or third parties who have forgotten what it's like to teach a full day's timetable, is another thing entirely.

Teachers across the UK, for example, have had to listen to countless politicians and experts advocate methods of teaching from overseas, comparing UK test scores in English, maths and science to those of students in very different cultures and contexts, to then proclaim, 'This is what our teachers should be doing.' If we continue to measure apples and pears, we will be none the wiser. There is nothing wrong with sharing best practice from overseas, of course. Lucy Crehan ends her epic journey of exploring the secrets of education superpowers by arguing:

> 'To attribute these countries' enviable outcomes to culture and therefore dismiss their value as models would be a grave mistake. Culture can change. And it is schools and school systems that have the power to change it.' (Crehan, 2016)

However, we must also be looking in our own schools to help develop professional discourse. It is my belief that we have the very best professionals in our classrooms already. I accept that I am biased, but I often think about teachers who choose to work in challenging schools in very difficult circumstances, with external judgements constantly being made like a noose around the neck. We need to create the conditions where all our teachers are celebrated, particularly those who choose to work in challenging situations. We need teachers. We don't have enough of them. We can't keep them for longer than two or three years. For those who do stick with the profession for 20 years or more, we don't pay them enough or reward them for continuing to do the job and supporting other teachers.

We need to continue to promote best practice in all classrooms, with the limited time and funding we have, by stripping back much of the nonsense that has emerged across the teaching profession over the past decade. Let's get our teachers to focus on what matters most: feedback, assessment, curriculum schema, lesson planning and high-quality teaching, with sufficient time and space to reflect on practice more regularly, with other colleagues around them. Without this, our teaching profession will always be on the back foot.

Mark. Plan. Teach. 2.0 is for all teachers and school leaders who wish to use their professional wisdom alongside evidence-based interventions that have the greatest impact on students, while avoiding government fads and in-school decision-making that drives up administrative work instead of placing classroom practice at the heart of what teachers do. We need to strip back everything and focus on the basics. We need to focus on classroom strategies from the ground up. This book is written for our current classroom teachers and our next generation of classroom heroes. We can be masters of our own destiny in whatever context and whatever country we are teaching in. You are reading this book because you want to be the best teacher you can be, despite all the rhetoric, guff and external accountability. Our schools need you, and more importantly, so do your students.

Educational research

After many decades of teaching, you might think that we would have discovered more about the best ways for teachers to teach and students to learn. We are getting there on the former, but we are still navigating the complex world of cognitive science to discover how best students learn. There is no shortage of research being undertaken in our classrooms but we need to raise the profile of educational research even further and continue to create the conditions for all teachers to conduct research in classrooms and corridors. We need to ensure this receives high praise from school leaders and external agencies. In England, we now have a network of Research Schools run by the Education Endowment Foundation (EEF), tasked with the mission to become a focal point for evidence-based practices and to communicate, model and innovate methods for improvement.

However, we must acknowledge that reliability is extremely difficult to achieve in educational research. This is due to the very high number of variables involved and unavoidable levels of bias, in terms of the selection and setup of experiments, the manipulation of subjective data and the communication of results. While quantitative scientific research deals with data that is objective and reliably repeatable under identical conditions, qualitative educational research deals with subjective observations and opinions. To justify its conclusions, educational research often adopts techniques and methodologies based on sampling, weighting, surveys and scale-based ratings. These produce numerical data that can be subjected to statistical analysis, or effect sizes, which can run into problems of manipulation, interpretation and how we see scientific research in a subjective world. The 'scientific' data derived from some studies has sometimes been used to sell specific educational products or methods to schools, for example, while other findings have been misunderstood. It is also frustrating that current governments across the UK have done very little to evaluate the impact of their policies. Education reform based on research data should influence education policy but instead it's often the other way around. Ideology trumps transparency and research is used to justify a particular approach.

Perhaps all the problems inherent in conducting meaningful, reliable educational research explain why in hundreds of years of education provision, there is still little consensus as to what and how we should be teaching our students. While we do need government intervention and support, you know as well as I do that the people who drive education forward are teachers themselves. In spite of its pitfalls, we must engage with educational research to examine and discuss existing practice, raise questions from a supportive but challenging perspective and search for possible solutions. The evidence that emerges should point us towards new or emerging practices and methodologies that might, in certain situations, prove worthwhile for some students.

Teachers yearn for a profession where they are free to make their own decisions and also participate with passion and purpose to enable deep and powerful learning to happen. It takes a brave school leader to protect their staff from external pressures, to reduce workload and to ignore various policies in the current climate of high accountability. If we are to do things that really work in schools, we need to start using one another's experiences in the classroom as evidence in itself. We need to enable teachers to meet more regularly and share ideas about what's working with the students in their school. Teaching ideas that lead to transformation are what matters. It's important to look at the research behind what common traits can be found in effective teachers and schools and what evidence-based strategies they use.

Mark. Plan. Teach. 1.0 was the outcome of a one-page policy designed to build consistency across my own school. Three years later, after speaking to teachers about my framework in over 200 schools across the world, I would advise: don't seek consistency; instead seek coherence through conversations with your colleagues on a regular basis. Build your own framework from the classroom floor, tinker with it and debate ideas with all staff on a weekly basis, making sure you look at what the research is saying along the way. Then we are truly creating the conditions and culture for our teachers to thrive. A one-page teaching and learning guidance document should become your hymn sheet, allowing teachers to veer away from accountability, avoiding absence and remaining autonomous, communicating expectations to all teachers and ensuring teacher happiness is supported through a culture of trust.

Each and every section of this book, therefore, builds upon every single conversation that I first had with the 110 teachers in my school over six years ago. The original edition has now developed with the work of 30,000 other teachers across the world, containing my experiences of over 20,000 lessons taught, 200 schools visited and tens of thousands of lessons observed, as well as all the wonderful teacher authors I reference in the bibliography on p. 180. This book is my action research. It shares my experiences of the classroom and is written to provoke, challenge and inspire every teacher across the world.

Mark. Plan. Teach. 2.0 offers my field notes to the rest of the teaching profession.

How to use this book

I have written **Mark. Plan. Teach.** in such a way that it can be read from start to finish to mirror the teaching process. The three sections each present ideas relating to one aspect of this process, all the while acknowledging how each stage of the cycle informs the next and cannot exist in isolation. Remember:

Of course, each section can also be read and put into practice independently, as can each individual idea. Equally, each section and each idea can be redesigned into a professional development session to train staff.

What will I find in each section?

Each section is divided into **ten** tried-and-tested ideas that can be implemented in the classroom. The ideas all begin with an 'idea snapshot', which provides an overview of the concept. Use these snapshots to dip in and out of the book and find the ideas and strategies you are looking for. You can easily pick out these snapshots by keeping an eye out for the camera icon as you flick through the book. Each section of the book ends with a short summary that provides a neat recap of all the ideas. Consider these summaries as essential synopses of the strategies in each section.

Each idea I present is supported by educational research or a psychological perspective, which helps to explain *how* and *why* the idea works. Look out for the following at the end of each idea:

Evidence

These sections draw upon a wide range of educational research relating to the ideas and how and why they work. However, regardless of this evidence, remember that context is everything and I am not suggesting that any of these ideas will work perfectly in *all* school settings and circumstances.

Psychology

In these sections, Tim O'Brien, Honorary Professor in Psychology and Human Development at UCL Institute of Education, focuses on particular aspects of my ideas and offers perspectives that consider the psychological processes behind the ideas. If you wish to reference anything from these sections in your own writing, please reference the section like this: (for example) O'Brien, T. (2017), 'Psychology and reflection', in R. M. McGill, *Mark. Plan. Teach.*, London: Bloomsbury.

Who is this book for?

Throughout the three decades that I've been working in schools – yes, I did start teaching in the 1990s when banda machines were the talk of the staffroom – I have been asked to implement countless strategies in my classroom, some of which haven't stood the test of time. Some training sessions have advocated providing trails of evidence for watchdogs, such as verbal feedback stamps, as well as 'research-informed' strategies that have later turned out to lack rigour and evidence. Today, we'd call this 'fake news' or at the very least 'educational myths'.

This book is for every teacher. I hope that by sharing some of my tried-and-tested strategies and supporting these with evidence and psychological perspectives, you will be tempted to apply some of them in your own classroom. This book is also for every leader of teaching and learning, who shares ideas with larger groups of teachers. It can be used as a training manual in professional development sessions to equip every teacher with classroom strategies to be used the very next day. For the past ten years, I have been working in very challenging school settings, where classroom ideas are difficult to implement across an entire school. We know that 'collective teacher efficacy' (see Section 3, Idea 3, p. 131) has a huge impact on student outcomes, but any idea – including those shared in *Mark. Plan. Teach.* – will only be as effective as the teacher who delivers them. Gone are the days of monotony and one size fits all. Teachers and schools need to be able to pick and mix strategies that work for them and their students, so use these ideas as a platform for inspiration, discussion and provocation with your colleagues.

Whoever you are, all I ask is for you to remember that context is king with everything you read in this book. I offer ideas that can stand the test of time, regardless of subject or setting. It is my intention to share every ounce of knowledge I have with you. I hope you enjoy the read and that this becomes a well-thumbed book on your classroom desk.

No matter how hard you look...

...you will NOT find the word 'Ofsted' in this book, other than in this sentence*. As in most of my writing, I will refer to this watchdog by my preferred nickname: the 'Grim Reaper'!

*and for accurate referencing.

Section 1:
MARK.

A long time ago, in a school far away (when I was less experienced)... I found marking to be a real burden. I never understood the value of assessment, and verbal and written feedback was something I just did. Over the last decade, research and the growth of social media for teachers' professional development have exposed misguided practice and allowed teachers and schools to work collaboratively outside of their silos. In this new digital epoch, I have academic research and evidence in the palm of my hand to help better understand how assessment and feedback can make the greatest difference to students.

Marking, or assessment, as is the real theme of this section, is the critical first step in the *Mark. Plan. Teach.* loop. In Section 1, Idea 1, p. 7, I explain what I mean by this in terms of developing a secure overview in order to plan a lesson more effectively. We must approach marking as an important aspect of assessment, but it is also important to add that this assessment can be verbal or involve internal data collection, and may not be something that is obvious on a spreadsheet or in written commentary in a student's book.

Assessment, feedback and marking form a crucial part of every teacher's daily routine, regardless of their experience, the subject they teach, or the ability and age range of their students. The importance of high-quality feedback has been evidenced by many academic studies, particularly supported through retrieval practice as a mechanism for quizzing pupils to support long-term retention. Today, I wouldn't waste my time marking; instead I would spend much more time quizzing pupils, or at least planning what to quiz them on.

The benefits of a rigorous approach to marking and feedback include the fact that assessing students helps teachers learn about their own impact. This can be seen in everyday classrooms where students are thriving and attitudes to learning and attainment are on an upward trajectory as a result of the quality of what teachers do on a daily basis.

> 'As a professional, it is critical to know thy impact. It may seem ironic, but the more teachers seek feedback about their own impact, the more benefits accrue to their students.' (Hattie, 2012)

All teachers struggle with the marking load at some point in their career; it's an occupational hazard, and my travel to schools across the world highlights that it is still the number one issue for all teachers, regardless of setting. School leaders must work hard to reduce the burden as well as reshape the narrative of marking, assessment and feedback.

We know there is a need for greater research in the area of teacher workload to help alleviate the burden. This is not to reduce the role of the teacher and some of the key things that all teachers should do, but we need to think very carefully about what is effective and how marketisation and increased accountability, at least for schools in England, have made teaching far more difficult than it needs to be.

I've updated this section of *Mark. Plan. Teach.* with the important yet challenging nature of assessment, feedback and marking in mind. I distil tried-and-tested gems and expose several gimmicks that I believe you can dispense with to equip you with strategies for marking and feedback that will reduce workload and increase classroom impact.

What is the purpose of assessment, feedback and marking?

Assessment, feedback and marking have three purposes:

1. Students act on feedback to make progress.
2. Assessment informs future planning and teaching.
3. Students learn to value their work and the quality of the work they produce.

Assessment, feedback and marking should improve the learner, not just a piece of work, and we will come across more purposes and examples in this section of the book, but for this short introduction, let's consider the above three points.

Making progress

Marking is a continuum between teacher and student, and student and teacher. It should be a dialogue, written or spoken, and something that students use to understand their learning better and how to improve. The aim of assessing work effectively is to get students to engage with the feedback in whatever form it is presented, and then take action in order to improve their learning. Ultimately, assessment and marking should enable students to act on the feedback received. We can therefore accept that a feedback-loop, which helps the student to improve each time, is critical to a student's success.

Assessment and feedback seek to highlight those elements of marking that have the greatest impact on learning, namely:

- Sharing the key marking points (the success criteria). A student is much more likely to be successful if they know where they are going and how to get there. This is what John Hattie labels as 'teacher clarity' in his study of over 800 meta-analyses relating to achievement (Hattie, 2009). I call 'teacher clarity' 'stickability' (which features in my 5 Minute Lesson Plan to help teachers focus on learning), or what knowledge, skills and understanding students must leave the classroom with and bring back to the next lesson (see Section 2, Idea 4, p. 81).

- Providing students with clear feedback about their work, for example comments-only marking or even just verbal feedback, but crucially making sure they *respond* to your marking by correcting the work or redrafting it using your comments to guide them to a higher standard. A simple way to achieve this is by using an excellent strategy to reduce workload and increase impact: zonal feedback (see Section 1, Idea 3, p. 18).

If we can keep these elements at the forefront of our minds, marking and assessment will be more focused and efficient and will help our students to progress.

Informing teaching

Consider marking from the basis of informing the teacher to be even better than before, not just the students. Abundant research says that the *quality* of the teacher makes the greatest difference to a child. It says nothing about how much or how little marking we should do and how hard we should work at it.

Report after report shows that teachers are working in excess of 50 hours every week during term time to keep on top of their workload. It is the number one reason why teachers leave the profession (DfE, 2020b). The teaching workforce experiences serious pressure on its mental health: the Teacher Wellbeing Index 2019 from the Education Support Partnership offers countless pieces of research data on some very important issues:

1. 72% of teachers describe themselves as stressed. This number reaches 84% for school leaders.

2. 33% of all teachers work more than 51 hours a week on average.

3. 74% consider the inability to switch off and relax to be the major contributing factor to a negative work–life balance.

4. Worryingly, 49% of teachers consider their organisational culture to have a negative effect on their mental health and wellbeing.

Why do I mention all this? Because marking is the number one factor contributing to workload in all of the schools I have visited since first publishing this book. Schools that are abandoning traditional forms of marking and data collection are bucking the trend but it's not everywhere and it is far from common practice.

So why have we created an unmanageable beast that is driving teachers to leave the profession or, worse, to depression, particularly when research suggests our focus should be on the quality of teaching, not quantity of marking?

Assessment, marking and feedback will tell you how effective your teaching has been and whether your students have grasped the concepts and developed the skills required by your assessment framework. It will also show you the progress your students have made over time. This will then inform whether you need to go back and re-teach any aspects of the curriculum (see Section 1, Idea 6, p. 35), whether you need to adapt the materials you are teaching them and what you could teach your students next. Assessment will help you understand the what, how and why of teaching (see Section 1, Idea 2, p. 14) and lead to a quality first teaching approach, which will ensure you are responding to your students in the best way possible.

The value of hard work

In schools where teachers are contracted to teach for 90% of their time, or in difficult schools where behaviour is challenging, finding any free time to mark outside of the classroom is a poisoned chalice. I personally believe that the hard work should be in the classroom, not away from it. Live-marking offers a solution (see Section 1, Idea 3, p. 18), but we should also remember that, when it comes to traditional marking, the hard work should be for the person receiving the feedback and not for the person providing the assessment.

Not only should your students engage with and respond to your feedback, but the onus should be on them to reflect on their own work, be able to recognise its flaws and fix them before you've even seen it! (See Section 1, Idea 7, p. 39.) There is a great deal of research on metacognition emerging across the profession. I would encourage you to read the contributions from Carole Yue (see Section 1, Idea 5, p. 30). Encourage a culture of self- and peer-assessment in your classroom (see Section 1, Idea 9, p. 47) and refuse to mark anything that isn't up to standard! (See Section 1, Idea 10, p. 53.) This will save you time and help your students take control of their own learning and progress.

Verbal feedback

In a blog post, Roy Blatchford, Founding Director of the National Education Trust, likens observing teachers making mistakes in the classroom to the surgeons who once removed a benign melanoma from his wrist:

> 'The lead surgeon began cutting precisely then passed over the scalpel to one of his juniors. Within thirty seconds he seized it back, clearly not content with the direction of the incision […] Ever since that moment […] I have rarely observed a lesson without interacting in some way.' (Blatchford, 2015)

Could the same be said for assessment? If we see a student going off on the wrong track, should we intervene? I would like to suggest that all teachers should. However, I believe that there is a far greater need for verbal feedback techniques to be used as the default mechanism for traditional forms of marking so that teachers can give immediate feedback that aids students in the lesson, rather than weeks later when a teacher has finally found time to provide written feedback.

You might not know that the Latin origins of the word 'assessment' is 'assidere' or to 'sit beside'. It is very interesting to see how this word has evolved to now mean teachers inputting countless scores of data into an online portfolio, often sitting beside a computer without a student, or on a kitchen table with a pile of books, rather than sitting with a child in a classroom having a conversation about their work and offering meaningful feedback. How far away are we from moving back to this as the sole experience in our classrooms?

I believe there is a greater need for verbal feedback as the default mechanism. Verbal feedback would also help combat workload, teacher mental health issues and ensure feedback is incisive, as well as 'manageable, meaningful and motivating', which aligns with the recommendations published by the DfE (2016; see Section 1, Idea 4, Evidence, p. 24). Using verbal feedback techniques would reduce the burden of marking in exchange for sharing initial feedback, mark schemes and common errors, and help teachers become better at what they are teaching in a feedback loop. I've been passionate about raising the profile of verbal feedback for at least six years now, and I was pleased when UCL commissioned me to conduct some research in disadvantaged state schools across England. You can read more about the results in Section 1, Idea 10, p. 53.

Issues at whole-school level

There are two problems that our schools and school leaders face when trying to improve assessment, feedback and marking. Examination boards and school inspections both impact on even the smartest teaching and learning policies designed to eradicate the marking burden.

Firstly, no matter how hard schools try to design a simple teaching and learning policy, there will be some teachers – particularly those teaching examination classes in Years 6 and 11 – who, in spite of their best efforts to follow school policy, will be trumped by external examination requirements asking teachers to mark drafts, redrafts and provide endless commentary.

The second issue is more serious for schools. At the time of writing, teaching and learning policies – or more specifically, marking policies – are not statutory law (DfE, 2020a). Schools are not required to have one or publish one for parents. Obviously every school hopes to communicate how students' work will be marked and how often, and no school would want to alienate their students and parents by keeping assessment a secret – this would be the polar opposite of 'teacher clarity'. However, schools are setting themselves up to fail – and don't even know it – if external partners who quality assure teaching and learning test what non-statutory policies say versus what is happening and then hold schools to account for it! Here's how it happens:

1. The school creates, consults (if you are lucky) and publishes a teaching and learning policy for staff, students and parents.

2. Teachers are trained (again, if you are lucky) – and then expected to mark or teach – according to a set frequency or framework.

3. School leaders monitor who is following the system well and who is not, then tweak it and repeat. They bring in capability procedures or poorly framed coaching strategies.

4. Parents, and perhaps fleetingly school inspectors, complain that a policy is not being followed.

5. Students remain complacent regardless of what happens at policy level.

6. The most able students make progress and the most disadvantaged children actually need more than a policy to help them understand why schooling is important to their future outcomes.

7. Over time, impending school inspections raise anxiety and school leaders start to crank up the pressure with comments such as 'the Grim Reaper is likely to want...'.

8. Teachers get stressed. They either pull their socks up and sustain a heavy workload for a period of time or buckle under the strain.

9. Capability ensues as school leaders anticipate what will be measured according to external partner methodologies and binary measures.

10. The result? Stressed-out teachers, headless school leaders and school inspectors judging how well schools can implement non-statutory policy.

It's a mindless cycle that leads to more cynicism and confusion. Of course, it's not like this everywhere, and the dialogue is slowly changing, but you will certainly find this in some toxic school cultures.

So what's the solution?

Schools should create a simple marking policy if they want. It's important to develop it as a guidance document through teacher training sessions where everybody has a say. The final guidance should be a coherent hymn sheet that offers clarity on a single page. The details should be given in teacher training sessions and the resources kept behind the scenes. My suggestions are:

- Teachers must have a secure overview of the starting points of their students, curriculum pathways and how students learn (see Section 1, Idea 1, p. 7).

- Assessment techniques must use diagnostic tools as a default process for improvement (see Section 1, Idea 2, p. 14).

- Feedback must be regular and proportionate to curriculum time (see Section 1, Idea 4, p. 24).

We should also remember that the value of organisations, school leaders and teachers assessing the quality of marking from books alone is limited. It is only one way to gauge student progress and is susceptible to interpretation and serious weaknesses if not conducted reliably (see Section 1, Idea 8, p. 42).

Imagine working in a school where you can publicly present your students' books, unmarked, in order to allow other colleagues to help you solve complex problems. That is a school I'd like to work in.

A secure overview

IDEA SNAPSHOT

Before you set an assessment and then sit down to mark it, you should first consider where you are in the curriculum and the purpose of setting and marking this specific piece of work. Think about the starting point, progress and context of each student. This 'secure overview' will inform how you spend time marking to improve teaching, learning and assessment.

J ohn Hattie's research suggests that 'goal setting' has a significant impact (d=0.68) on student outcomes because it helps students see the 'bigger picture' in their learning (Hattie, 2009). Hattie's work also suggests that 'conscious goals regulate human actions and influence performance levels' (Carroll et al., 2009). Imagine a map that is directing you where to go, with countless options ahead of you informing how you might get there. It is vital to have this 'bigger picture' in place as part of curriculum planning and assessment, not only so that students understand where they are going, but so teachers have a secure grasp of what needs to be taught and assessed.

In his book *The Slightly Awesome Teacher*, Dominic Salles suggests that setting goals is 'largely about workload and time management – getting through the curriculum' (Salles, 2016). As much as it saddens me to write it here in black and white, I agree.

Teachers are time poor and in constant conflict between what they would like to teach, what they have to teach and what they have to evidence for external stakeholders. Nevertheless, if we start everything we do with the end outcome in mind, surely we are at least in a stronger position as teachers? This will lead to smarter assessment, reduced workload and better outcomes for the students.

The difficulty for a school, and any individual teacher, is not knowing whether your colleague is doing exactly the same as you with the same students in the classroom next door. Of course, all teachers should be given autonomy to teach in a way that best suits their teaching style, but there has to be an agreed 'hymn sheet' to sing along to together. This means all students experience the same climate and culture across the school, in terms of expectations, behaviour and, to a degree, consistency in teaching and learning.

Teacher expectations and routines vary and there is scope for students to become confused between one teacher's expectations and another's. In any school, students will find the gaps – opportunities to misbehave or escape work – and many readers will nod their heads in agreement when I say how many times my colleagues have had students complain, 'But Miss, Mr McGill doesn't ask us to write down lesson objectives. Why do we have to copy them down in your lessons?'.

So how does any school address this if they want their teachers to be autonomous, yet consistent across the school? Well, it's a difficult question to answer and the context of the individual school will apply. What works in Early Years classrooms will be very different to what works with 16-year-olds.

The solution? Teach in a way that works for you and your students. If it works in the grand scheme of things, should we really worry about whether students are writing, speaking, reading or listening to the learning objectives, for example?

Communicate the written or verbal objectives with students effectively and make sure they understand them in the context of 'the bigger picture' of their learning, but remember schools shouldn't be demanding that teachers record objectives for observational and evidential purposes. Let's just focus on the learning!

Marking and feedback

So once we have a secure overview of the curriculum plan, what can school leaders and, more importantly, school teachers do with it in terms of marking and feedback?

Both the individual teacher's and whole school's approach to marking and feedback need to be well thought out, of high quality and appropriate for the individual school and setting. When marking and feedback is a regular routine in the classroom, it is always apparent: work is of a higher quality; students take more time over their work; work is better organised; students are able to talk about their learning and they have more opportunities to progress. Effective work can also manifest itself in non-routine aspects of learning, as well as routines evident through behaviour, punctuality, engagement in lessons, classroom displays and general excitement about work. Although these aspects are 'poor proxies for learning' (as in a shift in long-term memory), they do provide valuable data for the teacher.

When I developed *Mark. Plan. Teach.* as a deputy headteacher, the 110 teachers in my care collaborated to create our teaching and learning methodology over a sustained period of two years. Having shared the contents in over 200 schools in 15 countries, I am pleased to report that the clear, pragmatic and tested ideas work in any classroom. The challenge is how a teacher translates the ideas to suit their teaching style and the context of the pupils in front of them.

The work we developed together (I take no credit for the ideas in the book – after all, teaching is a team sport) was not a flash in the pan. It was a cultural process over a sustained period, developing a climate where teachers could develop their pedagogy, take risks and improve their subject knowledge. Sadly, this was not recognised by the Grim Reaper, who opted for 'chasing consistency', data and observational bias, instead of two years of staff training, reducing workload, and improving clarity and quality of department teaching.

The crux of the matter is that once you have a secure overview of the curriculum plan, you can mark all work with this in mind in order to inform whether your students have learnt what they have been taught and if not, what they need to do to get there. This means that ALL your marking will have an impact on student outcomes and will eliminate any needless work on your part, reducing your workload and maximising your impact as a teacher!

Why not try my **5 Minute Marking Plan** to help you do this? The Plan seeks to highlight those elements of marking that have the greatest impact on learning, including sharing the key marking points, because a student is much more likely to be successful if they know where they are going. The Plan also underlines the importance of ensuring that students respond to your marking by correcting their work or re-doing it in order to guide them to a higher standard.

Find my 5 Minute Marking Plan here:

www.teachertoolkit.co.uk/2013/07/01/5-minute-marking-plan-2

Knowing your students

How well do teachers know their students? This is a standout feature of teachers who have great relationships and also know their students' data, including their prior starting points and current pathways. However, this is incredibly difficult to achieve, for primary teachers who may teach just 30 pupils but need to know how they perform in ten different subjects and for secondary teachers who may teach in excess of 450 students per week!

So how can you know your students personally, as well as their performance? Over the past decade, schools and the way we teach have become more and more sophisticated, with data increasingly prominent in our conversations with young people. As a result, everything teachers do is richer, more efficient and more effective because they are better informed regarding how students are performing. This means the relationships they have with students are more powerful and meaningful when a) a good relationship with them is in place and b) the teacher can present useful data to students to help them progress.

It is this data, in the broadest sense, not just numbers, that will allow teachers to build a secure overview of the starting points, progress and context of all students, which is a huge help when marking.

This data may involve the following:

1. Information provided from previous schools or classes should be fully understood and used for planning. This includes:

   a. prior attainment data from primary school

   b. reading age

   c. how the student is doing in your subject compared to others

   d. how the student has done in the subject prior to you teaching them

   e. other vital information such as whether the student has English as an additional language (EAL), special educational needs and disabilities (SEND) or is gifted and talented (G&T).

2. Teachers should understand the student's overall strengths and weaknesses. In examination courses, a personalised learning checklist or a student-friendly knowledge organiser can often provide students with an overview of the course content and areas for assessment. This is an excellent signal that a teacher has planned well and intends on having a secure overview of every student in front of them.

3. Teachers should also be aware of the context of each class from:

   a. the relationships teachers form with students, in line with a behaviour or teaching and learning policy

   b. making a physical note of announcements about student welfare

   c. liaising with relevant pastoral teams and agencies where necessary to muster a deeper overview of the student; this is vital when working with disadvantaged or vulnerable students.

If we use the following simple step-by-step chart, we can build a secure overview of every student in our classrooms:

Step 1	Step 2	Step 3
Prior attainment and results	**Students' place in your course**	**Knowing your classes and kids**
What is it? • Results • Literacy • SEND/EAL • G&T • Pupil Premium • Ethnicity	**What is it?** • Student strengths and weaknesses • Knowledge organisers • Class tracking • Target groups	**What is it?** • Behaviour • Attendance • Pastoral issues • Likes and interests • Safeguarding
Examples of where we can find this information: • Whole-school datasets • Attainment data from feeder early years or primary settings • Attainment data from colleagues	**Examples of where we can find this information:** • Your marking and feedback • Your class datasets • Your observations in class • Curriculum maps	**Examples of where we can find this information:** • Your relationships with students and parents • School briefings, bulletins and end-of-day reports • Colleagues, pastoral teams and agencies

Remember: a student's context rarely means you should adjust your aspirations of what they can achieve. High expectations are critical in the classroom, yet sometimes there are events in a student's life that make it very hard for them to learn. This is where teachers can level the playing field. These students are the exception, not the rule, but we should never give up on them. I would rarely adjust my expectations for any child unless there were exceptional circumstances, for example a safeguarding issue is known and having the child in school is more important than asking them to complete a task.

Now you have a secure overview of every student in your class, make sure you keep this in mind when you are assessing their work. This will help you to focus on the key assessment points that will really make a difference to the learning of the individual student and guide them personally to a higher standard of learning.

Reflecting on your marking and feedback

Reflecting upon the value of marking and feedback to improve your own teaching is not a cardinal sin. Developing your understanding of the purpose of high-quality, focused marking and feedback and the way you incorporate this into your daily practice is an essential part of being a teacher. It will not disappear. Teachers will always need to mark students' work and it will be the bane of anyone's career if not done with aplomb.

Whether you are a class teacher looking to develop your practice or you are a school leader responsible for delivering CPD training for marking and feedback, *What Works?* (Major and Higgins, 2019) is an excellent book from the authors of *The Sutton Trust-EEF Teaching and Learning Toolkit*. In a podcast interview with author Lee Elliott Major (2019), he explains the dangers of research and says in his research with colleagues, as in my own, they have seen countless 'schools devoting extra hours to the marking of pupils' work under the false belief this would deliver effective feedback'. Quality not quantity of marking and feedback is crucial for learning gains, and feedback is not just marking. As Major and Higgins say, 'Marking is only feedback when it changes what learners do next.' This is the key to effective feedback, where assessment that is given, received and acted upon enables the pupil to develop subject knowledge, capability and confidence, and in time, reduces misconceptions. No wonder this quote stands the test of time: 'Teachers should focus on fundamental misunderstandings rather than waste time on careless mistakes' (Black and Wiliam, 1998).

In *What Works?*, Major and Higgins discuss three key principles. It would be helpful for you to reflect on your marking and feedback through the lens of these principles to determine what you're already doing well and what could be improved.

The Bananarama Principle

Named after the pop band Bananarama and their hit song 'It Ain't What You Do (It's the Way that You Do It)', this is essential advice for educators acting on the findings of research. This is often cited by many academics I have met and it's something I truly understand. Today, I am inundated with teachers and school leaders translating what I have written in this book as 'Ross says we should…', instead of 'I've read this and I have adapted it to suit…'. Context matters.

CONTINUES OVER PAGE

Teaching is a team sport and is a collective responsibility, plus there is a special place reserved in hell for teachers who do not share. Make sure that you share your knowledge, talk with colleagues and reflect on what you have learnt to improve your performance – and theirs – in your own context. So, what form of assessment is most beneficial for the students in your school? And how can busy classroom teachers implement this most effectively when they're working with 30 students at any one time?

The Goldilocks Principle

This is about getting things just right – 'not too much, not too little' – as in the fairy tale *Goldilocks*. What you do matters in teaching and I am reminded of the fantastic work of Mihaly Csikszentmihalyi and the flow model, balancing 'burnout' and 'boreout' (see Section 3, Idea 3, p. 131). When it comes to feedback, as Major and Higgins say, 'Too much challenge creates a chasm the learner can't cross. Too little challenge and the learner loses an opportunity to learn something new.' Judging how much you nudge students is what makes teaching highly complex, but timely and specific feedback and a secure overview of students can help.

The Matthew Effect

The challenge for all educators is how we can reduce the gap between disadvantaged students and their peers. This has never been more important, as the greatest concern on every teacher's mind is what impact the COVID-19 virus will have on our disadvantaged communities. We worry about young people without a secure environment, vulnerable children without the resources they need to access remote learning, and all four million families across the UK who are living below the poverty line. Our task as teachers is to work incredibly hard to rebalance the disadvantage gap. A belief I have held my entire teaching career is summed up by Major and Higgins: 'The prize of great teaching is progress for pupils from less privileged backgrounds. The most effective teachers succeed with all of the pupils in their class, regardless of their background.' And it starts with all teachers having a secure overview.

Psychology and...
a secure overview

In these Psychology sections, Tim O'Brien, Honorary Professor in Psychology and Human Development at UCL Institute of Education, will focus on a particular aspect in each of Ross's ideas and offer a psychological perspective.

Ross proposes that a secure overview allows a teacher to develop a secure base for teaching. They know where the students are in terms of their learning and where they are heading. This is vital. One critique of the current educational climate is that it has become obsessed with data. There is value in gathering data for a purpose but children and young people are not data – they are humans with vulnerabilities and needs. The needs of some students are evident to a teacher whilst other students develop strategies to camouflage certain needs. I propose that a secure overview should also include an awareness of psychological needs. When a teacher is aware of psychological needs, it enables students to develop a more secure base for learning.

One psychological need I shall consider here, varying in nature from individual to individual, is the need to feel a sense of belonging. Feeling that you belong creates a sense of emotional security and self-validity. So, how can you help a student feel or know that they belong in your classroom? At the risk of stating the obvious, it is a classroom and therefore access to learning is critical. Consider how you can adapt what you think, feel and do to increase the possibilities of removing barriers to learning – and not only for those students identified as experiencing SEND. If a student believes they can learn in your classroom, and knows that their learning will be acknowledged, they are more likely to feel that they belong there. Learning is an emotional as well as a cognitive activity, and recognition of the emotional aspects of learning, such as persistence and curiosity, can also create a sense of belonging. There are also strategies that can enhance an individual's sense of belonging when they are in a group. For example, when talking to the whole class, a teacher can openly communicate that they have high expectations for all students. Creating a sense of belonging is a psychological enabler for learning.

A student's sense of belonging can be nurtured, reinforced or amplified when they have a positive relationship with their teacher. Relationships are the heartbeats of pedagogy. Relationships matter – especially as research highlights that teachers will be involved in over one thousand interpersonal contacts every single day (Holmes, 2005). Realistically, for a teacher, it may be easier to develop positive relationships with some students more than others. So, make a conscious effort to notice the nature and quality of your interactions with all students. It is also worth being aware that research indicates that when teachers develop positive relationships with students, it is not only beneficial to the students – it also has an unambiguously positive impact on teacher wellbeing.

IDEA 2

Not yet...

IDEA SNAPSHOT

Use the powerful words 'not yet' in your marking to cut through complex grading systems and form a simple assessment framework that will motivate students to improve their learning and develop resilience.

Summative marking means evaluating a piece of work according to a success criteria and giving it a grade. **Formative marking**, on the other hand, is not about giving a grade, but rather providing commentary on the level the student is working at in order to improve learning. Despite this distinction, formative and summative marking are things that every teacher must do, and both often require the use of multiple assessment frameworks. Understanding multiple assessment frameworks is therefore critical, and communicating a grading system to students to help them understand the work they are doing, and more importantly, why they are doing it, is fundamental practice in the classroom.

When assessing students' work either summatively or formatively, you must think about how you are going to feed back. What grading criteria will you share? In 2015, government policy announced 'life without levels': removing levels in order to reduce time spent by teachers recording and tracking progress towards numerical targets, increase pupil motivation and engagement, and improve formative assessment in the classroom. However, the result was that most schools then adopted their own methods, which led to greater disparity. So stage, age, subject and country aside, how should we as teachers create a system where we can be masters of the classroom for the benefit of our students?

Obviously your school, department or subject will have an agreed system for teachers to use. I sincerely hope they do anyway. But you must also consider how well your students understand it. After all, they are the ones that need to know what it all means and how to improve, right?

So let's think about it this way: if you created a new project and scheme of learning from the outset that had no assessment framework to start with, what would you do and where would you go? Hopefully you will agree that the design of the curriculum comes first, but without an assessment framework, it is difficult for the teacher, never mind the students, to gauge performance and progress.

I propose that, as a starting point, both summative and formative marking should be **diagnostic**, namely we should make it clear to the student how to improve the piece of work and overall learning, rather than simply giving them a grade. This will help to remove the culture where thousands of students are transfixed on their grade and not on what they need to do to improve. If we can shift this approach, we can also improve teachers' workload and get to a place where curriculum drives assessment, rather than the other way around.

Using the words 'not yet'

One great strategy for diagnostic marking is using the two words 'not yet'. This is a fabulous method promoted by Professor Carol Dweck, who advocates the use of a 'Not Yet' grade. For Dweck, a fail grade tells a student, 'I'm nothing; I'm nowhere', but if they receive the grade 'Not Yet', they will understand that they are on a learning curve that gives a path into the future. Dweck asks, 'How are we raising our children? Are we raising them for *now* instead of *yet*? Are we raising kids who are obsessed with getting the top grades?'

According to Dweck, if we feed back wisely, praising students because of their efforts rather than their outcomes, we can develop a growth mindset culture in our students. Young people who engage show 'their effort, their strategies, their focus, their perseverance, their improvement [...] Just the words "yet" or "not yet" [...] give kids greater confidence [and] create persistence.' (Dweck, 2014)

The 'not yet' approach from Dweck has been the most valuable tip I have taken away from her research. It can be used in written feedback, but it is just as effective in verbal feedback. Try marking the first piece of work students produce in the lesson with a simple 'not yet because…' and see the immediate effect. You can't use this technique in your back garden on a sunny day, so why not leave your books at school and provide immediate, meaningful and motivating feedback based on Dweck's research? It's only your senior leadership team, examination boards and the 'observer police' who want to see reams and reams of written feedback. It shows you are working hard. But if it's not required, then why waste the time? Give students the feedback they deserve, today. This a great strategy for everyday use in the classroom.

Where is the best place for me to mark?

Being a reflective practitioner will help you answer this one. You might want to get all your marking done in school, either in your classroom, the staffroom or an empty office, so you don't have to take your work home with you. Or you might find it easier to mark at home in a quiet space that allows you to focus without the distractions you may get at school. We all have our own preferred space and time to work. *You* must choose the environment, the time and the space where *you* can get marking done, and the type of assessment being conducted will also be important.

Using 'not yet' to evaluate and improve your teaching

In my teaching career, I have found that marking for a new term – whether this is before or immediately after a holiday period – is a great way to use the 'not yet' method of diagnostic marking. I look back at my students' targets from the previous term and try to specify whether they have achieved targets set or whether they are 'not yet' there. This signposts students' progress and can be a keystone for planning the term ahead. Obviously context matters: think about the age of the student, subject and stage in the year. For the first lesson back after a period apart, consider what students have forgotten and what path you need to take them on next.

When evaluating the quality of teaching, learning and assessment, the following three things should be taken into consideration:

1. The **what** of teaching, namely what is being taught and when. This is determined by the curriculum and the curriculum should of course trump everything else.

2. The **how** of learning, namely the delivery that makes learning possible. How do we translate the curriculum into the classroom?

3. The **why** of teaching, namely why we are teaching the content and why we are teaching it in this way.

The **why** of teaching is the cognition process of lesson planning but it is often the last aspect on the minds of busy, time-poor teachers and is left behind in many of our day-to-day decisions in the classroom. 'I have lots of time to think about assessment and planning,' said no teacher, ever.

But it shouldn't be like this! If we can all consider the **why** of teaching, we may be able to equip ourselves, as well as our students, to acquire mastery in the classroom. Using the 'not yet' marking approach can be the perfect place to start. Once you know whether your students have achieved their targets, or whether they are 'not yet' there, you can plan which content to teach next term, how you are going to teach it and understand and explain to students the reasons why. See Section 2, Idea 2, p. 70 for more on lesson planning based on the **why** of teaching.

EVIDENCE

In her research paper, 'Even Geniuses Work Hard', Professor Carol Dweck argues that meaningful feedback on difficult classwork can motivate 'students to love challenges, to enjoy effort, to be resilient, and to value their own improvement'. This can all be achieved with the simple word 'yet'. Dweck states that 'yet' 'should be used frequently in every classroom. Whenever students say they can't do something or are not good at something, the teacher should add "yet"' (Dweck, 2010).

In terms of motivation levels, we want students to develop their own habits of self-regulation, and there is compelling evidence that people can learn, and therefore be taught, how to improve their levels of self-control. For example, Tougher Minds – a programme for learning and study to help anybody enhance their personal performance – has been proven to dramatically improve all aspects of school work. In a research project with a group of Year 7s in a school in which I worked, the Tougher Minds programme was shown to help students develop a better understanding of self-control and deploy sophisticated strategies to regulate their own motivation levels.

However, I should warn you that mindset isn't everything. In 2020, Burgoyne et al. found that the evidence behind mindset theory is perhaps not as convincing as previously believed, at least for university students. They concluded that 'the foundations of mind-set theory are not firm and that bold claims about mind-set appear to be overstated'. Their research claims that self-efficacy and need for achievement were found to have more of a basis.

It's also interesting to examine how much 'not yet' can apply for teachers. When it comes to professional development, I would argue that collectively we are *not yet* there in terms of all schools realising the true potential they already have within their buildings. One reason for this may be a lack of teacher agency or autonomy. According to Kirby and Mclaughlin (2016), 'demands to meet externally imposed agendas and specified outcomes have eroded teachers' capacity for agency' and teacher performance, data collection, pupil examination results, performance management and school inspection are examples of this. School accountability can often hinder innovation.

Coaching is often the key driver in teacher agency and evidence drawn from cognitive and behavioural psychology suggests that it improves teacher and student achievement (Sims and Fletcher-Wood, 2016). I know coaching is not yet in place in most schools, but in the happier and higher-performing schools I have worked with, leadership teams are making this happen for all their teachers.

IDEA 3

Live-marking

IDEA SNAPSHOT

Over the years, I've used 'live-marking' – marking in lesson time with the student by my side – to embed formative assessment in my classroom and reduce the workload burden. Why not try it to see if it works for you too?

Allow me to explain how live-marking can be managed and what impact it can have. Teachers are bombarded with marking because it is central to their role, and some teachers and schools yearn to mark every piece of work and record written feedback for the 'marking police'. These folk come disguised as fleeting observers who seek no context about the teacher or student and who flit in and out of classrooms in the blink of an eye and the flick through a book. Parents also expect to see reams of written feedback on their children's work.

Although the teaching landscape is slowly shifting away from this narrative, it is nonetheless more necessary than ever that schools have a clear feedback policy (be careful what words you choose) that is communicated to students, parents and colleagues so that marking is manageable and adds value. We know that feedback is one of the most effective ways to improve learning, but we should stipulate that not everything can be – or should be (see Section 1, Idea 10, p. 53) – marked.

I've been live-marking for my entire teaching career. You probably do too, without realising it. It is a technique that is hard taught and hard earned but it does have many advantages. It does not always have to be written and can be verbal, and there is the benefit of it being there and then in the classroom, rather than two or three weeks later or, worse, when it is too late to adjust decision-making during the learning process.

A research paper was published in April 2016 by the University of Oxford and the EEF, based on survey results from 1,382 practising teachers in 1,012 schools in the maintained sector in England (Elliott et al., 2016). The report found that evidence focused on written marking is of poor quality and that teachers and school leaders should create a marking policy that is effective, sustainable and time efficient. The report looked at seven different aspects of marking and considered the evidence and research currently available in the UK and internationally in relation to each.

The seven aspects were:

1. 'Grading'

2. 'Corrections'

3. 'Thoroughness'

4. 'Pupil responses'

5. 'Creating a dialogue'

6. 'Targets'

7. 'Frequency and speed'.

I will elaborate on three of these seven aspects – 'corrections', 'creating a dialogue' and 'frequency and speed' – in terms of live-marking and how they relate to giving feedback to students in the classroom. While you're considering these three aspects, it's also worth keeping in mind some advice from Major and Higgins in *What Works?* (2019): 1) keep it simple; 2) keep it direct; 3) keep them engaged. In order to reduce your own workload, they suggest asking yourself whether the activity directly contributes to the quality of teaching and learning, whether you have evidence that what you're doing impacts on pupil progress and whether there could be equally impactful approaches that take less time.

'Corrections'

The EEF report says, 'when marking a piece of work, it may feel logical and efficient to provide students with the right answer'. The report then looks at the evidence that discusses how valuable this really is and considers other methods of pointing out and correcting errors when marking student work.

Live-marking can help discourage teachers from providing students with the answers or correcting every single error in a piece of work. Over the last six years, I have seen yellow-box marking evolve into 'zonal marking' or 'zonal feedback' in the schools I have worked in, which has had remarkable results for teacher workload and the impact on students. Zonal feedback is a more targeted approach that ensures teachers and students focus on a specific area of the work (rather than the entire piece), that encourages teachers' feedback to be diagnostic and support improvement (rather than help students create a final product in every activity), and that reduces teachers' workload. See the box on the next page for an explanation of how this technique works.

'Creating a dialogue'

The EEF report discusses 'triple impact marking' (the teacher gives written feedback on a piece of work, the student responds to this feedback and the teacher then responds to this in turn) and 'dialogic marking' (where a written conversation develops between teachers and students). I would not expect any teacher to mark redrafted work unless it was required for external assessment. Does your school? If so, why should we insist that teachers mark the same work twice if we assume the average secondary school teacher has 300-500 students per week and the average primary

Zonal feedback

Choose one aspect of a student's work to assess – just one section – and draw a yellow box around it. Mark it well and in detail, offering feedback (verbally or in writing) that is sophisticated and, above all, specific and diagnostic (see Section 1, Idea 2, p. 14). Avoid assessing the work by giving it a grade because this helps students understand that their work is in progress and 'zooms in' on one area to improve. Zonal feedback focuses students to act on feedback with a clear and specific framework.

The result? You work less. You mark less. You provide specific feedback. The student knows where to work and what to target. Improvements can be identified much more clearly to help aid student progress and this is perfect for addressing bite-sized misconceptions and gaps in subject knowledge.

However, zonal feedback is only effective if:

- You allocate time for students to complete the improvements. This could be in class (as an excellent flying start activity – see Section 2, Idea 6, p. 89) or as a specific homework activity, either to complete one particular piece of work or ensure they are all up to date.

- It is important to re-assess the redrafted work in some form, whether this is a nod of the head or a quick 'Well done, have you considered XYZ?', and adapt the feedback depending on the type of work and age of the student. However, be wary about how many attempts the students need to get things right. 'Mastery requires both the possession of ready knowledge and the conceptual understanding of how to use it.' (Brown et al., 2014) If students do not have the requisite knowledge, you may need to re-teach it (see Section 1, Idea 6, p. 35).

Finally, the pens you use for zonal feedback don't have to be yellow – don't get bogged down with the choice of coloured pens!

teacher is teaching up to ten different subjects with 30 pupils? It is an impossible ask and we must be realistic about workload and the level of impact that can be made from re-marking students' work.

Although the EEF report concludes that there is 'some promise underpinning the idea of creating a dialogue' and that more research is required to test this, I would advocate using live-marking to put a greater emphasis on verbal dialogue that is scripted and targeted to help students improve their work. This means that students can instantly act upon the feedback, all the while significantly reducing written marking for the teacher. I use the question-suggestion-action approach, i.e. the teacher asks, 'Why might XYZ differ from ABC if you increase the amount of 123?'. The student responds. The teacher then provides a scripted response and a suggested action live in the classroom. Only when a student demonstrates that they have acted on that feedback should the teacher allow the student to move on to the next sequence of the lesson or learning. Remember, feedback should improve the learner, not the piece of work.

'Frequency and speed'

Defined in the EEF report as how often students' work is marked and how quickly the work is returned to the students, these are significant factors in teachers' workload and students' expected levels of progress. Couple this with the demands of working through curriculum reforms and teaching students so they can be successful in their exams and the conflict teachers face every week is clear for anyone to see. Should I ask students to redraft their work? Or should I move on and cover the next part of the curriculum? These are both important questions that all teachers will query on a daily basis, forever.

Only you can answer these questions but I would suggest considering them after each marking episode and ensuring that you build in regular opportunities for students to recap on work as part of your curriculum plan. 'Spaced learning' or 'spaced practice' is a learning process whereby content is taught repeatedly in short sessions that are broken up by intervals, during which students complete simple, unrelated activities (see Section 2, Idea 4, Evidence, p. 84). A separate report on spaced learning by the EEF, this time with the Centre for Evidence and Social Innovation at Queen's University Belfast, suggests 'teachers and pupils gave substantial positive feedback about the intervention'. A valid question raised in this study, however, is whether it is beneficial to provide less detailed comments quickly or to take the time necessary to provide more thorough feedback (EEF, 2017b).

Context is everything. What a teacher does with a four-year-old compared to a 16-year-old will always make teaching an interesting profession. However, I do believe that 'less and more often' is the better approach with the recent drive for verbal feedback and research that shows that meaningful feedback delivered in the lesson can make it easier for students to improve. Live-marking permits the teacher to give students concise, regular feedback that can be acted on immediately.

There is a lack of studies in schools on this issue, which suggests that more research would be valuable. The good news is that after five years of trial and error, the Verbal Feedback Project was published in September 2019, commissioned by UCL. The research concludes that 'verbal feedback, when applied well, has a positive impact on the engagement of all students (and gains in progress and achievement) and – at the least – appears to have no detrimental effects'. See Section 1, Idea 10, p. 53 for more details.

For me, the one issue stopping verbal live-marking rising through the pile of books stacked on every teacher's desk is having to provide evidence of marking. If demonstrating evidence is the one reason for marking rather than aiding students' progress, we have lost sight of the purpose of feedback.

Live-marking: pros and cons

As we've seen, there are many advantages to live-marking in lessons:

- It reduces teachers' workload outside of lesson hours.
- It encourages teachers to give feedback that is diagnostic, closing in on specific areas to improve.

- It allows for a dialogue between teacher and student, enabling the teacher to provide immediate feedback and a suggested action there and then that the student has to act upon before moving on to the next phase of learning.

- It gives students concise, regular feedback, making it easier for them to improve their learning.

However, there are some disadvantages to bear in mind if you try to implement live-marking in your classroom. Make sure you think about these points carefully before using the strategy in your teaching.

EVIDENCE

Research into teachers' workload by Peter Sellen for the Education Policy Institute suggests:

- Teachers in England work the longest hours and get paid one of the worst salaries in OECD countries.

- Long working hours are hindering teachers' access to continuing professional development (CPD).

- Long hours, low starting pay and limited access to CPD create a risk of teacher 'burn out', especially in the early stages of careers.

- There is no evidence that additional classroom assistants mean lower working hours for teachers.

- Teachers in 'outstanding' schools (defined by the most recent inspection at the time) tend to work the same number of hours as teachers in other schools, but when compared to 'satisfactory' or 'inadequate' schools, they are less likely to report their workload as 'unmanageable'. (Sellen, 2016)

I once watched a TED Talk that changed my working life. In his presentation 'How to Make Work-Life Balance Work', Nigel Marsh (2010), performance coach and bestselling author of *Fat, Forty and Fired*, said we need to redefine our meaning of success, and can't address the issue of workload alone in personal fixes to health and work. We need a cultural shift in attitude. It's definitely worth watching if you're reaching a crisis point.

As an educator, this is a belief I also hold. The moment I watched the video, it reminded me of the 60-hour weeks I was working, failing to spend time with my family. Bogged down in 15 hours of meetings every week and with a never-ending 'to-do list', I made a conscious decision to disconnect. That same day, I removed all the applications on my mobile phone that connected me to work. I promised to time my marking and mark faster, yet more thoughtfully, targeting

The disadvantages include:

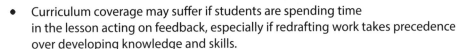

- The teacher can only work with one or a small group of students at a time.

- The teacher must monitor the level of detail provided to avoid spending too long with each group.

- Curriculum coverage may suffer if students are spending time in the lesson acting on feedback, especially if redrafting work takes precedence over developing knowledge and skills.

For me, the benefits outweigh the drawbacks and when used well, live-marking enables students to make progress.

the work I wanted to assess with students. I resolved to use live-marking and ensure students acted on feedback, doing essential work that focused on critical areas for improvement.

My attitude to work changed and I felt like I was back in control. But, I certainly haven't cracked the workload issue from watching Marsh's video. Taking back control and redefining my version of success in and out of the classroom must become a lifelong habit. It's a challenge I still have today running a small education company. Every decision I make is critical to my survival. And imagine if we all did it – we could reshape the workload landscape, particularly on marking, feedback and assessment, in every school.

We need to redefine what we understand as success. Teacher workload will not improve unless teachers' terms and conditions change to free them from 90% timetable allocations, as this would enable them to mark during the working day. This is a view I have held for many years and, with the emergence of emails and technology platforms in the classroom, teacher workload is increasing even further. If that's not possible, and it's unlikely given the cuts to education since 2010 (the DfE finally admitted in January 2020 that funding has decreased over the past decade despite years of claiming it was at 'record levels' (Gibbons, 2020)), marking and teacher workload will never improve. Any solutions will be a fallacy, simply because teachers are not given the time or the pay to do their jobs well enough.

Professor Becky Allen, Director of the Centre for Education Improvement Science at the UCL Institute of Education, says that with technology changing the way information is processed in teaching, 'it is time to step back and evaluate whether the time spent managing pupil attainment and pastoral data is proportionate to its educational benefits' (DfE, 2018).

Live-marking, like any other workload solution, is a by-product of a broken system, but it offers teachers a temporary classroom strategy that can have a positive impact on learning until the epidemic is fixed.

Marking code

IDEA SNAPSHOT

Ensure your students understand the key assessment points, then develop a simple marking code that works for both you and your students (and is in line with your school policy) to help them understand and respond to your feedback and, ultimately, progress in their learning.

Sharing key assessment points with students is absolutely critical, and this is the first step towards being able to use a simple marking code that students will understand and be able to respond to – and that will save you time.

As Professor John Hattie says, it is important 'for the teacher to communicate the intentions of the lessons and the notions of what success means for these intentions' (Hattie, 2009). Sharing this with students before they start the task you are planning to set them will really help to improve the work they produce and their overall learning. If student work is assessed in proportion to curriculum time, it means they receive regular feedback, have the opportunity to see how they have performed against the key assessment points and can improve their work with these in mind.

Here are some ways you can ensure your students understand the key assessment points. They will also help your students to assess their own knowledge before a final assessment:

1. An excellent approach is to give students different pieces of work and ask them to rank them and identify the main reasons why one is better than the other. (I've seen this work well in a controlled assessment research project I worked on with Goldsmiths College in 2004, where student coursework was ranked by comparative judgements rather than by an actual checklist – there is more information about this in my book *Just Great Teaching*.) Once ranked, students should be able to give you the key marking points that make one piece of work better than another. Once this is achieved, the assessment criteria can be provided to lock down understanding. In essence, it's worth testing whether holding back the assessment produces different results.

2. Self-assessment and peer-assessment work wonders. Students grade each other's work and identify the reasons as to why marks are secured or not, helping them to develop an understanding of the key assessment points. This must be done in the right conditions, however. It's impossible to achieve with a difficult class and

the climate for learning must be secure. This will also be a challenge for teachers working with younger pupils who are developing cognitive ability. See Section 1, Idea 9, p. 47 for more on self- and peer-assessment.

3. A 'spoof assessment' or a mock exam will help students assess their own performance against the key assessment points. After the assessment, two answers of different quality could be offered for students to assess using the key marking points provided.

Once students understand the key assessment points, you can use a simple marking code to mark students' work against them quickly and effectively.

Teachers must mark for impact, not for frequency, and this is where many marking policies fail. The frequency of marking must be proportionate to curriculum time. There is no specific rule, other than that marking, written or verbal, should be regular. This is a common-sense approach for schools to adopt across the board. Ensuring that feedback is proportionate ensures equality between departments in secondary schools, or teams of teachers working in different year groups in primary schools. Depending on the subject they teach, some secondary teachers may see their students once a week compared to others who may see the students three or four times a week. In primary schools, teachers see their children every day! So, there really is no one-size-fits-all solution. Whichever way you look at it, it is essential to provide regular feedback that builds in spaced practice and encourages students to engage with it and use it to improve their learning.

This is where a simple marking code can help. It will:

- ensure you can feed back to students more regularly and more quickly

- enable students to engage with your feedback quickly and easily so they can see how they have fared against the key assessment points and what they need to do to improve their performance.

Developing a marking code

I've developed so many marking codes over the past 15 years. Some have been awful and rarely used, while others were too cumbersome for teachers to understand, never mind the students! What works best is simplicity and clear symbols that have stood the test of time.

A quick note, though: while marking codes are typically very helpful, you should make sure you are still in line with your school's assessment policy. If teachers create their own marking code without taking school policy into consideration, they are generating further discrepancies and inconsistencies between classrooms, which can lead to students becoming confused and more workload for everyone! It's a fine balance.

The following is a typical – and simple and sensible – marking code for all schools. For me, the first four symbols would be what I'd want for the perfect set of symbols to use when providing written feedback on a student's work. They are standard protocol in schools across the world. After that, we get into specific grammatical codes for extended literacy and written pieces of work.

Symbol	Meaning
✓	Correct/good point/well written (in more practical subjects, such as PE, this could be a 'thumbs-up').
X	Incorrect/wrong point (in more practical subjects, such as PE, this could be a 'thumbs-down').
Sp	Correct a spelling mistake (these words should be redrafted as part of good retrieval practice exercises to support memory).
?	This does not make sense/the handwriting or sentence needs to be clearer.
^	You need to add a word.
//	You need to start a new paragraph.
e.g.	Provide examples.

NOTE: The above will need adapting to suit your subject and the age group you are teaching.

I don't believe there is much need for anything else for day-to-day classroom assessment. Anything more and it becomes confusing, adding to a student's cognitive load (unless you are teaching SPaG), and will make any marking code too difficult to use and, worse, too complicated for students and parents to understand.

So, what's missing for you? Or is there anything in the above that is irrelevant for your students to progress? Is there anything you could live without? Scribble your ideas for a perfect marking code for your classroom in the table below and share a photo with me on Twitter at #MarkPlanTeach.

The simplest marking code in the world

Symbol	Meaning

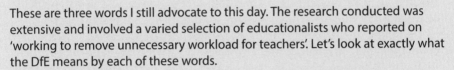

Fascinating research from the Department for Education (DfE, 2016) highlighted three simple words that best summed up useful marking, feedback and assessment:

- 'Meaningful'
- 'Manageable'
- 'Motivating'

These are three words I still advocate to this day. The research conducted was extensive and involved a varied selection of educationalists who reported on 'working to remove unnecessary workload for teachers'. Let's look at exactly what the DfE means by each of these words.

'Meaningful'

According to the DfE, 'meaningful' assessment will depend on the age group of your students, the subject you are teaching and the particular piece of work you are assessing. They suggest that teachers adapt their approach according to the needs of their students and 'incorporate the outcomes into subsequent planning and teaching'.

For me, 'meaningful' assessment basically means that it has to work and have demonstrable outcomes for you and your students. The feedback has to improve the learner as well as the piece of work. When students know the key assessment points, a simple, understandable marking code will help with this. Try using your marking code alongside the zonal feedback approach (see Section 1, Idea 3, p. 18) to reduce your workload even further and zoom in on feedback areas for improvement. But remember that 'meaningful' feedback can also be verbal and does not require evidencing for the 'marking police'.

'Manageable'

The DfE argues that the amount of marking a teacher does should be proportionate to the outcomes that it has for teachers and students, and schools should develop assessment policies that take into account 'the cost and time-effectiveness of marking in relation to the overall workload of teachers'.

I'm pleased to report that more and more schools are now evaluating their assessment policies against the number of pupils whose work a teacher needs to mark. I agree that this should be written into assessment policy, but I believe it should be guidance. Perhaps half the problem with teachers' workload is that we do not guide one another. Instead, we place unnecessary themes into school policy to hold good teachers to account.

CONTINUES OVER PAGE

The 2018 TALIS report suggests that teachers in England have one of the lowest rates of teacher autonomy in all 48 OECD countries (Schleicher, 2018). We need to move towards a position where our teachers are trusted. A marking policy is not statutory. It is something created by school leaders to support consistency. The danger is it becomes something to beat teachers over the head with and leads to *unmanageable* workloads. Quite the opposite to the advice from the DfE research.

So, how do we measure the costs of this workload?

Simple sums will tell you that a secondary teacher working a full-time timetable, with 15 different classes and 30 students in each, will have to mark the work of 450 students. With one period of a 25-period timetable costing the equivalent of £2,000 per academic year, teachers are supposed to spend 10% of their time on planning and assessment. That's two hours per week and equates to 76 hours during a 38-week academic year, or the equivalent, for every classroom teacher to use wisely throughout the year. If we take those original 450 students and divide this by 76 hours, that is the equivalent of 16 minutes per student per year! We can already see this is a huge and unrealistic expectation and costing a teacher's timetable is equally unhelpful.

Something has to change and keeping policies as simple as possible, with the onus on the student to understand the key assessment points and act on feedback, is a good starting point.

'Motivating'

The DfE advocates assessment that helps 'motivate students to progress' but acknowledges that 'sometimes short, challenging comments or oral feedback are more effective' here than 'in-depth' and 'universally positive' comments. The DfE also argues that a teacher 'doing more work than their students […] can become a disincentive for students to accept challenges and take responsibility for improving their work'. See the research from Mihaly Csikszentmihalyi in Section 3, Idea 3, p. 131 for more on why this is important.

How you motivate your students when giving them feedback is best left to you. You know your students better than I do, and we all know that students and their moods are often unpredictable. Routine is critical in the classroom but what they like one day might not be what they like another.

Nevertheless, 'motivating' assessment should help to engage students to make progress. 'Meaningful' and 'manageable' are key here. Brief yet challenging feedback that students can understand, such as a simple marking code, makes sure that the person receiving the commentary will complete more actions than the person providing it. This is more motivating for the student *and* the teacher. If not followed, we end up in a downward spiral where sanctions to complete work outweigh anything positive going on in the classroom.

Psychology and...
feedback

Feedback is a process and not a one-off event. Psychologically, whether you intend it or not, when offering feedback you will be engaging with a student's sense of self as a person and as a learner. Feedback is self-related, often in terms of self-development, and as a consequence, I recommend that feedback should be both motivational and developmental in nature. It should motivate a student to believe that they can make progress and do better. This is often achieved by reminding them of what they have already achieved – in terms of learning outcomes but also in terms of cognitive and emotional processes associated with learning. Feedback has to be developmental by providing clarity about next steps for action. Feedback should result in action. It is important to check the meaning that a student makes from your feedback: has the student understood, in exact terms, what the next steps are and what success will look like?

Feedback is also language dependent and relationship dependent. When giving feedback, teacher language becomes particularly important. You have to think carefully about the language that you use, as what you say is open to being processed differently by different individuals in different contexts. I suggest avoiding the phrase, 'I like it *but*…'. One of the reasons is that once a student hears the word 'but', they may disregard what you have said before the word 'but' – sometimes at an unconscious level – and only focus on what comes afterwards. This can result in the student assuming that you do not actually like their work at all, which was not your feedback intention. Instead, you could say, 'I like it *and*…'.

Firstly, this emphasises and validates what you like. The word 'and' is non-judgemental; it is not processed as dismissive. It also creates a better psychological space from which to engage the student in a discussion about what they think they could have done differently or additionally. There is a huge difference between how 'I like it *but*…' and how 'I like it *and*…' are psychologically processed, especially in terms of the emotional responses and behaviours they can elicit.

Relationships have a fundamental impact on how feedback is given and received and on whether it results in positive or negative outcomes. It is easier to receive feedback when you feel that the person giving it respects you and that it is being given with best intentions and your needs at the forefront. I believe there is one principle that should apply to feedback in all of its guises: feedback should be given for the benefit of the receiver and not for the benefit of the giver.

– Professor Tim O'Brien

Celebrate mistakes!

IDEA SNAPSHOT

We all learn from our mistakes. Making mistakes helps us to learn new things, builds confidence and encourages us to take risks as well as learning when to be humble and when to apologise. In the classroom, providing opportunities for students to take risks, as well as learning how to receive feedback, is critical for students to develop confidence, resilience and the motivation to improve their work.

I wouldn't be the teacher I am today if I hadn't made mistakes or tweaked my practice along the way or, even more importantly, hadn't been encouraged to take risks in a school where trust was given to me as a classroom teacher, a middle leader, then as a senior leader. I was confident that colleagues walking past or into my classroom were not assessing the quality of what I was doing from a thirty-second or twenty-minute observation, regardless of eyeballs and hands flicking through books with majestic grandeur. This was not the climate in which I worked and I hope it is not the one in which you work either.

Teachers make mistakes. So do students and so do school leaders. Yet, these mistakes are mostly miniscule and easy to fix in the classroom. It's fine to make as many of them as you can, as long as you don't repeat the same cataclysmic errors time and time again. And we've all witnessed those…

Encouraging students to learn from mistakes

So, how do we instil this confidence and ability to learn from mistakes into our students in time for them to become self-assured, risk-taking learners and eventually adults?

The answer goes back to the importance of diagnostic feedback. We looked at the 'not yet' strategy in Idea 2 of this section, which could certainly be used to help students understand the benefits of making mistakes, but let's consider here a few more helpful marking strategies that will enable your students to lose their fear of failure.

Delayed marking

In this technique, no grade or score is given on the work (although the teacher can record a grade in their private written or online records). Written comments from the teacher address the quality of the work in terms of the assessment criteria and give guidance as to how to improve. Students are given time to read the comments in class. After some time (e.g. one week), the teacher talks with students individually to discuss the work, the feedback, any improvements required and finally the grade or mark that was given to it.

Delayed marking helps students to focus on the feedback and how to act upon it, rather than simply being demotivated and demoralised by a grade or a score. When discussing the piece of work with each individual student, you can check they have understood what they need to do to improve and make this feel manageable and achievable.

Re-marking

This involves asking students to redo a piece of work for you after a lesson, focusing on how to improve it. Only accept the work if their improvements mean they would score a higher mark because they understand your feedback and have acted on it. This may be difficult to ascertain without actually marking the work, but a check to see if improvements are clear in relation to the original feedback should always be super quick to determine.

Similarly to delayed marking, your (hopefully positive!) comments on the students' second drafts will prove to them that it is possible to learn from mistakes and will encourage them to see the value of considering and acting upon feedback.

Responding to marking

This technique is similar to re-marking. You provide students with written feedback on their work and then ask students to redraft it based on your comments. The students should then write an appropriate response to the feedback, ideally signposting where to find any redrafting. The redrafted piece of work should **not** be marked until the student has responded.

The danger of re-marking in both of these techniques, however, is that it increases workload. We should be very careful about when we ask for redrafted work. It should be a carefully selected activity and we should make sure it is for improvement, not evidence for an observer. Also, to reduce workload when you do re-mark, you could try targeting only one area of the work for assessment by using the zonal feedback methodology. See Section 1, Idea 3, p. 18 for more details.

Peer-assessment

How does peer-assessment encourage students to develop critical thinking and reflection to evaluate their own work and that of others? In an interesting article, Ibarra-Sáiz et al. (2020) demonstrate how the practice of peer-assessment promotes students' competence. The research highlights that the assessment processes must be 'rigorous, credible, objective and participative' and students must give each other quality feedback throughout the process to increase their motivation and commitment and avoid judgements being perceived as 'unfair and discouraging'.

The research offers a model for peer-assessment that I believe is something worth considering to develop a culture of risk, embrace mistakes and develop resilience in all students:

1. Students participate in designing the task and assessment criteria.

2. Students must be trained in making 'evaluative judgements', namely analysing and making decisions about the quality of their own work and that of their peers.

3. Students offer one another peer-assessment and an evaluative judgement, making sure they give each other quality feedback as well.

4. Self-regulation is developed through this process and is also essential in helping students to develop knowledge and skills.

5. The process enables the student to move towards some form of competency.

Shaping student responses to teacher feedback

When it comes to effective engagement with teacher feedback, Sharon Hogan (2019) describes the importance of creating a classroom climate of trust, encouraging risk-taking and building positive relationships between the student and teacher and among peers. Part of Hogan's research focused on students participating in warm-up games in a drama lesson, with opportunities for collaboration appearing to enrich students' responses to teacher feedback. The research describes how the drama teacher offered feedback from inside of the dramatic action, taking on roles and acting with students. One student reported that he was more likely to take on board this feedback based on his relationship with the teacher and the willingness of the teacher to be vulnerable and take risks. Overall, the research highlights that for students to engage in teacher feedback, they must have a positive, safe, respectful, democratic and supportive classroom ambiance. This involves the need for safety, trust and shared power.

Therefore, if we want students to embrace our feedback and learn from it, we must build a space in which we can celebrate all mistakes, including our own. All teachers must work hard to develop a positive, safe and respectful learning environment. This starts with teachers themselves. I've been in thousands of classrooms where this doesn't happen, and this will be for a wide variety of reasons, with some because of the child, and sometimes, on rare occasions, because of the adult.

Metacognitive learning

Recently, there has been an emergence of metacognitive learning: helping students to learn more about strategies that are effective in terms of study and revision, and supporting them to become more aware of the things that they do not yet know. Carole Yue (2017) has published research on improving learner metacognition and self-regulation and she explains how teachers can help students to learn more effectively.

Yue offers three illusions to learning:

1. 'If it is easy to process, then it is easy to learn.' Yue suggests that this goes some way to explaining why some less effective study habits still persist. For example, re-reading (which we know is not effective for long-term retention) is easy to do, so students will therefore be less likely to engage in cognitive processes that could actually promote long-term learning.

2. 'If I test myself, I should only do it to assess what I've learned.' The research actually recommends students test themselves more often and earlier in the learning process.

3. 'If I know it now, I will know it later.' Testing is designed to get the correct answers, but this approach can lead to 'metamemory illusion'. Everyone understands that they forget things, but generally don't have a strong grasp of how much or how quickly they forget new information.

Yue concludes that 'although students are ultimately responsible for their own learning, there are steps a teacher can take to help make students aware of common errors'. This starts with teachers asking themselves about how they teach, as well as making students aware of how they learn. Students should understand the importance of formative assessment and self-testing to combat the above three illusions but this can only be done in an environment in which taking risks and making mistakes are encouraged.

Mastery marking

Mastery marking is the practice of only accepting a piece of work when it is of a specific quality. For example, ask students to continue to redraft and resubmit their work as many times as it takes for them to achieve an 'A' grade.

With the promise of an 'A' grade on the horizon, this strategy will not only enable students to practise learning from their mistakes independently, but also instil in them a sense of determination to produce the best piece of work they possibly can.

Plus, minus, equals (+, –, =)

Mark student work in relation to previous work, but this time only using your simple marking code (see Section 1, Idea 4, p. 24) or even better, only plus, minus or equals signs to indicate whether the quality of the work has improved and whether the marks would be higher or lower. For example:

- if the most recent piece of work is of the same quality as the last, it receives a '=';

- if it is better than the last, it receives a '+';

- if it is not as good as the last, it receives a '–'.

Hopefully, the redrafted work will be full of '+' signs, proving to your students the value of learning from mistakes. However, by using only a simple code of symbols, this technique puts the impetus on the student to look back at the changes they made in their second draft and understand why these had a positive or negative impact on the quality of their work. It will show them *how well* they have learned from their mistakes and help them build this skill even further.

These strategies will ensure your students understand that making mistakes and redrafting are part of the learning process and nothing at all to worry about. This will encourage students to take risks in an attempt to push their work to the next level of attainment, raising their self-esteem and confidence, and helping them to make progress in their learning.

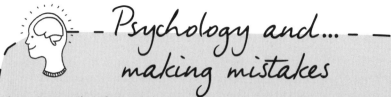

Psychology and... making mistakes

Learning involves forgetting and can be dependent upon remembering what you have forgotten. Learning also involves making mistakes and can be dependent upon how those mistakes inform new learning. Way back in 1978, Donald Norman proposed a tentative model of complex learning. This model focuses solely on the cognitive aspects of learning. Four cognitive stages were proposed:

1. **Accretion**: an organic process whereby new information is processed through multisensory channels. (It is worth noting that at this early point in the learning process, people can already experience cognitive, emotional and sensory overload.)

2. **Restructuring**: we begin to think about, make meaning out of and then act upon information. Accumulation becomes less prominent.

3. **Tuning in**: we 'get it'. The penny drops. Learning becomes meaningful to the learner.

4. **Automisation**: learning is now known. It becomes familiar and automatic. The learner is more independent.

Automisation and independence enable us to, for example, play with knowledge. However, learning can also become less familiar and increasingly unrequired and at this point, we no longer retain it; we forget what has been learned. This is one model, one way of looking at learning. I highlight this model here because when you consider it, you can see that there are stages – as well as transitions and connections between stages – where mistakes will inevitably be made. Learning is a challenge and making mistakes is an essential part of the learning process. I also include it because I assume that you might not be aware of the model. Therefore in understanding the model, you have to engage with the processes that are described within the model itself.

During the learning process, cognition and emotion engage in a complex dance. When we are learning, especially something new, we send out a party invitation to our emotions. Confidence might arrive for one student, anxiety for another. Anxiety can generalise and free-float in an unresolved manner but, given the opportunity, it can also arrive at breakneck speed and locate itself in the learning process. This can encourage some students to doubt their potential to succeed and entice them to do whatever it takes to disengage from learning. One of the tasks of a teacher is to help students to understand that it is possible to embrace mistakes and learn from them.

In 2009, Hattie highlighted the value of developing an environment in schools where mistakes are valued as an essential part of learning (Hattie, 2009). Of course, teachers can benefit from a culture where they are given permission to embrace their own mistakes too.

– Professor Tim O'Brien

Mind the gaps!

IDEA SNAPSHOT

Re-teaching or retrieval practice is a necessary part of any scheme of work if there is an important element of the module, topic or lesson that students just haven't grasped. Don't worry! It happens to all teachers, but the important thing is to spot the 'gap' in your students' learning through marking and assessment and then go back and address it again. How and when you do this is critical.

Psychologist Hermann Ebbinghaus, famous for his research on memory, related forgetting to the passage of time in his 'forgetting curve'. The curve shows that information is lost over time if no attempt is made to retain it (Ebbinghaus, 1885). Of course, a lot more research on memory has been conducted since, with many arguing that there are other factors that affect how quickly we forget information, including the nature of that information and its significance to us. Nevertheless, Ebbinghaus's premise that information is forgotten over time if we do not review it in the days after we learn it is one that many still stand by today and that we, as teachers, see happening before our very eyes (much more often than we would like!). Spaced practice and interleaving are both advocated by cognitive science.

Re-teaching is therefore crucial, but we must understand what, when, how and why we can re-teach to best effect so we can fit it into our jam-packed curriculums. This is where assessment techniques, such as focused feedback, can help.

Focused feedback

Focused feedback involves assessing students' work against one or two specific criteria, which reflect the key aspects of learning that the teacher wants their students to grasp. There may in fact be many different criteria that could be considered, but this technique allows the teacher to provide more focused and detailed feedback that relates to the most important learning points at a particular moment. Often, by breaking the marking down in this way, the teacher can spot the gaps in the learning of both an individual student and the class as a whole. Much of this is now automated in online assessments, but is useful for traditional exams on paper, for example. This is an excellent strategy to deploy when marking mock examination papers.

Closing the gap

So, how do we then go on to close any gaps we have identified? How can we help students acquire the desired knowledge in applying the skills to master a knowledge-rich and crowded curriculum? Perhaps we can find a better way to progress, rather than following a traditional teaching sequence. This would ensure curriculum coverage with enough slack to re-teach gaps in learning to individuals or the entire class when needed.

When I think about some of the best teaching that I have observed, I can extract a clear commonality. No matter how high the standards of assessment or how quickly the students needed to grasp a concept, there was always an explicit model provided and it was a step that *could not* be missed. Sometimes, a direct instruction or modelling in class opened the teaching sequence; sometimes the students had to experiment and investigate that perfect solution. Regardless, the students were *always* clear about what it was they were trying to achieve and what that could look like.

This direct, explicit form of teaching isn't a one-size-fits-all approach. Rather, it is about providing the right level of scaffold, support and inspiration for your students. When done correctly, it can allow you enough time in class to re-teach the aspects of the curriculum that your students are struggling to master.

Here are my top ten tips for using modelling to support students to help reduce gaps in learning:

1. Show what a good piece of work looks like, and how it is created, step by step, piece by piece. Demonstrate the whole process of creation, whether that is the perfect cartwheel, a neatly crafted butt-joint or a well-written argument.

2. Talk it through, and not only the things you decide to do, but also the things that you don't. The class need to hear you say, 'I know it can't be 17 because the answer's final digit is 0' or 'I need to say "sat" but I want it to show that I'm grumpy. I'll use "slouched"'.

3. Model out loud, speaking your thoughts. It is the very thoughts that our students cannot hear or see that they need to understand the most – those times of doubt and uncertainty when you question your knowledge base; the conundrums of which method would be best or which style of recording is most suitable; or those penny-dropping moments when the connections between ideas finally make sense.

4. Make mistakes! One of the hardest skills in the world is editing, especially when you're not yet wise or good enough. Work needs to be modelled. Students need to see that crossing out and making mistakes are part of the learning process and nothing to panic about. See Section 1, Idea 5, p. 30 for more on this.

5. Show students what to do when you don't know what to do. Model 'just drawing a line' when you are not sure of the word to put and don't want to waste ten minutes' thinking time. Demonstrate 'just having a go' at a problem when you don't know where to start. Talk through any doubts you have and how you sometimes just need to try to see what happens.

6. Don't use up all of your modelling tips at the beginning of a lesson. It can be equally (and sometimes more) valuable to stop the class after an initial experiment to address any common misconceptions found, or at the end of the lesson to build success criteria together and challenge thinking.

7. In a classroom climate built on trust and a belief that with good practice you can get better, a visualiser is your friend and a piece of work can be the next top model.

8. Never make assumptions about what the students already know and understand. Never. The most basic things also need modelling – from letter formation and counting slowly to 'what does good listening look like?'.

9. Model the learning in many ways – as imaginatively as possible. It is important that your modelling acts as a creative catalyst and not as an inhibitor, especially for the most inspired in your classroom. They need to see possibilities, not one solution.

10. Have at the forefront of your mind your goal – and within this should be the independent application of whatever it is you are teaching! Some students will be ready to run and make it entirely their own after one tiny exposure. Some may need a little guided work, some may need a confidence boost and some may need the same skill modelled in different contexts many, many times before those connections are forged. Only you will know what works for your students more than any other. A secure overview is essential (see Section 1, Idea 1, p. 7).

Use your marking to identify the gaps in your students' learning and put these modelling tips into practice to close the gaps and provide your students with quality first teaching (see more on this in Section 2, Idea 7, p. 94).

CLOSE THE GAP

Psychology and...
confidence

I would like to reflect on what Ross has said about learning gaps and the need for some students to have a 'confidence boost' to bridge these gaps. There is a fascinating and complex psychological space where teaching transforms into learning. Learning gaps can occur at various places in that space.

If a student spends too long in a learning gap, it rapidly starts to feel like a confidence-collapsing chasm. To boost someone's confidence, you have to know what you are trying to boost. Confidence begins inside your head. When it begins, it is invisible but it does not stay that way. We can see and feel confidence or lack of confidence in the way that people behave. To feel more confident and be more confident, you have to trust yourself and believe in yourself. You have to believe you can do it, trust yourself to step out of your comfort zone, take a leap of faith and then have a go and do it. Creating an environment where people are encouraged to have a go, whilst remembering the value of mistakes, is essential to promote learning. I must emphasise that being confident is not about flooding your mind with positive thoughts and denying the existence of negative thoughts. That is an illusory path to gaining or boosting confidence. To be more confident, you have to acknowledge negative thoughts and emotions so that you can process and deal with them.

Sometimes, the barriers to confidence are inside your head, but they can also exist outside of your head too. The same applies to confidence enablers. If a student needs a confidence boost to help them to overcome a learning gap, explore with them where, why and how the gap might be happening. This helps them to learn about learning. For example, if an emotional factor is relevant, you can encourage the student to identify and name the emotion or emotions that might be holding them back. As a teacher, in your mind, amplify the learning gap, dive in and take forensic rummage around so that you can see what it is that is creating a barrier to learning for a student. You may have to mind the gap but you also have to find the gap. Think in terms of the ecology of teaching and learning, and avoid assuming that a learning gap is inevitably due to a deficit within the student. Barriers to learning do not only occur inside someone's head, they can also occur outside of someone's head too.

– Professor Tim O'Brien

Find and fix

IDEA SNAPSHOT

Although it's important for teachers to identify gaps in their students' learning, it is crucial that we also encourage students to be independent in identifying problems with their own work and areas of the curriculum where they need support. A good strategy is to give students time in class to 'find and fix' their mistakes.

As highlighted in my **5 Minute Marking Plan** (see Section 1, Idea 1, p. 7), once a teacher has spent time adding comments to a student's piece of work, the student should go back and either correct errors or redo parts of their work that need improvement. Obviously this will depend on the context of the work and the age of the pupil. This is not required for every piece of work but it should be a regular exercise to help students learn from their mistakes, develop resilience and ultimately deepen their learning and understanding.

In previous ideas, we've looked at ways in which teachers can identify areas for improvement and encourage their students to correct and redraft their work. However, it is also important that we give students the opportunity to reflect on their work independently and think about where they have met assessment criteria and where they might need to improve.

This is a key part of the learning process (although admittedly harder for Key Stage 1 pupils). It helps your students to identify gaps in their own knowledge so they can improve their own understanding independently or seek support from you. Think about it: every student developing their own personalised action plan. They will be completely in control of their learning, with your guidance. Think about how this will increase their motivation. All the teacher needs to do is to identify which student needs to act on what and when.

So, how can teachers develop a reliable method to help students reflect on their work and build an action plan for their learning? Well, this is an interesting question, which will have countless permutations for different subjects, topics and styles of teaching, but allow me to offer five suggestions that will be timeless in the vast majority of classrooms.

Find and fix

The best strategy to help students reflect on their own work is to give them time to correct and redo their work during lessons. This can be a mixture of quick fixes and a deeper redraft to demonstrate that work meets assessment standards. To take this further, don't mark answers as correct or incorrect but simply tell students the number of answers that are wrong. Ask them to 'find and fix' their mistakes either individually or in groups.

Student marking (self- and peer-assessment)

Ask students to mark their own work and that of their peers using a student-friendly marking scheme. See Section 1, Idea 9, p. 47 for more on this.

Colouring in

Give students coloured pens and ask them to highlight on their work where they have shown evidence of different skills according to the requirements of the mark scheme. This allows students to reflect on their own learning but also shows you whether they understand what is required of them according to the assessment framework or if this is something you need to revisit with one specific student or your class as a whole.

Traffic lights

Ask students to leave red, amber and green coloured dots on their work to indicate areas where they have struggled and areas where they think they have done well. This targets the assessment for the students and the teacher on the areas that need it most. The colour ratings work as follows:

- **Red** indicates areas where the student has struggled, still does not understand or needs further support.

- **Amber** indicates that further work is needed to secure meaningful understanding.

- **Green** indicates that the work is meeting assessment criteria.

The beauty of this process is that students are highlighting to the teacher what *they* don't understand. The teacher can then look over the work, check whether they agree with the students' coloured dots and even give an overall red, amber or green piece of feedback for the work. The teacher then gives the student further support and guidance in any areas marked with red or amber dots and the student redrafts them in an attempt to achieve a green dot. The final assessment can be calculated from the number of green comments actioned against the assessment criteria.

Crack this one and student confidence soars, as does their motivation!

Aim for the next level

Students compare their work to exemplars that are at the next level of achievement. The students identify where they can improve their work in order to emulate these exemplars. They realise that they need to set themselves higher standards and find that it is possible to improve what they thought was already a good piece of work. It also makes the next level feel more attainable, particularly when the example has been completed by a peer.

Psychology and... motivation

It is tempting to think of motivation as being about our motives but it is far more helpful to think of motivation as being about motion: the desire to move from A to B. Inside our heads, we can be motivated to pull ourselves away from some situations – often for physical and emotional protection – and push ourselves towards others.

Learning involves challenges and students are expected to rise to such challenges. To be motivated to set about rising to a challenge, we have to be willing to accept that success does not happen in a straight line. The road to success contains bumpy terrain – it can involve unpredictable twists and turns and there is always the potential for setbacks along the way. This is one of the reasons why resilience is an important factor in achieving consistent motivation. Some students have a secure emotional base from which to rise to such challenges. Others, for a variety of reasons including, for example, the effects of emotional or developmental trauma, difficulties related to self-regulation or the rumbling presence of self-limiting beliefs, will need support in helping them to be convinced that they really can navigate the road ahead. This can even apply to taking the smallest steps on a learning journey.

Our feelings can be a predictor of the nature and duration of our motivation. A student can feel energised and inquisitive but they can also feel anxious and disheartened; feelings affect motivation and behaviour in differing ways. Internal motivation can be influenced positively or negatively by external factors too. The degree of autonomy that a person is afforded, or perceives that they are afforded, informs their sense of self-control and self-determination and will influence motivation. The sense of meaning or purpose a person attaches to the activities and tasks they are engaged in will inevitably influence their motivation.

There are many available perspectives and theories that aim to offer explanatory insight into what motivation is and why it might result in specific types of behaviours and outcomes. For example, biological needs, such as the need to survive, might motivate us to behave in particular ways, whereas psychological needs, such as the desire to be the best we can be, might cause us to behave differently. However, whether they are biological, psychological or social, our needs are interrelated and they will impact upon each other.

– Professor Tim O'Brien

'Fishing without the bait'

IDEA SNAPSHOT

Moderating student work as an individual teacher, a department or as an entire school is important for lesson and curriculum planning and assessing attitudes to learning and progress over a period of time. However, it should be a meaningful process for the student, the teacher and the school in question. It should also drive school improvement without increasing workload or being a process simply for evidence gathering; it is critical that time-poor school leaders learn how to conduct this process reliably and in a supportive manner.

When teaching, it is useful to ask yourself if there is a gap between the learning you *wanted* to happen and the learning that *actually* happened. This can be evaluated in the lesson through questioning and student participation, but it is often after the lesson – when looking at the work completed – that a teacher can really see what learning has (or has not) taken place. There is often a large disparity between teacher delivery and outcome.

Instead of spending hours assessing every single piece of student work in detail, you could use your time to moderate and review the work your students have produced, compare it to previous work and ascertain what your students have learnt. This will show you what needs to be changed in a scheme of work and what classroom activity you could try with your students next. It is also important to narrow the focus when evaluating 'learning'. In a maths lesson, if the subject is equations, what type? And are we evaluating all students, or just certain groups or a single child? Only once we gather sufficient context, can we begin to evaluate progress. The next question is to ask what benchmark we are using to evaluate: the start of the academic year, the previous year or the start of the lesson perhaps?

You should also regularly moderate and review student work with colleagues either in your department or in other parts of the school, so you can all look at work from students in classes other than your own. Triangulating pupil conversations, lesson observations, curriculum plans and work completed in books is a powerful way to improve the teaching programme and would be a useful departmental or whole-school professional development activity if schemes of work require refining in order to improve teacher delivery to meet student needs. It is vital to build frequent moderation into curriculum planning and assessment as a teacher or a department moves through a scheme of work with the students. It will also tell you whether a student is working better in someone else's subject and it may even give you some ideas of how you could teach or motivate that student more effectively in your own lessons.

In the happier, higher-performing schools I've visited, year-team and department moderation happens on a regular basis, where colleagues bring their students' books to help share complex classroom problems and turn issues into solutions. School leaders do not collect books, spend hours locked away evaluating teacher feedback and then return the books with no commentary and simply a colour-coded evaluation. However, in the worst examples, teachers are still provided with a grade on how they provide assessment! Talk about undermining each other.

Work sampling

Now, this is one to discuss with your school leadership team. There has been much discussion that work sampling – namely observers looking in students' exercise books to moderate quality of marking, assessment and teaching – has replaced the frenzy of grading individual lessons and having observers determine the quality of teaching. Thankfully, many school leaders, and the Grim Reaper, have now made a call for evidence to validate how reliable work sampling can be to judge quality of teaching. However, this 'scrutiny' dialogue has not yet seen its death. If anything, it's still viewed as a prominent source of evaluation in our schools, and worse, conducted poorly. I'm no hero! Like most school leaders, I learnt on the job and I have made many of these mistakes and worse. I am now here to share lessons learnt and pitfalls to avoid.

I would support the need for evidence in this area but for too long, schools have either conducted or been on the receiving end of work sampling *without* context. As former school leader and HMI Pam Fearnley would say, observers have been 'fishing without the bait'. They look in students' books at random without any context. The classes, students and teachers are not pre-determined. There are no conversations, even with teachers. No data is used and the process is very much a tick-box exercise.

We are all guilty of this – even me! As author Seth Godin said in 2012, 'Sometimes we can't measure what we need, so we invent a proxy; something easier to measure'. Work sampling is often left to ad-hoc procedures that lead to ad-hoc judgements and conclusions. For example, an observer arrives in your classroom, sits down quietly at the back where there is an empty seat and proceeds to flick through the book of Student A and Student B who are sitting next to them. Then, an assumption is made of the outcomes from what is seen or not seen.

Consider the classroom next door. Same project, same age group and similar ability, but students are working with a different teacher. For the sake of an easy argument, let's just assume both teachers are very similar in manner, style and performance. Another observer completes the same exercise. They arrive in the classroom, sit down quietly at the back where there is an empty seat and proceed to flick through the book of Student A and Student B. Only this time, Student B is absent and the work of Student C is sampled. Student A has lost their book and started a new exercise book last month. This explains why there is no work, but the observer – too busy and miffed that they are having to sample work in their free lesson because someone else is chasing their paperwork too – does not ask the student why the work is missing. There is no context, no conversation with the student or the teacher. Immediately, we are making a dangerously weak process even more unreliable.

However, all is not lost. I do believe work sampling is critical to the life of a school to help assess attitudes to learning and progress over a period of time, but only when completed in reliable conditions.

So what's the solution?

Well, first of all, it is critical that work sampling is conducted in the right conditions, with the input (purpose) and output (outcomes) communicated before, during and after the process. More importantly, the teacher of the student whose work is being sampled must be involved. An observer should never pick students at random for work sampling. They should instead select a range of students based on their prior data or starting points (for example, their Key Stage 2 results) and use this information to assess progress over time. It would be recommended to select a range of students, including high-, middle- and low-attaining students, students from disadvantaged backgrounds (or Pupil Premium students in England) and SEND, G&T and EAL students.

The observer should then:

1. Look at pieces of work by the targeted group of students, keeping in mind that this is *just one source of evidence* and that every book and every student has a story to tell.

2. Have a face-to-face conversation with the classroom teacher, so they can share information about the child and make observers aware of other factors that are not clear from the students' exercise books, such as absence.

3. Interview the students themselves.

When we have 'the bait' (the context), exercise books can show:

- teacher expectations
- classroom routines
- access to the curriculum
- use of the school's marking code
- attitudes to learning (i.e. if students take pride in their work; look for graffiti or ripped pages)
- the quality of written feedback
- if effort is recognised (i.e. if students are proud of their achievements)
- if students are acting on feedback
- if students are making expected progress.

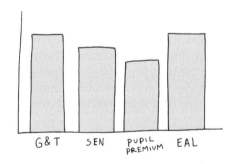

Critically, it's essential to narrow the focus to ensure that research is conducted reliably and any results are valid. However you conduct an evaluation, it's vital that the same methodology is applied in the classroom next door. For example, if you are asking pupils a series of questions in a lesson as part of work scrutiny, these exact same questions must be asked in the next classroom too. If they are not then, with immediate effect, your research is pretty much redundant. You must decide whether to ask open and closed questions. Think about asking an eight-year-old questions: how would your questions change when having to ad lib? What might be the responses from one child who can articulate themselves clearly and

answer complex questions, compared to another child who may need support? When we evaluate, the process must be bespoke so we can better learn what works and decide on interventions going forward.

Note that this process would need to be adapted for practical subjects where performance in plays, sports and music, for example, could be observed in application of knowledge and verbal feedback. Again, this is something the observer would have to complete in the lesson itself with the teacher and the students. The process should not penalise teachers and students simply because of the nature of the subject matter. It should be flexible, but also fair and robust.

It is good to see more and more schools developing their work sampling procedures, without judging individual teachers. Many schools are moving towards a professional development experience, with interventions evolving as a result of regular evaluation. Nevertheless, more work needs to be done to eradicate work sampling as a procedure for judging individual teachers in all schools. There's not much research evidence to suggest that having any marking consistency leads to an improvement in teaching and learning, yet a one-size-fits-all, binary 'marking compliance' is still applied in many schools. Little evidence of red and green pen in a student's book and the teacher is still likely to be viewed as underperforming, a maverick, lazy or non-compliant.

Much more research is needed to find out what evaluation system works best, what methodology leads to reliable assessments about the quality of teaching and if work sampling is a meaningful process for the student, the teacher or just the observer. If it's the latter in your school, then it's about time we all started to change the dialogue of work sampling for the benefit of teachers and students.

EVIDENCE

If you look at sources of research into assessment, particularly comparative research, it is clear that the reliability of marking is flawed when work is marked in different subject areas. In a study by R. J. L. Murphy, eight GCE examinations in a variety of subject areas were compared for marking reliability. The results showed that subject area, the number of questions on the paper and the type of questions asked all had an effect on the reliability of marking in these examinations (Murphy, 1978).

On Google Scholar, there are only 227 entries for 'marking reliability' in England. It makes me wonder if marking in the classroom, and not just in public examinations or in studies conducted in a university environment, is equally unreliable. How often have you moderated work with colleagues in your department, only to find one of you is wildly off the mark? I'm sure we all have. There could be a million and one reasons for this: time, accountability, type of assessment, distractions, workload, and whether the work is high stakes or not.

This means that moderation is essential, whether as a department, a whole school or more broadly. However, teachers are not very comfortable with being judged by another professional, largely because of what it can do to your confidence and worse, your career. It is therefore necessary that if we, as a profession, are to use students' work as a measure of teaching and student performance, we need to improve our methodology for doing so.

And what of school inspectors? Can they really look through pupils' books with any degree of reliability? I've been conducting 'deep dives' in secondary schools my entire career. It took several years of senior leadership even to get close to something I would call 'reliable' and that involved many months of development, trial and error and triangulation. How anyone can conduct this process with any degree of reliability in 1.5 days is beyond me.

The Grim Reaper has chosen to use Cohen's kappa, a very insecure data set (see McHugh, 2012), to develop their deep-dive methodology and implement this nationally. This was based on earlier research (DfE, 2019a), in which they tested with nine (just nine!) inspectors whether their approach to workbook scrutiny was a reliable method for assessing the quality of education.

I'm not saying that we shouldn't look in students' books. Of course we should want students' work to be reviewed and standards disseminated, but we must consider the methods used, and the focus and expertise needed to draw conclusions. We must think about the observer's subject specialism, what questions are asked of pupils and whether these questions are consistent and public knowledge. Was there a conversation with the classroom teacher before, during and after the lesson? And what happens if there is insufficient evidence? What constitutes evidence in classrooms that have no books?

Smarter not harder

IDEA SNAPSHOT

Introduce self-assessment and peer-assessment into your marking routine to ensure your students are working harder than you are! Take some time at the beginning of term to teach them how to do this effectively and you will reduce your workload and make your marking smarter for the rest of the year.

As Nigel Marsh, performance coach and bestselling author of *Fat, Forty and Fired*, says, 'If you do not define your own work-life balance, your employer will' (Marsh, 2010). This piece of advice transformed my life as a school leader and is great advice for all teachers too. Students should be working harder than the teacher. Marking is driving teachers crazy in all types of school and college settings. In many respects, the term 'smarter not harder' is unhelpful. However, even though external assessment is, I believe, the root cause for the marking burden, there are things that schools and teachers can do to assess pupils' work more effectively.

Teachers like to maintain high expectations and it's all too easy to be snowed under with workload, but we must be flexible, not just in the classroom but with our own workload and wellbeing. To do this, it is vital that schools reduce the quantity of checklists and encourage staff to work smarter, not harder. This can also be achieved by individual teachers in the classroom, but it is not possible without taking something away so we can replace it with something new.

Teachers should not only be defined by student outcomes, which is our current problem in education. If education is to make any progress with teacher work-life balance, we need a serious debate. Success in education cannot be defined by examination results alone and the sooner we realise this at government level, the sooner we will start to rescue teachers who are reaching unprecedented burnout levels.

To have mastered a skill or concept, a student must possess a deep understanding and be capable of applying that skill or concept creatively and in a range of different contexts. Therefore, a good teacher does not work harder; they simply work smarter and more effectively to ensure a greater impact on students. I know, I know. There I go again and you're about to throw this book against a brick wall or bash it across another colleague's head! What you want to know is how can I work smarter when...

- My line manager has told me to mark this way.

- Our school policy says…

- The Grim Reaper is due any day!

- Our leadership team are conducting a work sample next week. I must mark, mark, mark…

- [Student name] has asked me to mark their work tonight and I can't let them down.

- A parent has just emailed me and they want a reply before they arrive at reception in the morning!

- I'm leading department moderation this week. I must take an exemplar set of class books to show off!

- I teach 450 students every week.

- [Any other reasonable excuse.]

One strategy I would recommend all teachers adopt is a deeper understanding of memory and cognitive load theory (see Section 3, Idea 4, p. 134). When teachers understand memory and how knowledge is retained, I believe they can work at a smarter level. However, in terms of assessment, it is also wise that teachers invest heavily in equipping their pupils to be able to self- and peer-assess in lessons.

The importance of self–assessment and peer–assessment

Self-assessment and peer-assessment are not simply tools we may choose to use but are the foundation of the reconceptualisation of the roles of the teacher and student and the entire process of education. Part of the learning process is equipping pupils to be able to address their own misconceptions. Ultimately, the role of a teacher is to develop the whole child, encourage them to self-regulate their behaviour, their choices and the learning.

As we saw in Section 1, Idea 1, p. 7, all assessments should be related to the curriculum that is being taught in the school. Most schools in the UK will have started the process of developing a revised assessment framework in line with the curriculum reforms that have taken place or will have adopted one that has been created externally. Those readers who are finding that this process of change is still the order of the day will know that it requires time-consuming, ongoing evaluation and adjustments.

Nevertheless, we should now be looking for greater depth in the assessment that takes place. As Tim Oates, Group Director of Assessment Research and Development at Cambridge Assessment, said in 2014:

'Study fewer things in greater depth, so a deeper understanding of central concepts and ideas can be developed. Assessment should focus on that.'

We must work hard to teach pupils schematic content that allows them to develop a network of concepts, rules and facts in relation to one another. This mental model, alongside concrete experiences, will allow pupils to develop metacognitive approaches to their own learning. We are some way off all our teachers and families being aware of this approach, but we are already on this journey in our schools.

Self- and peer-assessment provide the perfect opportunity to build depth into assessment. Learners need to develop assessment skills and it is worth investing time in this, particularly as part of a whole-school, department or phase approach. So how can we ensure that self- and peer-assessment are valid tools that will decrease workload in this context?

Self–assessment and peer–assessment explained

If used well, self- and peer-assessment can improve students' understanding of a topic. It is essential that teachers provide their pupils with a clear assessment criteria, and in some cases, this may be developed alongside students. Providing a range of assessment strategies, as well as modelling a response, is supported by research. Time to think as well as the quality of feedback will help you get your class working more efficiently and intelligently.

You should never use self- and peer-assessment simply because your school or an observer insists that you do. It should form a concrete evidence base for students' learning and be a motivational and reflective opportunity for each individual child in your class. Both self- and peer-assessment are skills that need to be taught so that they become a routine in your lessons. They are part of the permanent dialogue between teaching and learning. They also form within the learner an ongoing process of:

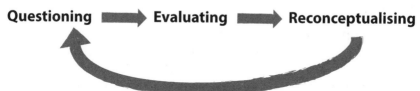

Questioning ➡ **Evaluating** ➡ **Reconceptualising**

This is an inquiry cycle that develops the cognitive process. However, given what we know about memory and cognitive load theory, how pupils evaluate and reconceptualise feedback (which then leads to improvement) would be another book in itself!

Self- and peer-assessment can sometimes be unreliable, with the largest deviation found among students who do not understand the success criteria or the objectives. But whose assessment has more value? Is it the teacher's assessment or the learner's assessment? Arguments could be made for both. So, in order to provide a more accurate snapshot of the child's learning, perhaps a balance between the two is required. Of course, the next question is: what is the correct balance?

Before you mark an important piece of work, you should try to get to the point where it has gone through the following cycle of assessment and improvement:

Self ➡ Peer ➡ Self

Then you should take in the piece of work and assess it from your point of view, as the teacher.

But how do we get our students to self- and peer-assess successfully? A simple way of doing this is to use C3B4ME: see three other pupils before coming to me (the teacher) for feedback. Here are some other strategies you can use to get started.

Student–friendly mark scheme

Create a student-friendly mark scheme at the beginning of term and ask students to mark their own work and that of their peers against it each time you want them to self- or peer-assess. You could also share with them your simple, five-symbol marking code that you developed in Section 1, Idea 4, p. 24 so they are marking in the same way as you! This may take a bit of time at the start of term but will save you plenty of marking later on.

Highlighting

Give your students a set of coloured pens. Ask them to highlight on their work where they have shown evidence of different skills according to the requirements of the mark scheme you gave them.

Margin marking

To get students used to assessing their own work, put a mark in the margin indicating how many mistakes there are in a particular paragraph or section. Then ask students to look back through their work to find the mistakes and correct them.

Retrieval practice

In the excellent book, *Powerful Teaching*, Pooja Agarwal and Patrice Bain (2019) share their deep insights and research into the power of retrieval practice as a method for transferring knowledge and providing meaningful feedback and as a form of assessment. The critical thing that must be stressed is that retrieval quizzes must not have a score or a grade. When we remove the summative assessment, we reduce the stress associated with learning. Retrieval practice should be about self-assessment, not testing. As Agarwal and Bain write, 'Retrieval practice is when we embrace mistakes rather than emphasize perfection.' Agarwal and Bain offer ten benefits for teachers using retrieval practice. They say it:

1. Improves learning and retention of information in the long term.

2. Increases higher-order thinking and transfer of knowledge.

3. Identifies gaps in knowledge, providing formative assessment for teachers.

4. Increases students' metacognition and awareness of their own learning.

5. Increases student engagement and retention.

6. Increases use of effective study strategies.

7. Increases advance preparation for class.

8. Improves students' mental organisation of knowledge.

9. Increases students' learning of related information that isn't initially retrieved.

10. Increases students' learning in the future by blocking interfering information.

How and when you use your quizzes matters to retrieval. A simple fix is to ask students what they learnt yesterday, rather than today. At all times, make sure they *think* first and then write something down or say it out loud. This ensures thinking has a concrete response. Michael Chiles (2020) offers some further ideas for retrieval practice:

- **Revision clocks:** Students condense knowledge into a one-page summary using a visual graphic similar to a clock face. This layout makes information easy to reference using dual coding as a process to support long-term retention. Keywords can be replaced with symbols or acronyms, with diagrams and pictures used to support detailed explanations. The clock face can be used over time to increase desirable difficulty to improve retention.

- **Graphic organisers:** Graphic organisers use design thinking and dual coding to present ideas and knowledge in coherent maps. For example, chunk, compare, sequence, and cause and effect methods allow information to be presented to support the development of schemas. Comparative information can be presented as a Venn diagram or cause and effect models can be presented as an input-control-output method to demonstrate the sequencing of information.

- **The Leitner System:** This is a spaced practice method using flashcards to improve memory. You could have an equation on one side of each card and the solution on the other, or a country on one side and its capital city on the other. The Leitner System is designed to increase the level of difficulty by increasing the number of times you test between each answer. The key point is to quiz yourself regularly on the answers you do not yet know, but still coming back to those you do, albeit less frequently.

One great thing about retrieval practice is that it's the perfect opportunity to offer students verbal feedback (see Section 1, Idea 10, p. 53). If we could get everyone to accept verbal feedback as an immediate and valuable method of marking in the classroom – that does not need to be evidenced with written comments or stamps in books – we'd all be starting a revolution!

EVIDENCE

In their article 'Formative Assessment and Self-regulated Learning: A Model and Seven Principles of Good Feedback Practice', David Nicol and Debra Macfarlane-Dick report on research they conducted in relation to formative assessment and feedback. They suggest that students should be seen 'as having a proactive rather than a reactive role in generating and using feedback' and offer seven recommendations for teachers that will help students take control of their learning:

1. 'Clarify what good performance is

2. Facilitate self-assessment

3. Deliver high quality feedback information

4. Encourage teacher and peer dialogue

5. Encourage positive motivation and self-esteem

6. Provide opportunities to close the gap

7. Use feedback to improve teaching.' (Nicol and Macfarlane-Dick, 2006)

As highlighted in the research, students can only achieve learning objectives if they understand what these goals are in the first place and if they take some ownership of and can assess their own performance. In order to facilitate this, teachers must create structured opportunities for self-assessment and provide feedback because teachers are 'more effective in identifying errors or misconceptions in students' work than peers or the students themselves'. However, the report recommends that feedback should be more of a dialogue to ensure students understand and can act on it. Verbal feedback and 'live-marking' would be good examples of this.

The report also draws upon research (including Carol Dweck's) that suggests that 'high-stakes assessment' can have a negative impact on students' motivation and self-esteem because it focuses students on performance and not learning goals. The report therefore suggests that several 'low-stakes assessment tasks' are more beneficial in helping students to self-regulate. Time and time again, research points to regular low-stakes quizzing rather than one-off, high-stakes performance to improve learning. I do wonder if our examination system undermines everything we know about learning.

Crucially, the report provides five key strategies to 'close the gap between current and desired performance', all the while reducing teacher workload. These include: allowing students to resubmit work; using two-stage assignments where feedback on the first stage informs the second; modelling; providing action points; and asking students to identify their own action points in groups. Finally, it's essential for teachers to have good progress data.

Verbal feedback is good enough!

IDEA SNAPSHOT

In previous ideas, we've seen that feedback is one of the most effective ways to improve learning, but we should recognise that not everything can (or should) be marked. To strike a balance between quality and quantity of marking, let's take a look at what work we should not be marking and how verbal feedback can help.

Why are we so fixated on marking every piece of work that our students produce? What influences this? Is it assessment policies, school leaders or external inspectors? Parents or teacher habits? I do wonder whether what examination boards require teachers to do to evidence for qualifications trumps even the best teaching and learning policies, at least in terms of marking. Often, by the time a teacher has made it through a pile of books, weeks or months after students have submitted them for written comments, the opportunity to discuss and improve the work in class will have already passed us by!

How do we move forward in the future and strike a balance between quality and quantity? What will add most value to the teaching and learning process? Where does assessment fit within the curriculum? After all, the curriculum should be driving teaching and assessment, not the other way around. You will see evidence of this not being the case in schools where every classroom is testing students at a particular time of year, rather than according to the needs of the curriculum. Of course, school seasons follow a particular rhythm, but learning does not.

I have never been a fan of marking. I know some teachers are. However, I do recognise that marking, or at least assessment, is a teacher's greatest planning tool. There is a good reason why 'mark' comes before 'plan' in this book. Assessment informs our planning, and planning informs our teaching. The teaching provides us with assessment data, and hence, here is our *Mark. Plan. Teach.* loop.

The more I have delved into policy and teacher workload, the more I have been thinking seriously and cognitively about assessment. Dare I say, I actually enjoy marking and assessing much more now that I understand it at a deeper level than I did as a newly qualified teacher. What if our initial teacher training providers equipped all teachers with a better understanding of not only their subject knowledge, but also assessment and how we learn?

In terms of written feedback, marking should:

1. develop high-quality assessment

2. develop diagnostic feedback across all subjects

3. be realistic in terms of teacher workload

4. be approached with common sense by the school leadership

5. work for students and teachers from the outset.

What should not be marked?

With all this in mind, let's take a brief moment to look at what teachers should not be marking to give them more freedom to mark less but with greater impact. The first thing I should mention (again!) is that context is king. Secondly, teachers should never be afraid of telling a student that their work is not yet good enough for them to spend time providing written feedback. Of course, how this is communicated is essential for student motivation and C3B4ME is a fantastic verbal feedback strategy to lessen a teacher's workload and place more impetus on the student to improve their work before submission.

Here are some other suggestions for reducing the quantity of work we mark in favour of the quality of our marking.

- Do not provide extensive or unnecessary written dialogue. In particular, you should avoid 'triple marking', whereby a teacher first marks the work, then a student responds to a teacher and the teacher is expected either to re-mark the work or reply to the student's actions. Research from the EEF says 'there is no strong evidence that "acknowledgement" steps in either dialogic or triple impact marking will promote learning' (Elliott et al., 2016).

- Do not bother leaving comments such as 'well done' or 'good' on students' work. It is a waste of time. Say it in person when returning the work to the student and only write clear action points in their book. Better still, reduce your workload and try zonal feedback (see Section 1, Idea 3, p. 18) or simply give instant verbal feedback.

- Do not promise students, parents or colleagues a particular frequency of marking work. It will mean you are marking for the sake of adhering to this schedule. As discussed in Section 1, Idea 4, p. 24, marking should be regular and proportionate to the curriculum. It's that simple.

- Do not mark every single page of work and avoid tick-and-flick. Instead, simply leave the work blank and communicate to the student exactly what will be assessed.

If you are still desperate to mark as much of your students' work as possible, we can increase the amount we mark, while still reducing the amount of time we spend on marking, by swapping extensive written feedback for verbal feedback.

Verbal feedback

Why do we assume that written feedback is the best and only kind? Written feedback is not the most valuable type of assessment, and nor is it the best evidence of a conversation between pupil and teacher. Worse, just because it is evidenced in a student book doesn't mean that it counts towards progress. This philosophy is slowly changing, but we are not there yet.

For me, the sooner that schools move towards verbal feedback techniques, the better for teacher workload and for every child. At the same time, schools should be working hard to change perceptions so parents understand that if something is not written down in their child's book, it does not mean that the assessment has not taken place.

Verbal feedback stamps

I have been calling for the abolition of stamps on students' work since 2014. Stamps indicate that a teacher has provided verbal feedback and are a by-product of an accountability system that requires teachers to evidence feedback to internal and external observers. I'm not afraid to say that they are absolute nonsense!

Unless a student is able to recall that conversation exactly, the stamp is also meaningless to the student. It may serve as a visual reminder between teacher and student that something did happen, but I suspect its impact is negligible. While working with 30,000 teachers across 15 countries using methods from the first edition of this book, I have asked thousands of teachers, 'Where is the evidence that verbal feedback stamps improve outcomes?' In a profession that seeks evidence and research, we are still waiting.

Of course, context matters. Every school requires some flexibility and 'stamping' student books with 'smiling stars' or a 'thumbs-up' can be a useful motivational tool, but 'verbal feedback given'? I'm not so confident. If we want to provide the conditions for teacher autonomy, where teachers are trusted to get on with the day job and school leaders are free to create the conditions in which teachers can thrive, we must help one another remove these poor proxies.

Imagine this: instant verbal feedback, provided there and then, with a meaningful and motivating return to the student, but without a single pen stroke! And how would we know it was working? Well, allow me to introduce you to the Verbal Feedback Project...

Verbal Feedback Project

It is with great satisfaction that I present this classroom-based research project, published in September 2019 in collaboration with UCL, as evidence that 'speaking with pupils' (using a range of in-class assessment techniques) does make a difference to pupils' outcomes. The findings of this research, conducted in seven disadvantaged state schools across England, are clear:

'Our findings suggest that verbal feedback, when applied well, has a positive impact on the engagement of all students (and gains in progress and achievement) and – at the least – appears to have no detrimental effects.'

The aim of the report was to identify what common approaches to verbal feedback led to positive outcomes for disadvantaged students. Please read the original report, disseminate the findings with your leadership teams and challenge any inspectors who visit your school, telling them that day-to-day marking – in its traditional form – is no longer king!

I am often asked, 'How do I evidence verbal feedback?' and 'How do I convince my school to abandon written marking?' The research project offers a detailed list of benefits, shown in the table below alongside the related evidence as reported by the teachers involved in the study.

Benefit	As seen by…
Improved engagement	• Involvement in lessons, homework, discussions and practical work • Attitudes to learning • Effort grades • Self-regulation • Being on task • More active in lessons • Enthusiasm • Independence and resilience • Raising hands
Improvements in attainment	• Attainment grades improving across the year • Achieving at or above targets • Responding to feedback • Expanding their areas of knowledge • No detrimental effect on progress • Better-quality work • Choosing the subject at GCSE
Increased confidence	• Students said they were more confident • Reported in lesson observations • Willingness to join in discussion • Regularly volunteering
Improved attendance	• Overall average improvement in attendance
Better completion of work	• Improved completion in lessons • Better presentation • More writing in assessments • More willing to stick at tasks
Improved relationships	• Higher level of participation in group discussion • Listening to others • Student–teacher relations • Peer-to-peer relations • Having a sense of community

Source: McGill and Quinn (2019)

For me, the biggest takeaways from the research are that:

1. Improved lesson planning allowed the teachers to provide better-quality, more creative and more focused delivery in the classroom.

2. The teachers became more confident with the pupils and shared their findings with other teachers across the school.

3. Almost all teachers reported a reduction in their workload. They spent less time on marking and as a result their teaching improved because they knew their students better and developed better relationships.

What if all teachers sat beside their students in lessons, rather than on their own after school hours marking books at their desk (or worse at the dining room table) or uploading assessment data onto an information management system? What if we could empower all teachers to sit beside their pupils more often in lessons, delivering scripted feedback in micro-conversations to reduce the burden of written feedback?

EVIDENCE

In May 2017, the EEF published a research summary on 'Feedback' as part of its Teaching and Learning Toolkit (EEF, 2017c). In consideration of the evidence, the report concluded:

- Effective feedback 'should be specific, accurate and clear (e.g. "It was good because you...", rather than just "correct")'.

- Feedback should be about 'challenging tasks' because this will 'emphasise the importance of effort and perseverance as well as be more valued by the pupils'.

- Teachers should consider 'the challenge of implementing feedback effectively and consistently'.

This supports the idea that not every single piece of work a student produces needs to be marked. As teachers, we should be more selective about the tasks we choose to give feedback on because marking some tasks will have more impact than marking others. This will reduce the amount of marking that we do, giving us more time to ensure that our marking is genuinely useful when we do decide to feed back on a task. There is no point simply giving a cursory tick or cross or scribbling a hurried 'good' on every piece of work. We must sacrifice quantity for quality, allowing ourselves the opportunity to provide in-depth feedback that will help our students to progress.

Section 1: Summary

· ·

What we have been looking for in this section of the book are smarter ideas to reduce workload and improve the impact of our marking. No one can argue with that, surely? We know that marking will never disappear from the life of a teacher but we also know that the landscape of teaching is in flux and how we go about assessing students and equipping them in the classroom is evolving. Remember, too, that there are psychological factors, such as motivation, understanding needs and reflecting on the cognitive and emotional aspects of learning that underpin your practice.

Unfortunately, the research we need is not yet in the eyes and ears of every school inspector or school leader, so if you are lucky enough to be part of action research in your school or you discover a hidden gem to help combat teacher workload and change the marking dialogue, share it widely and loudly.

To conclude this chapter, here is a summary of the ten high-impact, evidence-based ideas I have suggested to improve your marking:

1. Develop a 'secure overview' before setting and marking an assessment. Consider where you are in the curriculum, the starting point, the progress and the context of each student and the purpose of setting and marking this specific piece of work. The curriculum should determine your assessment strategy, not the other way around, and this will help ensure your marking impacts on teaching and learning.

2. Use the powerful words 'not yet' in your marking to motivate students to improve their learning and develop resilience.

3. Create a culture of live-marking in your classroom to help your students progress more quickly and to reduce your workload outside of lesson time.

4. Ensure you are using a marking code that works for both you and your students and remains in line with school policy to help your students progress and save you time.

5. Encourage a culture of redrafting in your classroom where not every piece of work is the finished article and mistakes are used to improve learning.

6. Use marking and assessment to spot the 'gap' in your students' learning, then go back and re-teach anything that students haven't quite grasped.

7. Ask students to identify gaps in their own learning and understand how they can 'find and fix' mistakes and problem areas themselves.

8. Moderate student work and marking as an individual teacher, a department or an entire school to inform curriculum planning and monitor progress, but never do so without taking context into account.

9. Make your marking smarter and ensure your students are working harder than you are by introducing them to self-assessment and peer-assessment. Take time at the beginning of term to teach them how to do this effectively and you will save yourself time for the rest of the year.

10. Don't give extensive written feedback on every single piece of student work. Be selective about the tasks you choose to mark and use verbal feedback to provide your students with quality, not quantity, in your marking. The research is now clear: when applied well, verbal feedback strategies have a positive impact on students, with gains in progress and achievement, and appear to have no detrimental effects.

Section 2:
PLAN.

When I was a young and inexperienced teacher, I spent hours and hours planning lessons. It's a shame to see this still being expected of teachers twenty-five years later, especially among those with experience. Schools I have worked in would insist that teachers write lessons out in detail and then submit the plans to observers one week in advance. And as a newly qualified teacher, this was expected for every lesson. I've also heard of primary school teachers having to complete weekly overviews and being asked to submit these ahead of each week of teaching.

Even though the dialogue is shifting in most English schools, can you believe some schools are still forcing their teachers to do this? I can understand why it is requested in primary schools or in some secondary schools where classes are shared between teachers, but doing this for every lesson regardless of context really adds to teacher workload. It's like asking all drivers to resit their theory test every time they jump into a car to drive it away. It's worthy knowledge but we know drivers generally get better with road practice, and theory is useless without the practice. And why do we still insist in all routes into teaching that trainee teachers provide detailed lesson scripts that lead observers through lesson sequences, when the observers are not the ones actually teaching the lesson? Of course, teachers will always need to plan lessons and those new to the profession have to learn that process, but there are alternatives. Some initial teacher training providers are now looking at reshaping lesson plan scripts and also reconsidering evidence collection for qualified teacher status.

Is there a need for lesson planning on mass-produced templates or can teachers simply develop a lesson plan sequence that is coherent and clear and gets the best out of their pupils? Forcing teachers to complete a lesson plan on a particular template does not promote teacher autonomy. It simply increases workload. I've seen some large multi-academy trusts offer templates that are a useful starting point for reducing workload, but the key question is: can a teacher then adapt the content to suit their own style and context? Is there a need for any teacher to write – never mind submit – a lesson plan, other than when going through initial teacher induction? It's a crazy mindset we have in our profession. I'm all for developing and tweaking practice, but where is the freedom to trust teachers and help reduce their workload as they develop a repertoire and gain experience? After many years in the classroom, teachers should be permitted to rely on this experience to save them time when it comes to preparing for lessons. When I started to think deeply about writing this section of the book, I was inspired by a blog written by Jude Enright in 2013. Although Jude's blog dates back several years, it is still just as apt as it ever was before. Jude writes about how little time she had to plan lessons as a member of the senior leadership team in her school, meaning she relied on 'door knob lessons' – lessons she planned while turning the door knob to enter the classroom:

> 'When I joined [senior leadership], my lessons were invariably door knob lessons. You have so much extra to worry about, to solve, that you have very little time to spare and plan lessons.' (Enright, 2013)

I would argue that school leaders should also plan lessons, but of course, leadership workload gets in the way, and there are sometimes emergencies. Nonetheless, whether teacher or school leader, classroom lessons should be everyone's number one priority. All this goes to show that instead of asking each other to waste time writing things down, we would do better to trust experienced teachers to do what's right for them. We should also involve all teachers in planning for curriculum coherence.

In this section of the book, I provide you with a range of options to consider for lesson planning. We will question what we've always done, as well as consider cognitive processes to help better understand the mechanics needed behind planning to inform not only what a teacher needs to teach, but how and why.

For the past fifteen years, I've been using the **5 Minute Lesson Plan** to frame the process of planning on one page. It's perfect for working smarter and definitely reduces workload. There's a good reason why it's had nearly two million downloads on my website! All you need to do is trial it – nothing works for everyone, remember – and if you like it, suggest using it in your school as a framework for all lesson planning thinking, and perhaps curriculum planning, to help remove any unnecessary bureaucracy and burden placed upon you and your colleagues. It's a great model and it has evolved deeply over recent years, and now has a digital version too, not because of changes to 'external accountability' or other phrases often bandied about in the education sector, but because I've rediscovered the importance of planning lessons the right way. For me, this means finding the balance between effective use of time and impact in the classroom, as well as what the research recommends about cognitive science and learning.

Find my 5 Minute Lesson Plan here: www.5minutelessonplan.co.uk

The right way

When we think about the right way to plan, we must consider countless scenarios, for example age, subject, time of year and how the curriculum will be assessed, and also what we know about cognitive load, memory, and social and emotional aspects of learning.

The main issue with lesson plans is that what is written in the plan is not what happens in the classroom. We know that students can be very unpredictable, which is why it's important that teachers learn from experience and are always adapting to meet the needs of their students in every lesson. It is vital for teachers to plan, but it's impossible to be able to predict every detail of a lesson. What teachers can do instead is roadmap the lesson as a whole, scripting out the highlights from an already mapped-out curriculum plan, and targeting what students can learn on this intended journey.

Lesson planning must be a memo to self, to help a teacher reduce their cognitive load by having the key points of the lesson sketched out ahead of them. Today, with the emergence of online curriculum planning tools, much of this can now be stored online in a scheme of work. This can include hyperlinks that lead to PowerPoints, resources and videos.

I remember vividly when an experienced middle leader came into my classroom to observe me as a deputy headteacher. 'Do you have a lesson plan?' he asked. I smiled, said 'no' and carried on teaching the class. I was modelling to colleagues what I also wanted from them – to plan their lessons for the students in front of them, not for a passing observer.

So, despite my obvious desire to quash detailed lesson plans, this does not mean we should all ignore the process of planning or encourage new teachers to ignore it. Planning is a fundamental section in this book: it is part of the teaching cycle that connects marking (or assessment) to teaching. Without a plan, your teaching is guesswork. It's impossible to map out every single lesson in a detailed plan, but it is important to have the key concepts written down somewhere. The hard work of planning should already have been done when mapping out the curriculum, syllabus and medium-term schemes of work. We should encourage our teachers to have 'planning schemes', drawing out learning pathways from greater curriculum plans that map out key aspects of the knowledge and skills to be taught. This grand scheme can then be used to filter what needs to be learnt in class. 'Stickability' – or 'what learning should stick' – is what lesson planning should hinge upon and is something I explain in much more detail in Section 2, Idea 4, p. 81. This all feeds into a lesson plan of sorts, but not a one-off lesson plan written out in detail on paper.

The thinking process taking place in your working memory when you plan lessons provides a lot of detail that doesn't necessarily need recording. Writing things down does reduce any extraneous load on working memory, but you don't need to record everything in minute detail. Instead, you should try to capture the key elements of learning in a simple planning framework, such as the 5 Minute Lesson Plan. What I believe is great about focused and simple lesson planning is that it helps us concentrate on what's important. We are not necessarily focused on *what* we are teaching, but *why* we are teaching it (see Section 2, Idea 2, p. 70). More explicitly, we are thinking about the learning itself, rather than classroom activities.

The planning process

Planning is a process, not a product. It has one purpose: to enable high-quality delivery, which meets the needs of students. So, before you start reading my ideas on the process of lesson planning, take a moment to reflect on what you think teachers should be planning for in the various stages of a lesson. Use the table below to record your thoughts.

The planning process	What you will be doing and what the students will be doing
Start of lesson	
After initial start	
While students are working	
Towards the end of the lesson	
End of lesson	

Did filling out this table help you to frame the process of lesson planning or did it at least make you start questioning your planning habits? Once you've read the ten ideas I present on lesson planning in this section, revisit your completed table and see whether you'd do anything differently in light of my suggestions. Let me know using the hashtag #MarkPlanTeach.

Now, let's get started!

A cognitive process

IDEA SNAPSHOT

Planning a lesson is a cognitive process – a reflective process – and is not a form filling exercise. It is important that teachers always think about the bigger picture. How does your lesson plan fit into your scheme of work or the topic that you are teaching? What knowledge are students coming to the lesson with and what would you like them to take away? In this idea, I encourage readers to reflect on what students should *learn*, not what they should *do*, as the starting point in the process of lesson planning.

L esson planning is a learning curve and teachers will often adapt methods handed down to them by their mentors or enforced by school policies. There is no single solution for planning, no silver bullet or exemplar methodology, other than a teacher trying out different techniques and learning from their successes and failures. This pattern of trial and error will be repeated with each new intake of students and every time a teacher moves to a new school. Crucially, when evaluating a lesson and considering ways to move forward, teachers must remain reflective. This is an essential characteristic in our profession.

It is vital that teachers understand planning as a course of action, a process of unfolding teaching and learning into something that is accessible for those sitting in the classroom. It is a thinking process, and developing good habits of thought about lesson planning is of fundamental importance for all teachers. How to master lesson planning is a lifelong journey.

When you start planning a lesson, you should first think about the bigger picture. It's important to consider what's going on in the classroom before the actual lesson, and where you see yourself currently with the students. Breaking down what you want students to learn can often reveal skills or knowledge they have to acquire and that need to be taught.

As obvious as it sounds, your planning must first consider *what students should learn* before giving any consideration to what you want the students to *do* to reach this goal. Throughout each stage of lesson planning, ask yourself 'why?' and connect the learning episodes with the intended outcomes in mind (see Section 2, Idea 2, p. 70 for more on this).

What you should not do

All too frequently, planning starts from the wrong place. Teachers find an excellent activity or resource and do their utmost to integrate it into their lesson plan, re-engineering the schemes of work in order to make their lesson workable. It's backward planning and takes away the hard work already done in curriculum planning. There's nothing wrong with integrating enticing resources and activities into lessons – it's what makes teachers creative and enjoy their work – but it should never be in place of planning lessons with curriculum sequencing and retention in mind.

In *Lean Lesson Planning*, Peps Mccrea suggests that the planning process should have a 'lean mindset', meaning it should be all about quality and not about quantity. All too often, teachers start planning lessons by thinking about *how* students will learn something, without first considering where students are and what goal they need to reach next. The bigger picture is often not examined. Mccrea, an experienced lecturer in teacher education – someone who has the responsibility to impart lifelong habits for great lesson planning – says that there are two 'classic traps' that teachers can fall into:

1. 'Activity-focused planning'
2. 'Coverage-focused planning' (Mccrea, 2015).

In the first edition of **Mark. Plan. Teach.**, which drew upon the action research conducted in my former school, we added a third: 'over-planning'. It's hard to argue against these, so let's look at each in turn.

'Activity–focused planning': when did you last do this?

You come across (or try to find) a good activity and then reverse engineer the lesson objectives to match the likely outcomes of the activity. Over time, this can become an exercise in keeping students busy and leads to more *doing* than *learning*. This is known as 'Parkinson's Law'.

'Coverage–focused planning': how much do we rely on others?

This begins with using another teacher's learning objectives (from a colleague or a textbook, for example), rather than considering your own students' needs and how the objectives could be interpreted or adapted for them. Over time, this can become an exercise in getting through the curriculum or covering everything required for an assessment, rather than understanding your own lesson planning and the students in front of you. There is a need for off-the-shelf lesson planning to help improve teacher workload, but this shouldn't be used as an excuse for teachers who can't be bothered to read the curriculum plans or who rely on ready-made PowerPoint presentations.

'Over–planning': how often have you done this?

Too many activities? Too many objectives? I have definitely been guilty of this before and I'm sure every teacher has too at some point in their career. You fail to break down lesson objectives (and no, they don't need to be written down on the whiteboard or in students' books, or worse, checked off at the end of the lesson to see if students almost hit the lesson plan targets) and then realise during the lesson that you are trying to cover too much. Over-planning generally leads to under-learning; the pressure to match what you had intended to teach with the actual outcomes of thirty individuals every lesson already only has a one in thirty chance of being successful. That's very slim odds.

How do you like to plan your lessons?

How important is it to you to have every learning episode planned out? Do you stick to your plans most of the time, or are they simply a tool to help you crystallise your ideas? How do you store, organise or reuse your plans? Do they end up in a folder tucked into a drawer or hidden away somewhere on your computer to then be forgotten about or regurgitated next year when teaching the same project with another class?

Dialogue has shifted significantly for most teachers in terms of recording individual lessons, but many newly qualified teachers still find themselves having to record lesson plans on paper for their own benefit or for an observer. Once teachers reach a certain level of experience, I believe lesson plans, however you prefer to work, should be roughly sketched out but generally kept in our explicit consciousness. However, with over twenty individual lessons to teach per week, this becomes a real challenge in terms of an individual's cognitive overload.

The 5 Minute Lesson Plan, which was published on my website in 2007, is still the number one resource accessed by teachers across the world. Some action research I conducted with Angel Solutions, the organisation that helped me build the digital 5 Minute Lesson Plan in 2014 (www.5MinuteLessonPlan.co.uk), sampled 500 lesson plans. 44% of the lesson plans included a total of four learning episodes, with more student-led episodes than teacher-led episodes. Lessons with four learning episodes were more likely to be led by a teacher in the first episode and by students in the last episode. More often than not, the teacher facilitated the beginning of the lesson, and this was then followed by a period of student-led learning.

Research by TeacherTapp, an online mobile application that analyses teacher behaviours, found that only one in five teachers deviate from their planned lesson. I would be curious to learn the demographic data of this survey to gauge what teachers were working in such contexts, but the blog post suggests the results were higher for teachers in disadvantaged areas, where prior knowledge may be patchy, and for newly qualified teachers who are developing their subject knowledge.

Lesson planning varies dramatically for teachers who teach A-level students and teachers working with Reception classes. So for me, what's important is the process of planning, regardless of how many learning episodes you plan, whether you keep your lesson plans in your mind or put them down on paper, and what you do with them after the lesson has been taught.

What you should do

To avoid these traps, ask yourself not 'how can we get to X, Y or Z?' but 'where are the students starting from?'. Once this is established, planning can help shape where you want students to get to in the lesson, and subject knowledge, resources and activities can be introduced around the purpose of the lesson. 'Wait', I hear you ask, 'how will I know when students are there?' and 'why is it vital that they reach X, Y or Z?'. Once a simple framework is established in the mind of a teacher, the final eureka moment is knowing how to engineer a method for students to reach the goal of a lesson.

If this all needs to be written down in a lesson plan, it can hopefully be for your benefit only and not for any observer. Even better, if the script needs to be recorded for the lesson itself, it should take less than five minutes to do because in your working memory, the hard work has already been completed. This also helps you to communicate your lesson plan to your students effectively.

If you cannot describe your lesson plan in less than thirty seconds, it's already overcomplicated. You should aim for excessive clarity and precision in your mind, so you can articulate what you want your students to learn and the interventions you have selected in class for them to use. Explanations should be phrased in such a way that students will quickly understand what they are aiming for. This is the bigger picture; hard graft, namely the process of planning, filtered into a succinct thirty-second lesson plan. As Jim Smith says in his book *The Lazy Teacher's Handbook*, one of the key sources used to develop ***Mark. Plan. Teach. 1.0***, as you reduce the amount of time you spend actually teaching, you can start to observe the learning more (Smith, 2010).

Lesson planning: an art or a science?

I've always believed that teaching is an art form but that over the years, I have adapted my techniques considerably and have made my teaching style a science. But my views could be challenged easily. As Alexander Makedon argues in his paper 'Is Teaching a Science or an Art?', 'whether teaching is an art or a science depends on which definition of teaching we adopt, or what we think the goals of teaching should be'. He does, however, suggest that this is a question worth pondering:

> 'If art is not different from science, then it makes no sense that we should have two different terms in our language to describe essentially the same thing [...] There must be certain underlying principles or practices in science which we can't reject without at the same time becoming unscientific, and the same may be said regarding art.' (Makedon, 1990)

So, is lesson planning an art form or a science? Perhaps it's both? Or neither?! For Mccrea, planning is a form of 'architecture', an 'exercise in design [that is] a stormy marriage of process and creativity. Where science and art collide.' Mccrea writes *Lean Lesson Planning* as a deliberate attempt to make the lesson planning process simple with a roadmap of three acts:

Act I: 'Lean foundations' introduces the 'meanings, mindsets and habits underpinning the lean approach'.

Act II: 'Habits for planning' details the 'core habits of lean planning'.

Act III: 'Habits for growing' provides strategies for growing excellent classroom practice.

Act II begins with a chapter on 'backwards design', which is poignant for us in terms of the cognitive process of lesson planning. Mccrea argues that 'backwards design' leads to better solutions. This is something I have grappled with in my senior leadership roles in school. School leaders need to be well ahead of the workforce in terms of whole-school deadlines, providing resources and guidance to their staff in time for various new initiatives or professional development to take place or new deadlines to be met. We have to plan events or activities with the end goal in mind. This is very similar to what we do as teachers in the classroom, and although the time we spend teaching decreases as our responsibilities increase, the habits I acquired in the formative years of my career were still very much evident in how I managed senior leadership processes.

In fact, I discovered a strategy that enhanced my planning while undertaking my master's degree in 2004. It is something I apply in all aspects of school life. 'What?', 'Why?', 'How?', 'What if?' and 'When?' are the simplest, yet most effective, questions to ask yourself when forward or backward planning. This simple questioning technique can be implemented when planning lessons or teacher training days, when producing policies or when leading school meetings.

Planning with the end goal in mind enables planning for optimum learning. It's a matter of changing the lens and sharply focusing everything you do on *learning*, rather than on activities you want your students to do. Instead of 'what do I need the students to do?' or 'why do I need the students to do this?', ask yourself, 'why do I need students to *learn* this?'. This self-regulatory reflective thought really does sharpen the teacher. Once you've made this leap, you can then start to hone in on the cognitive processes of lesson planning, meaning you can reduce cognitive load and think more coherently.

Following on from this idea on cognition, I will unpick the stages required for lesson planning and suggest a process that all teachers should consider.

Psychology and... reflection

If 'I teach and you learn' was as simple as it sounds, then absolutely anyone without any qualifications could be a teacher. But it's not that simple. Teaching and learning are complex. One of the challenges of being a teacher is responding to individual differences and dispositions within groups. To do this, you need a plan. To create a plan, you need to reflect – you need to be a 'reflective practitioner'. The process of reflection is of critical importance in any needs-related context.

Teachers are called upon to be reflective practitioners – raising consciousness of the meaning of their own experience. Reflection is a higher order psychological activity that involves the perceiver interacting with the perceived: it is a form of subjective critique where we step back from our familiar world in order to establish new meanings and construct new responses. When reflecting, teachers are encouraged to problematise experience – to become deliberately puzzled – so that they can build new repertoires for teaching. A teacher can engage in 'reflection-in-action' or 'reflection-on-action'. The former is an analytical response that occurs in situ and the latter occurs retrospectively post activity; both are context dependent and context respondent.

Schön (1983) is a key initiator of the discourse of teacher as reflective practitioner but his model is open to critique. Firstly, he posits reflection as an individual activity but teachers do not exist as individual entities; they exist in communities of practice. Therefore, group reflection that is participatory is required alongside individual reflection. Also, a reflective practitioner may well think about the 'doing' of practice but this does not necessarily mean they are a reflective theoriser. It can also be proposed that teaching is so complex that it calls for constructions and responses that are not based upon the intellectual processes of critical reflection at all. The proposition here is that teaching involves an anatomy of intuition and reflection, as a process can stifle intuition and block creativity.

The process of reflection, with its emphasis upon the critical analysis of predicaments, challenges and dilemmas, ensures that both experience and pedagogy remain under constant scrutiny. As teachers become more reflective, they also become more reflexive: continually engaged in researching their own practice and interrogating their own theoretical frameworks. By definition, the job of a reflective practitioner is never finished.

– Professor Tim O'Brien

The 'why?' test

IDEA SNAPSHOT

Once you have identified what you want students to learn in your lesson (Section 2, Idea 1, p. 64), you should then turn your attention to how your students will get there. You should apply the 'why?' test to all the learning activities you plan to include to ensure each one will deliver the learning you want your students to achieve, in the time you have allocated to it. As teachers, we must establish a mechanism for our students to understand *why* they are learning things, rather than just *what* they are learning. This will not only help to deepen their understanding but will also increase engagement in the classroom.

As adults, we can all recognise the time in a child's life when they repeatedly respond, 'Why?' to everything that you say. As a parent, this can be very frustrating – particularly when trapped close together on a car journey – but it is, thankfully, a phase that normally only lasts for a brief period of time. Nevertheless, after years of frustration and trying to quash this exasperating habit, it is strange for me to admit that asking 'why?' is something I would promote for all teachers – and for every child!

'Why?' is a higher-order thinking question than 'what?'. It seeks a greater understanding of the world around us, challenging our working and long-term memories to switch declarative knowledge into procedural knowledge. This is simply building schematic maps in our memory to articulate and use facts and rules and turn this knowledge into action. This means it's easy to explain what scheme of work you are teaching, but it's much harder to explain why. 'Why?' helps us to unpick concepts and problems using a higher order of thinking and deepens our learning. Although we don't know the exact science behind how we learn best, we do know that understanding – or at least asking ourselves – 'why?' requires a greater depth of thought than simply being asked to recall via 'what?'.

Let's look at how this applies to lesson planning.

The dangers of over-planning

As we saw in Section 2, Idea 1, p. 64, over-planning can be a very common problem among teachers, especially when they are going to be observed. This tends to lead them to focus on activities in order to satisfy observers and their checklists, rather than on episodes that are intended to have a genuine impact on students' learning. But how can you recognise that you are falling into this trap? Well, the first quality control check is simple: ask yourself whether you believe that you are spending too much time lesson planning.

If the answer is 'yes', what external factors are influencing this? If it's likely to be line manager or school expectations, then workload and teacher mental health must be questioned. If this isn't the problem, then you should make sure your lesson activities are focused on learning and not on control. Over-planning and teaching to the middle (rather than differentiating successfully) can be signs that student behaviour is hindering teaching and therefore impacting on the quality of the learning that can take place. Worse, when teachers are dealing with a difficult class, control can feel like the best (or only) way to share knowledge.

In this case, simplifying planning is easier said than done. Particularly in the first few weeks of teaching a new class, simplification is something that is etched into the dreams of all newly qualified teachers. They often question how more experienced teachers can waltz into lessons with no more than a board pen and have children lapping up their every word and powering through reams and reams of work.

All teachers need some time to gel with their students. Detailed lesson plans often go out the window in the first few lessons, even for the most experienced teachers. But regardless of the circumstances, a focus on learning should always be your long-term aim. Rather than teaching to control, in order to then be able to teach, let's think about how planning can lead to a heightened sense of confidence in being prepared for a lesson and in keeping students readily engaged. When I say engaged, I don't mean making a lesson loads of fun and including various wacky tasks involving you and your students singing and dancing on the tables. Getting students engaged in their own learning is hard earned and can only be secured with routine, rigour and recognition of hard work. This is where the 'why?' test comes into play.

Using the 'why?' test in lesson planning

When planning a lesson, ask yourself 'so why are we doing this?' about every single activity you include and question the length of time you allocate to it. This will help you check that the activities are supporting you to deliver the learning you want to achieve and whether there is a more efficient way of doing it. If an activity is not making a significant difference to the teaching and learning in the time you've allotted to it, then drop it. If this becomes habit, you'll start to master the art of planning for learning. Once this technique is embedded, you'll find yourself enjoying a sense of freedom in your day-to-day time management, as lesson planning will feel much more worthwhile and less onerous.

You should also make sure you can explain the 'why?' behind each element of a lesson, clearly and succinctly to your students. This will improve their understanding of their own learning and help keep them engaged for longer, as they will appreciate the importance of each task. How you do this without increasing unnecessary information is critical. See the MINT strategy and redundancy effect in Section 3, Idea 1, p. 76. You can support the 'why?' of a task through modelling and exemplar work and if you can bring these two things together, you will start to cultivate the roots of a very special classroom. Let me explain how this can be done.

Learning objectives

How often do you question your learning objectives? The precision of your language really counts in making learning stick but this does not mean that students should copy down objectives or that you even need to have any objectives at all. I know, radical, right?

A practice commonly subscribed to by teachers is to 'publish' learning objectives at the start of a lesson and collectively share them so that everyone knows what the purpose of the lesson is. There is no harm in this and of course context matters. However, in some cases, when chasing consistency for work scrutiny, teachers ask students to routinely copy the objectives out into their books and there's your evidence. Objectives covered.

However, as Dr Debra Kidd points out in her brilliant book, *Teaching: Notes from the Front Line*, this isn't always the best use of lesson time:

'Across schools all over the country, little clones write objectives in their books copied from boards plastered with two letters, LO, or two words, WALT (We Are Learning Today) and WILF (What I'm Looking For) […] Even if in every lesson, just two minutes are spent on this, that is 10 minutes per day, 50 minutes per week and 32.5 hours of learning lost per year!' (Kidd, 2014)

Surely it would be best just to get on with the learning. Instead of starting your lesson waiting for students to copy out objectives, why not start it with a retrieval practice exercise? Remember, this should not be a high-stakes assessment and can be as simple as asking students, 'What did you learn last lesson?' By making students think longer term, you're asking them to retrieve information and this helps it stick.

Retrieval practice can also help us to sequence our lessons and our curriculum plans. In *Powerful Teaching*, Agarwal and Bain offer a three-step methodology for students to better retain information in their long-term memory: 1) encode: getting information in; 2) storage: when information sticks; 3) retrieval: getting information out. Take a look at your current schemes of work and highlight which parts of the curriculum plan are deliberately designed to: 1) put information in; 2) help information storage (using storytelling and schemas); 3) consciously quiz pupils to help get information out. Think about these three different elements when questioning the 'why?' of your lesson planning. Try using the grid below to get you started.

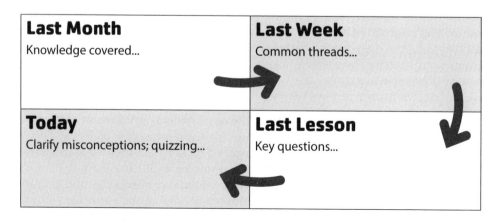

Last Month	**Last Week**
Knowledge covered...	Common threads...
Today	**Last Lesson**
Clarify misconceptions; quizzing...	Key questions...

Modelling

Finding ways to get students to meet and master lesson objectives is tough. Goal setting or sharing lesson objectives can have a meaningful impact on student progress, but not if how you share or record objectives is prescribed in a specific way that adheres to checklists or that is used to beat teachers over the head. To improve teacher autonomy, it would be my advice that every teacher chooses what suits their students and subject, and selects when (and when not) to share, copy or record lesson goals. Regardless, in all examples, whether for a one-off lesson or for a series of lessons for a project, teachers must *model* the success criteria, namely why we are learning what we are learning, in some shape or form.

This has been a feature of some of the best teaching that I have observed and is cited in numerous research papers by the EEF, Rosenshine and Hattie, to name but a few. No matter how high the expectation, how brilliantly the students were working on their own or in groups, or how good the students' work was, there was always an explicit model of the success criteria for the lesson or project. Students must always be clear about what they were trying to achieve and exactly what that could look like.

Why this is so important is fundamental. How often do you hear students say, 'Do we have to, Sir?' or 'Why are we doing this, Miss? Can we do this instead?' In terms of planning, teachers teaching to set curriculums must have answers for 'why' students need to learn, for example, trigonometry or the American Civil War of 1861, so that they understand the cognitive need for learning, develop a deeper understanding of these topics and can see how they can apply this knowledge in the future, rather than just being able to regurgitate facts. This relates to cognitive load theory, which links the amount of effort being used in the working memory to how well we learn and retain information in our long-term memory. Understanding 'why' requires students to put in some hard work. It also requires teachers to ensure they offer explanation and detail.

If any teacher can master this, then it's a classroom environment I would love to observe. It is largely an unknown area for teachers and an approach, in terms of a new era of evidence-rich teaching and neuroscience to understand what works and why, in which we are only just scratching the surface.

Tips for modelling success criteria

Here are a few strategies for teachers to model success criteria (the lesson objectives or the 'why?' of learning) and tackle this aspect of teaching:

1. Show what a good piece of work looks like. Talk it through and share your thoughts.

2. Celebrate mistakes. Show students what to do when you don't know what to do.

3. Build a classroom climate based on trust and a belief that with good practice, you can get better.

4. Never make assumptions about what the students already know and understand. Ask lots of questions and seek feedback.

It isn't one size fits all. It's about providing the right level of support and inspiration for your students. That's the true craft of teaching, and it begins with planning.

EVIDENCE

Do we really want our students copying learning objectives off the whiteboard and into their books? Every lesson, every day? Is copying out 'L.O. I can… so that…' the only means of sharing with children what they are learning and why they are learning it? These are things that teachers have become accustomed to in recent years, as teacher agency has been squeezed across the UK, but surely the answer to all these questions is no.

Do school leadership teams want their teachers to write lesson objectives on the board and have them on display every lesson? I don't. However, if I were to seek consistency because it may be viewed favourably by external agencies, then how would I answer that question? Well, my moral answer would still be no. We must ask ourselves whether this habit is present in our schools because we fear what external watchdogs want. If we want to deliver on our teachers being trusted, we have to create better conditions for our teachers to be autonomous. Does having a student regurgitate what they are learning in a lesson to a visitor prove that learning is taking place? Of course not. Instead, we should be doing what's right for our students.

As we saw in Section 1, Idea 1, p. 7, John Hattie's research suggests that 'goal setting' has a d=0.68 impact on student outcomes. This equates to progress of approximately half a grade over an academic year, so learning objectives clearly do have some impact. However, this doesn't mean simply asking students to record objectives or recite them every lesson. Doing so does not demonstrate progress or learning and simply supports evidence chasers, who want to appease observers when they examine students' books. It is not something that should be asked of students anywhere. Instead, we should be making sure students understand *why* they are learning what they are learning to help build a deeper understanding, encourage the application of knowledge and improve engagement. So do share and demonstrate learning objectives, but for goodness sake, don't write them down for anyone other than you or your students.

A little research into the matter...

In 2020, I caught up with John Hattie after he published a new meta-analysis of educational research on feedback: 'The Power of Feedback Revisited' (Wisniewski et al., 2020). The research considers his earlier findings from *Visible Learning* (2009) and takes into account assumptions from his work *The Power of Feedback* (Hattie and Timperley, 2007) and the importance of interpreting different forms of feedback as independent measures.

The early research of *Visible Learning* found the type of feedback made a difference to its level of impact, with praise, punishment, rewards, and corrective feedback all having low or low to medium effects on average, but corrective feedback being highly effective for enhancing the learning of new skills and tasks. Feedback using video or audio and computer-assisted feedback were found to have medium and high effects, with written comments being more effective than providing grades. If we approach this research from the point of view of learning objectives or success criteria and how teachers could set goals, it is critical that we look at feedback as a loop for learning to reinforce what should be taught next.

Hattie and Timperley (2007) argued that feedback can have different perspectives:

1. 'feed-up' (a comparison of the actual status with a target status)

2. 'feed-back' (a comparison of the actual status with a previous status)

3. 'feed-forward' (an explanation of the target status based on the actual status).

Wisniewski et al. write, 'Additionally, feedback can be differentiated according to its level of cognitive complexity' and later in the paper, they claim, 'One of the most consistent findings about the power of feedback is the remarkable variability of effects.' It has been shown that the majority of feedback in classes is task feedback, the most received and interpreted is about 'where to next', and the least effective is self feedback (feedback about personal characteristics) or praise feedback.

The researchers in this new paper say they are digging deeper into past research and removing duplicate studies that may influence overall effect sizes or recommendations. So, where does this leave teachers now in terms of feedback? Well, the academics conclude that feedback must be recognised as a complex and differentiated task; feedback has many different forms with, at times, quite different effects on student learning; and most importantly, feedback is more effective the more information it contains.

Put simply, feedback, on average, is powerful, but some feedback is more powerful, and this is what teachers must now consider when setting goals and using pupil responses to re-teach.

Storyteller...

IDEA SNAPSHOT

Lessons that are well pitched use imaginative teaching strategies. A colleague (she is now my wife) once told me, 'tell the students a story'. I knew this and had already been doing it subconsciously, but until I'd heard it spoken out loud, I'd never really tried to make it part of my lesson planning. I use this strategy in school assemblies and teacher training events. But how can we integrate engaging strategies into our lesson plans to hold our students' attention while also supporting their learning? Having a clear rationale to work with is essential, and it can make all the difference with lesson planning and delivery in the classroom.

Misbehaviour has no place in the classroom, yet it would be naïve to think it doesn't crop up for every teacher at some point or another, even for the most experienced and even in the least challenging schools. Misbehaviour rears its head in many forms, including non-verbal and non-physical manifestations, which sometimes start outside the classroom (or online) and then arrive in your lesson for you to deal with.

Every teacher must consider how they can secure students' attention in class and ensure all are safe, focused and ready to learn. It can be a challenge for teachers to impart any topic – from the simplest to the most difficult – to thirty students at a time. Whether in a one-off lesson or in a series of lessons as part of a longer-term project, every teacher needs to be able to hold the attention of all their students at any given moment.

It's important for teachers to use engaging teaching techniques at the right time so they can capture the minds of students. Think of a teacher as a television presenter, an actor or a comedy compère standing at the front of a large audience in the West End. How do they hold the attention of the crowd? What are these unwritten rules that just say, 'they've got it'?

For me, teachers who can hold an audience are all of the above. They are comic geniuses, actors and actresses, presenters and politicians all at the same time. They are storytellers who capture the attention and imagination of every student, even the hardest to reach…

Nevertheless, 'engagement' takes a great deal of unnecessary criticism in schools because it's a misnomer for 'having fun' in class. Politicians seek to impart their experiences of school onto classroom policy and processes, assuming what happened thirty years ago will suit the students of today. There are so many myths associated with teaching among the general public. Most rely on their episodic memory, a section of our long-term memory that can be emotional and unreliable. Our memories of school will fail us. People recall personal stories in their lives, rooted in time and place – a bit like a film where you are the star of the show. The problem is these types of memories are not enough for academic learning and, dare I say, for people outside of education to hold a reliable view of what teachers and schools should be doing. Teaching is not a mass-production conveyor belt with templated teachers ready to be deployed into any school following a bite-sized teacher training course. Teachers need time to grow and refine their practice, and what external agencies fail to recognise is that every teaching technique, style or resource should be used appropriately, with context and at the right time to ensure maximum impact for students.

For example, there is no point using a tablet just for the sake of completing 'online research' for a project. Nor is there any point in a teacher standing on a row of desks like Robin Williams (a.k.a. English teacher John Keating) in *Dead Poets Society* to 'seize the day', if there is absolutely no chance they could develop students' knowledge and understanding of *A Midsummer Night's Dream* by doing so. They may be able to 'engage' students in the lesson, but are they learning?

However, this is certainly not to say that technology or imaginative teaching strategies should never be used. There is a time and a place for all classroom strategies but we should make sure they will actually help the student make progress before we decide to use them.

Teaching with a story

Have you ever considered teaching with a story? If you haven't already, watch *Dead Poets Society* and think about what the late and the great Robin Williams does as John Keating to engage his students. He encourages them to 'make [their] lives extraordinary'. It's certainly not a one-off, whimsical idea. Keating's ability throughout the film to engage with his students is hard earned and gradually leads to a place where he is deeply touched by their infamous parting gesture, 'Oh Captain! My Captain', which is the moment he realises his teaching has made a lasting impact.

Stories will help you gain your students' attention at the start of a term and throughout all the lessons you will be together. They build relationships that are exciting and meaningful (without you working too hard) and you can use them to lure students into learning. It's not needed every lesson, as we all have our bad days, but a good story is often enough to secure the minds of even the most challenging. It's all about connecting on the same level. After all, that is what makes teaching, teaching. Our life experiences can enrich our classrooms and that should *never* be ignored.

Linking a story to lesson content

In the fabulous book *Connect the Dots*, Tricia Taylor (2019) argues that 'children benefit from experiencing a concrete, episodic experience prior to learning more abstract concepts'. When it comes to telling stories, they will be more powerful for pupils when holding objects, attending school plays and going on field trips, rather than just experiencing the theory. Pupils remember more when emotional memories are backed by hard concepts and facts. So, what evidence do you need for your school leadership team to get the school trip to the local theatre approved?

However, it's essential to have a clear rationale about how the story you want to tell will be used in class and how it links to your lesson content. Remember, this is not about finding exciting activities and building an entire lesson plan around them. As I suggested in Section 2, Idea 1, p. 64, always start by thinking about the learning you want to take place in the lesson. Jot this down for some upcoming lessons in the table below, then note down some of your favourite films, books and/or personal experiences that might help bring this learning to life. In the third column, think about how your story might then link to any activities or resources you intend to use in the classroom to develop learning further. I've included an example for a design technology lesson to get you started.

Learning/curriculum content	Film/book/experience	Classroom suggestion
Example: Problem solving and mechanisms (design technology)	**Example: *The Man Who Touched the Sky* (book)**	**Example: Making rockets**

Show me a photo of your completed table on Twitter using the hashtag #MarkPlanTeach.

Engaging students with stories and real-life experiences doesn't need to be something that is done consistently across the school, but it could make everyone's job a lot easier, particularly if used in aspects of teaching that are common practice, for example as a flying start activity (see Section 2, Idea 6, p. 89). It can help the determined teacher capture the minds of the most challenging, as well as the most gifted, students in the class.

If you are using storytelling in your classroom, make sure you ask yourself the following:

- Do your lesson plans incorporate links to real-life experiences or examples?

- If so, do the links then feed into the resources you intend to use in the classroom?

- Is there a strong basis for planning? If so, how could storytelling be built into the initial lesson structure?

- If the scheme of learning is written by another teacher, how could you adapt the plans to suit your own personal experiences and the stories you have to tell?

Storytelling and literacy

If you can embed storytelling techniques into your lesson planning and delivery, then you are also promoting a love of reading, speaking and listening in the classroom. This is something that every teacher hopes to impart as part of their professional duties. In 2019, the National Literacy Trust conducted a study into the impact of their Stories in Schools pilot programme, in which professional storytellers delivered literacy workshops targeted at reluctant or struggling readers over six weeks. The study found:

'4 in 5 (79.7%) of pupils who took part in Stories in Schools said that as a result of taking part in the workshops they now want to read more books, while more than three quarters (76.9%) felt more excited about reading and 7 in 10 (71.4%) better at writing their own stories.'

Reading enjoyment is connected to behaviour and motivation, so it's important to engage your students in the magic of stories and give them every opportunity to read aloud in class, so they become more confident and more avid readers. You might even find it reduces the amount of time they spend connected to digital devices.

There is extensive evidence in this area from a range of studies over the past thirty years. Below I have quoted the 'Reading Comprehension Strategies' summary from the EEF's Teaching and Learning Toolkit, which suggests that approaches to improve reading comprehension include:

'a range of techniques that enable pupils to comprehend the meaning of what is written, such as inferring the meaning from context, summarising or identifying key points, using graphic or semantic organisers, developing questioning strategies, and monitoring their own comprehension and identifying difficulties themselves.'

The summary goes on to report that several of these techniques can be 'usefully combined with phonics, collaborative and peer-learning techniques' (EEF, 2017d). It is therefore clear that, when carefully selected according to the needs of your students via lesson planning, telling stories in class can develop techniques of reading comprehension, all the while providing effective engagement and challenge in relation to the lesson content.

In this section, I have referred to storytelling. Professor Tim O'Brien once introduced me to the concept of a different type of story – one that people continually tell to themselves and that exists inside their head. He calls it an 'inner story'. Read on to find out more about why inner stories are so relevant to us as teachers.

Psychology and...
inner story

You have two stories inside your head. One is about your life. The other is controlling your life. I call the story that controls your life your inner story. You may want to read a book I have written about it (O'Brien, 2015). Your inner story is created in your mind and you are living it every moment of every day. It is an internally constructed narrative about what it means to be you. The more you tell yourself your inner story, the more you become that story. One way that people offer an insight into their inner story is when they start a sentence with 'I am the sort of person who...'. Please complete the sentence a few times and see what you notice.

As a teacher, when you interact with a young person, you are always interacting with their inner story and they are always interacting with yours. Your influence on their internal narrative is very powerful. What you say and do – and how you say and do it – makes a contribution to shaping who the young person thinks they are both as a person and as a learner.

In any mass education system, every learner's inner story is potentially at risk. This is particularly the case if the young person experiences learning difficulties in systems where deficit-focused labels abound. In such systems, 'the problem' is seen as being located within the child and therefore children who experience difficulties, especially those who experience SEND, are in danger of being treated as if they are broken washing machines that need fixing. However, the problem might not be the problem. The notion that the adults or the environment should change, in order to enable the young person to change, can often be absent from the agenda.

Inner stories do not have to be bad to get better. Think of any young person that you teach. How do your interactions with them contribute to shaping their inner story? What can you do to help change their inner story for the better? Think of a colleague and ask yourself the same questions. How about you? Is your inner story empowering you or is it holding you back? What could you think, feel or do differently to change your inner story for the better? Answer the question. Start now. Make a change.

– Professor Tim O'Brien

Stickability

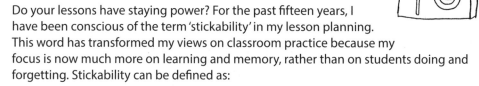

IDEA SNAPSHOT

Do your lessons have staying power? For the past fifteen years, I have been conscious of the term 'stickability' in my lesson planning. This word has transformed my views on classroom practice because my focus is now much more on learning and memory, rather than on students doing and forgetting. Stickability can be defined as:

1. What learning should 'stick' in the long-term memory of students?

2. What key point(s) do you want students to remember and bring back to the next lesson?

This idea will show you how to integrate stickability into your lesson planning.

'Stickability', or 'sticking power', is a term used in the 5 Minute Lesson Plan (see Section 2, Introduction, p. 60). Such is its importance that 'Stickability' was even going to be the title for this book, but it didn't quite stick with the publishers! Teaching ideas that stick – or ideas backed by cognition and pragmatic application – is the same as setting students up with learning objectives. The only difference is that the focus is on the actual end goal and success criteria, not just on what we hope to achieve. By aiming for 'what learning should stick' when you teach a lesson, the focus of your planning will be to help students reach that goal, rather than on offering a haphazard hit-and-hope objective at the beginning of a lesson.

Living and dying by the ideology of stickability then, what one thing would I want you to take away from this book? Well, here goes:

When the shift in lesson planning moves away from *doing* in favour of *learning* and hones in on the key points students must take away with them, lesson planning becomes sharper. A greater commitment is made in your teaching to ensure students leave your classroom with what has been *learnt*, not what has been *done*.

Stickability is fundamentally what learning and lesson planning should be all about. With relation to lesson planning, stickability can be defined as the following:

1. What is the fundamental aspect of the lesson that you need students to learn?

2. What key skill, knowledge or understanding should students grasp?

3. What should students leave your classroom knowing or understanding? What should students return to class knowing or understanding?

4. Why should this skill, knowledge or understanding stick with students? And how will you make it stick?

5. How will you know that it has stuck? And if students become unstuck, then what?

There are clearly a lot of sticky questions to answer, so I will try to offer some guidance.

As we've seen in previous ideas in this section, good teaching focuses on the learning and not on the activity. This is fundamental; once we are clear about what learning we want to stick, lesson planning can remain loose and adaptable. A curriculum without learning at its heart is rigid and has more emphasis on a fixed, detailed lesson plan and the activities students must complete.

From curriculum plan to lesson plan

If we don't require written lesson plans, but do consider planning in some form to be important, how can we enable curriculum plans to feed into day-to-day lesson planning without it becoming a burden on the teacher?

We should expect that long-term planning exists – although in my experience, you cannot always assume this to be true. It is always worth digging into schemes of work to see if they are current, relevant and are providing challenge and development for all student abilities. A PowerPoint is not a scheme of work, nor is a document or a project you have been teaching for over ten years.

Curriculum reform is happening in many of the 48 OECD countries and it's important that schools, teachers and subject departments are working within the latest guidance. There are benefits to curriculum reform. A paper by the OECD notes that 'changes in the educational system or in pedagogies can help customise the educational process'. However, curriculum reform is brought about in different ways across OECD countries:

> 'Out of 26 analysed education systems, 13 relied more on schools than on central level in bringing about curriculum innovations, while 8 out of 26 expected innovation to originate from centrally driven processes than from schools. Five OECD countries applied a mixed approach to curriculum innovation.' (OECD, 2014)

It may not come as a surprise that England reports one of the worst scores in all 48 jurisdictions for teacher decision-making on curriculum course content (Schleicher, 2018). I would argue that teachers need curriculum autonomy at a local level and some freedom to interpret curriculum mapping into classroom resources for their students. Lesson planning should then stem from schemes of work that feed into short-term planning in a teacher's day-to-day lesson planner. The TALIS 2018 report looks at the high levels of autonomy given to teachers in Sweden, Iceland and Norway in terms of determining course content, and the report attributes this to the high levels of trust between teachers, school leaders, parents, students and the authorities.

Unfortunately, the level of autonomy granted to teachers when it comes to curriculum reform is out of the hands of most classroom teachers, but we can define how lesson planning looks. In my opinion, the journey from curriculum to scheme of work and from lesson objectives to goal setting can be simplified as stickability. Stickability is the end product. It is the cognitive aspect of lesson planning, namely working out how to build into our lessons the mental action or process of acquiring knowledge and understanding through thought, experience and the senses, and adapting elements of teaching plans based on the 'why?' test (see Section 2, Idea 2, p. 70). This is how we can improve autonomy for teachers, help to reduce workload and steer planning so it zooms in on learning.

I hope by now you will agree that there is no point in planning if we are not focused on learning and are simply producing reams and reams of lesson plans for evidence-mongers. Schools should not expect teachers to produce individual lesson plans for observed or unobserved lessons, but sadly this is not the case in many of our schools, and it is partially to blame for the teacher workload crisis we are currently experiencing in England.

Two of the five secondary schools in which I have worked did not expect teachers to produce individual lesson plans, but did expect 'evidence of planning' over time. The need for detail was removed and replaced with an overview, and the teacher planner could contain the difference between the scheme of work and the lesson a teacher intends to teach. More importantly, trusting that teachers were considering the 'why?' of their teaching and what must stick in lessons was the *ordre du jour*. The impact? Well, surely it's obvious (depending on whose side you're on…).

The 5 Minute Lesson Plan (see Section 2, Introduction, p. 60) is a useful tool for recording the thinking behind a lesson plan on one page, removing the need for laboriously writing lengthy notes. It's perfect for teachers who may wish to plan or for those who still need to develop their planning in order to teach more confidently.

Collegial support

When it comes to lesson planning, collegial support (collaboration between teachers, schools and other providers) is essential. As part of my role as a school leader of professional development, I facilitated teachers to work in paired departments to review lesson planning as part of teaching and learning policy implementation. Each department was paired with another and they were provided with resources to facilitate planning as a whole – from curriculum plans and schemes of work, right down to the teacher planner.

The impact of this collaboration on lesson planning is clear:

- It allows progress against whole-school thinking to be reviewed.

- It provides teachers with opportunities to think about best practice and to share their ideas with others.

- It enables teachers to review how the curriculum feeds into schemes of work and lesson planning, and how overarching plans feed into their colleagues' individual teacher planners.

If you were able to introduce a similar collaborative approach to lesson planning in your school, it would be the perfect opportunity to explore how stickability could work for you and your colleagues. Schools that have no recruitment issues and report higher levels of teacher satisfaction are allowing their teachers to collaborate on a weekly basis in small teams or at a whole-school level. It really isn't that difficult for school leaders to develop power from the floor. Simply facilitate opportunities for them to talk in a structured way on a regular basis.

Making learning stick

In *Make It Stick*, Peter Brown, Henry Roediger III and Mark McDaniel remind us, 'the most successful learners are those who take charge of their own learning and follow a simple but disciplined strategy' (Brown et al., 2014). The issue for teachers is that we

EVIDENCE

Making learning stick can, of course, be considered at all levels – marking, planning and teaching – but in terms of planning, a technique called retrieval practice is recommended and is supported by evidence and research. Retrieval practice means quizzing yourself from memory on information you have just read or listened to and it can be used as a primary study strategy.

So, how can teachers incorporate this into their lesson planning? Well, we must coach students on how to study. This might seem quite simple to you and me, but it's not so clear for the students we teach. The following is a concise version of the information retrieval model suggested by Brown, Roediger III and McDaniel in *Make It Stick*:

1. Read a text.

2. Pause.

3. Ask questions.

4. Quiz yourself.

5. Write down the answers.

6. Set time aside to revisit the content and quiz yourself again. (Brown et al., 2014)

Introducing a pause in-between reading the text and testing yourself on it is a form of 'spaced practice'. Cognitive psychological scientists Yana Weinstein and Megan Smith of The Learning Scientists blog define spaced practice as:

'the exact opposite of cramming. When you cram, you study for a long, intense period of time close to an exam. When you space your learning, you take that same amount of study time, and spread it out across a much longer period of time.' (Weinstein and Smith, 2016)

are so bombarded with external pressures to achieve X number of grades and levels of progress, that curriculum coverage leaves us with very little time to teach students how to be disciplined or how to learn and revise.

Teaching students how to make learning stick is essential and we should make the teaching of study strategies a habit, allocating them structured time in our lesson plans and pursuing them regularly. As Brown et al. (2014) suggest, we should:

'Embrace the fact that significant learning is often, or even usually, somewhat difficult […] These are signs of effort, not failure.'

We should be encouraging teachers to promote effort, not completion (see Section 1, Idea 2, p. 14), among all our students. If we can achieve this, making learning stick lies within our control.

You can also gradually intertwine various topics to force the learner to recap on past knowledge in-between learning new information. This is known as interleaving. We saw the importance of recapping on knowledge with the Ebbinghaus Forgetting Curve in Section 1, Idea 6, p. 35. Spaced practice means placing wider gaps between learning the content and repeating the content, and as Alex Quigley says in *The Confident Teacher*, 'the brain is forced to do a harder job at remembering' (Quigley, 2016).

So, now we know a simple method for retaining information, how can teachers weave this into their lesson plans to help make learning stick and to stop students leaving revision to the last minute? Here lies the challenge, particularly when curriculum coverage and time pressures ensue.

As teachers, it's important that we give students opportunities to retrieve and elaborate on their studies by building time for recall into schemes of work, while also taking into account curriculum and syllabus coverage. If this is left as a bolt-on, it can make day-to-day teaching and learning difficult for all. Secondary teachers can use the fact that they teach in block periods, often separated out by several days, to plan lessons in a sequence that balances learning new content with recapping to consolidate prior learning. In my opinion, this is more challenging for primary teachers to do because they are with their pupils all of the time.

Every teacher must discover what works in their classroom. The subject and age group will determine what is taught and what must be retaught, but there is one aspect of making learning stick that is essential in all settings, namely explaining to students how learning works. This is often left to the latter years of school life when examinations are pending but by then, bad habits will already have formed. We must instil in our students the importance of information retrieval throughout their education with careful curriculum design and lesson planning. It is a key strategy to help improve memory and learning.

The struggle zone

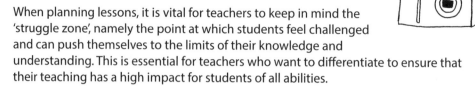

IDEA 5

IDEA SNAPSHOT

When planning lessons, it is vital for teachers to keep in mind the 'struggle zone', namely the point at which students feel challenged and can push themselves to the limits of their knowledge and understanding. This is essential for teachers who want to differentiate to ensure that their teaching has a high impact for students of all abilities.

I n *Making Every Lesson Count*, Deputy Headteacher Shaun Allison and co-author Andy Tharby of Durrington High School in West Sussex have formulated a very popular teaching approach based on six principles: 'challenge', 'explanation', 'modelling', 'deliberate practice', 'questioning' and 'feedback' (Allison and Tharby, 2015). These principles inform their school's teaching and learning policy. I would recommend using this approach specifically when lesson planning and when assessing students' progress.

Allison and Tharby believe that 'expert teaching requires challenge so that students have high expectations of what they can achieve'. When it comes to planning, it is therefore essential for teachers to include some form of struggle or challenge. Keeping students in the struggle zone means walking the fine line between students becoming apathetic due to boredom and students giving up because of stress or a feeling that they are incapable. Allison and Tharby see the struggle zone as sitting in-between the 'comfort zone' and the 'panic zone'. They describe it as 'High challenge. Low stress. Thinking required. Effective learning.' (Allison and Tharby, 2015)

So how can a teacher plan to provide high challenge but low stress? How can they require students to think hard in order to achieve effective learning? Well, it's a tough ask for any teacher and it's even tougher to do every lesson.

First and foremost, teachers must consider the comfort and panic zones of all students in their lesson. It is of course vital that teachers know their students and they can do so through the relationships they have with them and the current data they have available. However, another way of knowing where students are going and when they are struggling or bored is through assessment, such as questioning. Assessment is all about challenge, pitch and delivery. Knowing how to use assessment to guide students and help them to improve without causing them anxiety is something every teacher must learn.

Planning for assessment

Planned questioning is rarely discussed in teacher training sessions and lack of development in this area can lead to teachers not knowing how to assess student progress on the spur of the moment. Dylan Wiliam and Paul Black, both Emeritus Professors at the UCL Institute of Education, have written a short, yet revered, document on assessment: *Inside the Black Box: Raising Standards through Classroom Assessment*. It's a powerful read – who says great things don't come in small packages? Wiliam and Black warn us that:

> 'There is a wealth of research evidence that the everyday practice of assessment in classrooms is beset with problems and shortcomings [...] For primary teachers particularly, there is a tendency to emphasize quantity and presentation of work and to neglect its quality in relation to learning.' (Black and Wiliam, 2001)

I wonder how much this is still prevalent today, despite many teachers becoming much more aware of research, learning theory and better methods for assessment. In my experience, this does still apply in some schools. It is relevant to secondary teaching too and is perhaps an indication of how education has lost its way and has become a victim of evidence trails and accountability on a grand scale. Teachers have lost sight of what it is they are supposed to be doing with children because they have become so fixated on *what others think* of what they are doing.

Many schools no longer require lesson plans but do want to see evidence of planning. I would go one step further and declare that there should be no expectation on teachers to provide lesson plans for any observations either. This will help teachers manage their workload. Of course, this is not to undermine the need for planning full stop or for the newly qualified teacher – or the experienced soul who has just changed schools – who needs to use existing curriculum plans and lesson planning frameworks to help settle into a new way of working. But whether we write lesson plans or not, how do we know where students are going? Planning for assessment could be one of several ways. As Allison and Tharby say:

> '[Assessment] also helps to shift your view of students – rather than thinking about them as low ability, think of them as having a low starting point.' (Allison and Tharby, 2015)

So, when planning to keep all students in the struggle zone, ask yourself:

- How do you assess where your students are at during the lesson?
- Do you know where you want them to go?
- What teaching strategies are you going to use?
- What key questions will help you to lure students into learning?
- What classroom strategies will you use to keep students on task, motivated and working to their potential?

A careful plan that takes into account all the above can make a significant difference in helping you to deliver a perfectly pitched lesson that meets the needs of all students. It's difficult, but not impossible to achieve.

Psychology and...
The Zone of Proximal Development

Ross referring to a zone that promotes learning prompts me to discuss the Vygotskian concept of 'The Zone of Proximal Development' (ZPD). Lev Vygotsky, a Russian psychologist, was particularly interested in how human learning potential is socially mediated. I shall characterise his view as: learning takes place better between two or more heads than it does inside one. Vygotsky asserts that an important index of a person's learning and development is not their actual level – where they are right now – but their potential level. He describes the difference or distance between a learner's actual level and their potential level as the ZPD.

The teacher should teach within the ZPD, aware that a learner's processes are in a state of developing maturation. To help learners move through the ZPD, a teacher must believe the learner has the potential to be different. The learner needs to interact with supportive people, who assist learning by knowing what the learner does not currently know and enabling cognitive apprenticeship. On most occasions, that supportive other is a teacher. The teacher needs to have a notional idea of the actual level of the learner, be clear about where they want the learner to go in terms of a potential level and develop a plan of best interactions, including scaffolding, that will enable a learner's potential to be realised. Scaffolding does tend to be conceptualised as a one-way process but it is also possible for it to be negotiated between teacher and learner.

I suggest that a deepening awareness of metacognition, by the teacher and the learner, is a valuable component of scaffolding within the ZPD. In 1979, John Flavell, a developmental psychologist, coined the term 'metacognition'. It referred to the knowledge a person has about their own cognition in relation to learning processes. Metacognition, a higher order activity associated with self-regulation, enables us to, for example, learn about learning or think about thinking. Some researchers believe this to be a deliberately conscious process, whilst others assert that metacognition involves unconscious processes too. I recommend that specific opportunities to focus and reflect on metacognition be built in when teachers are planning. It offers teachers insight into a learner's ZPD. It also enables students to learn about how they learn and become more resilient when approaching and encountering cognitive and emotional challenge within their own ZPD.

– Professor Tim O'Brien

A flying start

IDEA SNAPSHOT

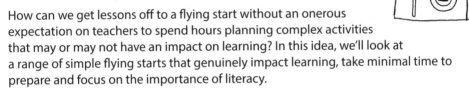

How can we get lessons off to a flying start without an onerous expectation on teachers to spend hours planning complex activities that may or may not have an impact on learning? In this idea, we'll look at a range of simple flying starts that genuinely impact learning, take minimal time to prepare and focus on the importance of literacy.

A flying start to a lesson engages students from the outset and will help build up to the main parts of the lesson and the challenges that lie ahead. A flying start can also provide an opportunity to remind students of classroom expectations and routines. If tasks are established time and time again, students will know what is expected of them as soon as they arrive in your classroom. They will become accustomed to your expectations and be quicker to respond to them. This will help you to manage behaviour and set the tone for the lesson to ensure optimum conditions for learning. These activities also support retrieval and engagement. On the whole, students will participate no matter what the teacher asks them to do because this will be the norm, even when the teacher takes risks.

Simple flying starts have the greatest impact. I would recommend routines, one-off performances, quizzes, retrieval practice exercises, for example using mnemonics, and simple strategies to recap on the previous lesson and introduce what's coming up. Unusual and unpredictable resources can often hold the most interest, as well as current affairs and news stories. Of course, teachers reading this book will most likely be equipped with numerous ready-made starter activities and strategies to deploy with any class, but here's my two pennies' worth in this idea.

Meet and greet

Flying starts can include meeting and greeting students at the door as they enter the classroom. The teacher welcomes the students one by one and asks them to sit down and work independently while the remaining students arrive. The students could be asked to get on with work put in front of them or consolidate information from the previous lesson, so they understand that this lesson is a continuation of the last. You could also ask them to complete a redrafting exercise, such as zonal feedback. See Section 1, Idea 3, p. 18 for more on this.

Stickability

Use techniques to break down the learning objectives or what learning you want 'to stick'. See Section 2, Idea 4, p. 81 for more on this and try using the retrieval practice grid in Section 2, Idea 2, p. 70.

Technology

Two fantastic pieces of software I'd recommend are Classroomscreen and also Whiteboard.fi. Classroomscreen is one of those websites that brings everything into one place for free, perfect for time-poor teachers who are always searching for countdown timers, random name pickers and whiteboard annotation tools. Whiteboard.fi is another free online whiteboard tool for teachers and classrooms. The software allows all pupils and teachers to gather remotely and annotate the same screen. Pupils can be divided into groups and it's perfect for online collaboration.

Keywords

You will often see teachers using oral recital to help improve retention. This is a fantastic strategy! For the vast majority of teachers who are teaching key subject terminology, a mixture of quizzes, word displays and focused exam questions will support retention of knowledge. Given what we know about cognitive load theory, avoid instructions becoming too complex, as this may lead to complications and misconceptions. It also makes what a teacher is trying to teach too generic and, as a result, this will reduce its intended impact.

I recommend that all teachers try teaching the etymology and root meaning of a keyword. Break the word down into parts so that students not only understand how to spell the keyword but acquire a secure grasp of its meaning and origin throughout history. And this is not just for teachers of English. I find it fascinating that even when teaching in your own subject, there is a whole new world waiting to be discovered when breaking keywords down into more refined details.

The snowball technique

You could also try the 'snowball' technique to recap keywords at the beginning of a lesson. Ask students to spell three words of your choice on a piece of paper. They then scrunch the paper up into a snowball and throw it across the room. Students find one of the snowballs, open it up, spell check the words written on it and write down three more keywords of your choice. The snowballs are then thrown a second time. You can do this as many times as you like, with as many keywords as you want, but I usually stick to ten. You can also increase the pressure with a countdown clock.

Reducing the number of words to recall can support long-term memory. Teachers can therefore start to use more difficult words and concepts with younger students. Even better, if this strategy becomes a routine, then students are likely to use keywords in their speaking, listening, reading and writing activities in class. I have discovered that adults love this strategy too. When we consider teacher professional development, it's no different to what happens in the classroom when we ask pupils to develop their subject knowledge and improve their progress. This simple snowball technique works perfectly in teacher training sessions to recap on past knowledge, introduce new concepts and keep the training engaging, purposeful and memorable.

The importance of literacy

Several of my ideas for an effective flying start to a lesson relate to literacy. I believe that literacy should feature heavily in our lessons, so why not start as you mean to go on and introduce it right at the beginning of class? Literacy is central to teaching across the curriculum. According to the Teachers' Standards for England (DfE, 2011), a teacher must:

> 'demonstrate an understanding of and take responsibility for promoting high standards of literacy, articulacy and the correct use of standard English, whatever the teacher's specialist subject.'

Every classroom teacher should take a moment to think about how assessment in their subject links to literacy and how they are currently embedding literacy in their lesson plans. What do you already do and what's missing? Use the following questions to reflect on and start to identify how you could develop your teaching of literacy further. I know there are many areas where I could improve…

1. Why is literacy central to teaching?

2. Why should learning and literacy be considered very closely related?

3. Why is learning that takes no account of literacy never going to be better than poor teaching?

4. What role can language play in the development of children's learning?

5. Why might specialist language be critical to securing a teacher's long-term subject confidence?

6. How could literacy link to your subject?

7. How well do you know your students' literacy levels and reading ages?

8. Is there an expectation in your school that every child has a reading book?

9. Is there an expectation that every teacher shares what they are reading with their students?

10. What opportunities do you give for extended pieces of writing in your subject?

It is critical to support a student who is walking a fine line between failing and succeeding at literacy (particularly if they are a reluctant student), so they understand and see the potential benefits of dealing with these challenges. Every child knows they need to be able to read, but if students are reluctant, at what point should the teacher step up to support them and what can they do to help?

When it comes to literacy, role models are key, as are opportunities to be part of activities that enrich a student's life. Students take inspiration from great writers, poets and people from their communities – role models who provide a level of openness and expertise that most busy classroom teachers cannot offer. Students often express their feelings more freely with adults who are not their teachers. This can open many doors and can develop a student's confidence to speak out.

EVIDENCE

In their book *How Learning Happens*, Kirschner and Hendrick (2020) analyse learning techniques that really work. They lament that, despite over a century of research into learning and memory, many students (and even some teachers!) don't know which strategies are effective. Referencing Dunlosky et al. (2013), the authors document and discuss ten study techniques:

1. explaining why a fact or concept is true
2. explaining processes step by step or how new information and known information are related
3. summarising
4. highlighting and underlining
5. using mnemonics
6. forming mental images of texts
7. re-reading
8. self-testing or practice testing
9. distributed practice
10. interleaving.

All of these techniques are effective to support the retention of knowledge, so think about how you might integrate them into a 'flying start' for your lesson.

A great example of an enrichment opportunity, which I have had the privilege of seeing some of my pupils experience, is the UK Youth Parliament, with young people, aged 11 to 18, elected in 369 seats as MYPs (Members of Youth Parliament). They are elected in youth elections across the country and come together to organise events, plan projects, run campaigns and influence decision-makers on issues that matter to most young people. Some of my students have gone on to great things after this incredible opportunity. Politics aside, encouraging young people to speak up about critical issues in our society through Youth Parliament and other organisations such as Debate Mate is an essential school activity.

Of all the various opinions about teaching and learning, there is one common thread that educators will agree on, namely that literacy is the one thing that has the greatest impact on learning. A student's level of language, fluency and love for reading will have a significant bearing on their overall attainment. Without a good level of literacy, students are unable to access learning in a large variety of circumstances in the classroom. If additional effort is needed to decode text while reading in class or independently, access to learning will be more challenging for the student and for the teacher. In fact, many of the techniques listed above rely on students' literacy skills in order to be effective.

But, of the ten techniques listed above, how many could actually support the development of literacy? From this list, practice testing and distributed practice were recommended as the two best techniques. The former is where students must retrieve information that was previously studied from long-term memory. The latter is where a student or teacher spreads out the study instead of 'cramming'. Cramming can be effective in the short term but spacing is significantly better for long-term retention. These techniques can absolutely be used for teaching complex subject terminology and embedding this in long-term memory.

It would be my recommendation to every teacher wanting to improve any interventions, whether study skills, literacy or students' understanding of subject knowledge, to commence all lessons with a flying start. No matter what this task looks like, ensure that literacy features heavily and that you keep all students in mind – from the most vulnerable to the most able – when you plan it.

Quality first teaching

IDEA SNAPSHOT

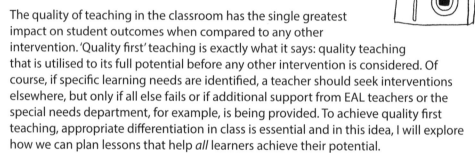

The quality of teaching in the classroom has the single greatest impact on student outcomes when compared to any other intervention. 'Quality first' teaching is exactly what it says: quality teaching that is utilised to its full potential before any other intervention is considered. Of course, if specific learning needs are identified, a teacher should seek interventions elsewhere, but only if all else fails or if additional support from EAL teachers or the special needs department, for example, is being provided. To achieve quality first teaching, appropriate differentiation in class is essential and in this idea, I will explore how we can plan lessons that help *all* learners achieve their potential.

High-quality teaching should always be considered the first wave of intervention. Research from the Education Development Trust (EDT) suggests:

'Teachers are one of the key elements in any school and effective teaching is one of the key propellers for school improvement.' (Ko et al., 2014)

It is therefore paramount that we invest in our teachers and give them the time they need to develop their practice and achieve their goals. With the decimation of specialised services, teachers are increasingly expected to do every intervention possible, when in fact doing everything will yield limited impact. We need our teachers to be research informed, so they can:

- be clear on lesson objectives and communicate these to students across a range of abilities

- become knowledgeable about curriculum content

- make use of available resources to support learning

- teach cognitive strategies to their students to support their learning

- provide appropriate and timely feedback.

For any school, part and parcel of this challenge is ensuring there is consistency in all classrooms. If every teacher adopts all of the above except for Mr McGill in the classroom next door to you, who is long in the tooth, believes he has 'seen it all before' and 'just wants to teach', the entire school will still have a problem.

It's important that schools establish consistency in their approach to quality first

teaching and as the EDT suggest, 'engender a culture of professional debate and developmental lesson observation' (Ko et al., 2014). I have found that happier and higher-performing schools bring teachers together on a weekly basis to talk about pedagogy. Quality first teaching can only be achieved in a culture of trust. Sadly, this is hard to find in some of the more toxic and challenging schools we teach in today. The external machine drives schools to regularly monitor and evaluate what they are doing and although this is apparently a voluntary stipulation, they are punished for lack of leadership, direction and evidence of improvement if they fail to provide reams of evidence. This pressure to perform and always be improving filters down to individual teachers and students. It's not possible for all students to achieve the best grades in the current English examination system because allocation of grades is distributed. We need to ask ourselves whether we wish to continue with this methodology for another century, but in the meantime, peddling myths that *all* students can achieve the top grade is simply unhelpful.

As former headteacher, author and educational consultant, Tom Sherrington, writes in his blog post 'The Bell-Curve Cage: Something Must Break', the problem with external accountability on schools and teachers is:

> 'If you're using the same mechanisms – i.e. our national examinations – to measure both improvement and standards, you're stuffed. You can't keep a firm hold on standards with a bell curve cage and, simultaneously, proclaim improvement.' (Sherrington, 2017)

Sherrington adds that this 'pressure to improve' is a 'head-on car-crash collision' waiting to happen because 'everyone must improve but not everyone is allowed to'. These external pressures reach all the way down to every child and their performance. Sadly, three years later in 2020, our education system has not yet moved on, dabbling with school accountability over three-year averages but not yet making a commitment to change.

For the past twenty-five years, I have worked in difficult schools with some of the most disadvantaged children in this country. To achieve a degree of consistency with over one hundred teachers in any of these schools was a huge challenge. I've seen this problem manifesting itself in all types of education settings all around the world. I've argued recently that schools should stop chasing consistency and instead seek clarity and coherence to improve teaching and learning standards. The priority has always been the child, but often what precedes the needs of the child is the quality of teaching in each individual classroom. How do schools achieve consistency when working in challenging environments? Teaching is incredibly complex, and as educators we do ourselves no favours whatsoever. I return again to the mantra of this book. Teachers and school leaders must return teaching to its simplest form to allow complex ideas to become manageable. If we do less, we can increase our impact. It is vital for all teachers to approach quality first teaching as a differentiation strategy and one that will be delivered over time, not as a one-off, quick-fix solution.

Quality first teaching and differentiation

So, with the needs of your own students in mind, how can you plan for differentiation to ensure quality first teaching?

Differentiation is not a one-off exercise. You should not be overexerting yourself with endless planning for individual lessons, especially for something that is incredibly challenging to achieve and often completely unrealistic to attain. This is neither effective nor sustainable and has a wholly negative impact on workload and productivity.

Aside from marking, differentiation is one of the most viewed topics on my website, which exceeds 12 million readers. Differentiation still continues to be a challenge for newer teachers, with myths perpetuating across the education sector. Differentiation should be planned over time to ensure a quality first approach that meets the needs of all students and maximises the use of any additional adults in the room. Taking a graduated approach to differentiation and ensuring quality first teaching for all students are both embedded in the SEND Code of Practice for England (DfE, 2014). The most useful form of differentiation is in-class assessment, which helps you to adapt lesson plans to the needs of individual students and groups in your class. In staff reviews for appraisals I have conducted throughout my leadership career, I have found this is often cited as the most challenging aspect of teaching.

So, what else could we be doing to differentiate our lessons over time? Below are a few suggestions.

Conversations

Give yourself time to speak with students and colleagues outside of lessons. It never ceases to amaze me how powerful a brief conversation with a student can be when you speak to them in their 'territory', just before a lesson. Checking in with students to discuss the expectations you have when they first arrive in your classroom can have a huge impact, especially if there is an issue that needs to be resolved from the previous lesson.

Modelling writing

For students who struggle with language, modelling written tasks, by completing them alongside the student, can be hugely beneficial. This is the most obvious idea, but one that's difficult to achieve with 29 other students in the classroom. A solution is displaying work via a video link, enabling all students to see you doing the work alongside them as a teacher. I'd guess that if you are doing it too, the students will be more likely to value the work and invest in the activity or task being asked of them.

$$7 \times ? = 28$$

I am a huge fan of non-verbal communication. Imagine the equation $7 \times ? = 28$ on this whiteboard. Now imagine if I am saying this equation out loud, facing the whiteboard with the back of my head to the students, compared to me facing the students, allowing them to lip sync non-verbal signals through my eyes, my voice and my lips, as well as moving my finger along the equation on the board and adding a double tap underneath the question mark. Go on, try it for yourself! You'll be amazed how subtly effective this technique can be.

Scaffolding oracy and writing frames

Scaffolding oracy and providing writing frames for students of varying abilities can embed learning at all levels over a period of time. This can support students of all abilities and allow them to work independently, freeing you up to assist individual students. Where possible, you can also systematically check understanding in the lesson through self- and peer-assessment techniques (see Section 1, Idea 9, p. 47).

EAL students

Following the advice of Dr Jim Cummins, the cognitive challenge of some tasks will need to be lowered when students are new to English and are learning a lot of new vocabulary. This doesn't mean we should lower our expectations, but it is certainly something we should consider when teaching a large number of students with EAL. Cummins suggests that we can keep cognitive challenge high for EAL learners, if we provide students with **context**. This could be through visual hand signals or facial expressions (such as those mentioned in 'modelling' above), graphics or collaborative opportunities that allow EAL students to work with peers.

To support EAL learners further, we should consider using culturally accessible materials to help them sequence learning. If you're lucky enough to have a specialist in your school, you could also ask them to translate a text into the students' home language, so students can – with dictionary in hand – highlight keywords with you and practise extrapolating the spelling and meaning of these words in English.

Seating plans

To differentiate successfully, you must build a seating plan that takes into account students' starting points and pathways. I would advocate the use of seating plans in every classroom, even with older students and even if you're an experienced teacher. They provide stability, ensure students know who is in control and mean that every learner will be working in a place where they can be supported and challenged most effectively. I'm always surprised at how many teachers fail to use such a simple strategy for quality first teaching.

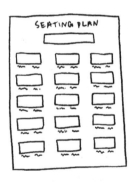

Seating plans have many advantages:

- They can be a good source of evidence that a teacher has processed the data available for the class. This data also acts as a memoir in the lesson.

- They help establish authority over a new class. Where students sit should always be up to the teacher. 'We always work better when we sit together, Sir/Miss' is most frequently an indication that they do not!

- Changing the seating plan at the start of every term is easy and the new dynamics keep things fresh.

- A boy–girl seating plan rarely fails, difficult though it can be to implement in the more boy- or girl-heavy year groups. For single-sex schools, use data, assessment in class and pastoral needs to determine what is best for your students.

- They can be easily accessed by another member of staff, who you may need to help with the class, such as a pastoral leader, head of department or supply teacher.

- They can show you things you may have inadvertently missed, such as whether all your Pupil Premium students are sitting together at the back or where a gifted and talented student, who wants you to forget about their high prior attainment, is sitting.

- You could consider having a 'home' and 'away' arrangement, with 'away' being an alternative seating plan you use from time to time, for group work, for example.

Creating a supportive environment

No matter which differentiation strategies you decide to use, to provide quality first teaching over time, you will also need to create a supportive and inclusive classroom environment for all students, regardless of ability and background. Environment impacts on sensory memory, and as a result, this influences our ability to 'pay attention'. It also impacts on our working memory, which hinders our long-term retention and schemas. Ask yourself the following questions to ensure you are including techniques in your lesson planning to allow all students to access subject knowledge and to support their language and literacy development:

1. Do you seek opportunities to use first language at the initial stage of learning?

2. Do you model and encourage risk-taking (see Section 1, Idea 5, p. 30)?

3. Do you create opportunities to engage with new arrivals in the classroom, including early-stage EAL students or students with SEND?

4. Do you consciously interact with learners who do not speak English?

5. Do you support students to build on previous learning and experiences?

6. Do you provide thinking and rehearsal time before students speak up?

7. Do you regularly monitor student understanding and allow opportunities for individual explanation?

8. Do you use visuals and identify keywords for clarity in your lessons?

9. Do you explicitly teach the subject-specific vocabulary?

10. Do you clarify keywords, provide synonyms, and rephrase key content?

11. Do you use group work for cognitively demanding tasks?

12. If receiving EAL specialist support in lessons, do you plan your teaching tasks and target setting collaboratively?

It's also vital to consider the impact of creating a supportive environment if you find yourself teaching via video link. To ensure that certain students are not disadvantaged, consider all of the above with extra determination. Use technology to survey students' opinions and understanding, facilitate retrieval practice, and encourage online group work. Interact with each student privately, listening rather than talking. That way, you will be able to spot the students who are progressing and those who need a helping hand.

EVIDENCE

In spring 2015, the EEF published 'Making Best Use of Teaching Assistants', a research report that sought to establish why teaching assistants (TAs) were 'not being used in ways that improve pupil outcomes'. In their book, *What Works?*, two of the academics behind the EEF's research, Lee Elliot Major and Steve Higgins (2019), describe the onslaught of rage they received when they originally unveiled their findings that TAs, on average, 'added little to pupil achievement'. However, all became clear when they explained in more detail that 'TAs properly managed, prepared and trained and working alongside teachers had significant impact on children; those without support, and allocated pupils with severe learning needs, struggled.' Based on these findings, the EEF's report made seven excellent evidence-based recommendations to help schools maximise the impact of TAs. Read the headlines below and think about what you could do differently when working with TAs to enable effective differentiation and provide quality first teaching in your classroom.

1. 'TAs should not be used as an informal teaching resource for low-attaining pupils.'

2. Teachers should 'use TAs to add value to what teachers do, not replace them'.

3. We should 'use TAs to help pupils develop independent learning skills and manage their own learning'.

4. Teachers should 'ensure TAs are fully prepared for their role in the classroom'.

5. TAs should be used 'to deliver high-quality one-to-one small group support using structured interventions'.

6. Schools should 'adopt evidence-based interventions to support TAs in their small group and one-to-one instruction'.

7. We should all 'ensure explicit connections are made between learning from everyday classroom teaching and structured interventions.' (Sharples et al., 2015)

NOTE: The first four points are recommended when using TAs in everyday classroom contexts; points five and six are for TAs delivering structured interventions out of class; and point seven is recommended for linking learning led by teachers and learning led by TAs.

In my experience, the fourth point above is the most challenging to achieve. The nature of school timetables, funding and teacher allocation all limit the amount of time a TA and teacher have to plan together. Often, schools deploy TAs to one particular student. This does ensure consistency for the student but often to the detriment of teacher–TA consistency, meaning the student is receiving support but often with a different adult to the one who is teaching them.

Inspiration

IDEA SNAPSHOT

We are all so bombarded with hogwash from inside and outside of our schools that we often take risks and teach 'off the cuff'. It is simply impossible to plan every lesson out in minute detail and even when we do, not everything will go according to plan 100% of the time. In this idea, I will look at how you can take care of your professional development and work with colleagues to stockpile resources and strategies to help you prepare for any eventuality.

f I think back to when I very first began developing my *Mark. Plan. Teach.* methodology in 2014, I remember that the teaching profession had only just discovered social media. Graded lessons were about to become a thing of the past and teacher training days still received a bad reputation. Fast forward six years and teacher salaries, at least in England, are still below the OECD average and teacher workload is well above, with marking still the number one issue in all schools.

However, there is hope.

The teaching profession today is increasingly immersed in planning coherent curriculums mapped alongside schemas, in cognitive science approaches and in research-rich pedagogy. It's an exciting time, with highly energetic newly qualified teachers entering the profession (although not enough of them). When I visit schools, I am inspired by the breadth and depth of teaching experience and enthusiasm of teachers hungry to discover and use cognitive science approaches in classrooms and collegially.

As a deputy headteacher, I worked alongside teachers in my school to develop the *Mark. Plan. Teach.* methodology to tackle the marking burden. We developed speed dating sessions and a marking marketplace to bring teachers together to talk about complex problems, sharing best (and worst) practice, discussing many of the issues that we all encountered and developing a culture where it was OK not to be perfect, but far from OK not to want to engage or be better. In any school, those teachers who want to be better are reflective, open to feedback, and seek support from fellow professionals. On the other hand, teachers who close their doors and disengage with their own professional development, never mind the school's evolution, seriously risk undermining the teaching profession.

I have always argued that if teachers want to be trusted and respected by the general public, the media and politicians, then, first of all, we have to respect one another, and our range of strategies and opinions about 'what works'. We cannot always agree with one another, but we can listen better to each other's problems. This starts with a school providing the conditions in which teachers can participate in professional development with their colleagues in their teams and those outside of them, but an organisation and leadership team can only do so much to facilitate a teacher's own development. A teacher does not become a teacher after qualification, nor from being spoon fed. 'Wanting to be better' starts with the individual teacher, no one else.

In this chapter, I'd like to give you a set of ideas that will not only help you to take care of your own professional development and therefore improve your lesson planning but also enable you to plan for your medium- and long-term future to ensure that you create the conditions in which you can grow professionally.

Five things teachers should be doing for professional development

Let me start with five basic things all teachers should be doing in today's education sector to support their own professional development:

1. Be at the forefront of your subject.

2. Be up to speed with the latest behaviour management theories and fine-tune your safeguarding knowledge on a regular basis.

3. Make sure you have access to a teaching union, an organisation that shares journals, one (or more!) of the latest education books and a social media account to build a teacher network.

4. Find a colleague or coach you can go to for support and challenge inside or outside of your immediate team. Arrange to meet them on a fortnightly basis at least.

5. Protect what little time you have to visit other schools on a regular basis. I know this won't be possible for everyone but make any excuse to visit a teacher, attend an event or simply look around the corridors and get some ideas for displays, resources or how the latest software is working in practice.

Do not underestimate the importance of getting out of your silo to understand how other teachers work. Of all the things I have done throughout my career and the things that I now do on a weekly basis, visiting schools and speaking with teachers is the number one thing I recommend all teachers do.

Check the finances

When I was a deputy headteacher, we invited over 500 teachers to our TeachMeet events on an annual basis. We arranged other internal and external events too, even though they weren't a regular feature. However, we should have worked harder to organise more events for our own teachers during school hours; this is a challenge for all schools but isn't it time for school leaders to make the best professional development happen during the school day?

I am reassured that this is happening in some schools, but it's not happening everywhere. It's certainly not a job for one person, and I am reminded of many financial discussions I've had with school leadership teams, in a time when schools lack significant funding, as to how much money they protect for teacher professional development from their overall budget. As a ballpark figure, your school should protect 0.1% of its overall budget for staff training. This doesn't sound very much, but if we take some broad figures, say from a primary and a secondary school in inner London, the primary school's overall turnover will be just shy of £2 million for a population of around 300 to 400 pupils and 30 teachers. The secondary school, with approximately 1,500 students and 100 teachers, will have £9 to £10 million turnover. It may sound a lot, but it's far from enough and it's not an easy challenge, especially when approximately 70% to 80% of this money will be used for teacher salaries (and even that is not enough for our professionals in comparison to other graduates). Yet 0.1% of these school budgets equates to £2,000 for the primary school and £10,000 for the secondary school. Now, divide that figure by the number of teachers they have in those schools and this is the cost that they should be protecting for each individual teacher.

Go on! Ask your headteacher what your annual turnover is, or if you're not comfortable with doing that, just look it up on the government website. It's easily available if you're working in the state sector, as it's public money, but a bit harder to find for other school settings. Whatever the figure is, do the sums and see if your school meets the 0.1% benchmark for teacher training in your school.

Professional development on a budget

As I've mentioned, when schools strip back silly marking and data collection ideas, teachers gain this time to plan better lessons. Alongside this, they use the time to read, research and plan collaboratively, not only to meet the needs of individual students but to focus on their own needs. Here are some cheap and cheerful ways schools on a budget can enrich their professional development environment for teachers. These solutions are perfect for finding inspiration for lesson ideas and resources that you can share and stockpile as a teaching team to improve your planning and keep in your back pocket for when things don't quite turn out as expected.

1. Find one or two social media champions to curate content and share this with their department or whole school on a weekly basis.

2. Contact well-known researchers, academics or other colleagues and ask them to share two- or three-minute videos via social media; perhaps they could pre-record a short video to be shown at the start of your professional development sessions.

3. Contact local publishers, subject associations and teacher-authors like myself, and ask for book donations to build up a staff professional development library.

4. On that note, contact fellow teachers in other schools, colleagues working as consultants, academics and even celebrities to see if they would be willing to give up their time to work with your teachers for an hour after school.

5. Create a menu of workshops for teachers to attend, organised by your own teaching staff and published on a half-termly basis, so that sharing ideas becomes part and parcel of the school culture.

6. Organise a public conference that external visitors can attend. If you could make it part of your own professional development days, even better, because your own staff can then attend during their working week and you immerse them with external audiences and create a feedback loop of professional development.

7. Ensure that your school has signed up to key organisations to receive online access to resources, subscriptions and magazines.

8. And for goodness sake, make sure your staffroom is a warm and inviting place for teachers to get together, relax for a short moment, offload, find a place of privacy away from pupils, and access key resources from a central location.

EVIDENCE

In the book, *Why the Brain Matters*, by Jon Tibke (2019), there is an interesting chapter on how schools can become involved in and influence research. As more and more teachers become fascinated with accessing research-informed ideas to enhance lesson planning, the challenges for many of our teachers are limited time, limited income and often countless other priorities getting in the way. As Tibke writes, 'There can be little doubt that for teaching and learning to gain from neuroscience research there needs to be continuing progress in how neuroscientists and educators communicate.'

I'm reminded of a recent podcast I conducted with Professor Barry Carpenter, the UK's first professor of mental health and education. Barry's extensive career spans 40 years and his expertise is working with vulnerable children, particularly those who were born prematurely and those with autism. Carpenter uses his experience and expertise to influence a culture of 'mental wealth' in our young people to make them emotionally strong. He predicts that in ten to fifteen years' time, all headteachers will be given an MRI scan for children on admission to school to help inform how best to teach them and meet their needs. His rationale? Why waste years getting to know a child and passing on information from file to file and teacher to teacher, when neurological signals, maps of the brain and emotional responses to environment provide teachers with data they can use to support children at a much younger age? Carpenter says this would not only help our most vulnerable children but also equip all teachers with the power and knowledge to support young people cognitively and emotionally in the classroom.

In the meantime, it's important that opportunities to engage with research form a large part of a school's professional development offering to teachers. Of course, we cannot access all the research that's out there, nor will we ever be aware of it all or remain fully up to date, so we must be more selective and focused. It is important to keep sight of improving education within your own circle of influence and this should be your key priority. Think about your own professional development and that of those around you both in the short and long term.

All change please!

IDEA SNAPSHOT

In the previous idea, I discussed how you could stockpile ideas to use should external events or mistiming put your lesson planning up the spout, but what if behaviour is the reason that your lessons flop time and time again? How can we adapt our lesson plans to deal with disruption in the classroom and how do we prepare for these last-minute changes?

Although poor lesson planning, classroom resources that fail to deliver and external events (such as extreme weather or a fire alarm) are all cited as common reasons for lessons to flop, behaviour is often one of the main issues that disrupts perfectly planned lessons. We've already seen that there are many factors involved in teachers delivering consistently good lessons and, once we have mastered them, positive relationships and well-planned lessons catering for the needs of all students will help us to trump potential bad behaviour. Nevertheless, even the best of us can hold our hands up and admit that factors outside of our classroom can arrive on our doorstep and quash everything we've worked so hard for.

A case study

I am reminded of an ex-student (let's call him Sean) and what it must have been like to be him in a classroom. He was finding life particularly difficult and was struggling to meet expectations. He had been excluded a few times for several misdemeanours. He was under-performing across the board and disliked school.

Imagine, just for one moment, that you are this 14-year-old student in a large secondary school, moving from lesson to lesson on the sound of the bell once an hour, every hour. On the sound of this klaxon, you are expected to stop learning French and then walk calmly along the corridors – past hundreds of other spotty, hormonal teenagers – and arrive on time, smart and ready to learn maths, for example, the moment you step foot across the classroom threshold.

How would you feel if I told you to put this book down right now, even if you were really enjoying it (though maybe you are not…!), and asked you to start reading on another, completely unrelated topic? What if I then said to you that you couldn't pick this book up again until the same time next week? You'd probably find it pretty frustrating.

Is this model for schooling what we expect education to look like in the next ten or twenty years? Is this how I see my son learning at school over the next decade, even though we understand the brain and cognition a little better than we used to in the nineteenth and twentieth centuries? I hope not. As David Price says in his book, *Open: How We'll Work, Live and Learn in the Future*, learners now 'find themselves in the driving seat' because with the growth of technology, they can choose what to learn and when to learn it. School is no longer the only option available and Price recommends that educators 'have to look at the way [students] learn outside' the classroom if they are to keep them engaged in the classroom. He says:

> 'We in the West want to be more like those in the East, who, in turn, want to be more like we in the West. We call for learning fit to meet the challenges of the 21st century, while recommending teaching methods belonging to the 19th century […] In short, we're really, really confused.' (Price, 2013)

This all makes me wonder if our current model of schooling needs a revamp. It is too early to say what the long-term impact of the COVID-19 pandemic will be on education, but many have been reflecting on an alternative future for schooling. As headteachers have developed emergency plans, training for teachers to work remotely and new methods of delivering classwork, there have been opportunities to master online resources and develop online teaching content. One conclusion from this period is that quality of teaching is more important than how lessons are delivered. It will take government decisions for us to move away from the methods we have always used, and whatever issues we choose to reform, we will all need to agree! However, we must be open to new ways of working. I've been privileged enough to see schools operating in 15 different countries, and I am pleased to report there are other ways that we can teach our children. With the increased profile of mental health, the need to explore how students can learn in different places and at different times will provide students with opportunities to have more agency and give teachers more autonomy.

All that said, differentiation and the impact on disadvantaged students have been serious concerns. There is evidence that remote learning can have a positive impact, but very few research studies have examined this in relation to disadvantaged pupils. How can we prevent them from becoming disengaged when they might not even have access to the Internet or a suitable digital device at home? And how can teachers keep tabs on students' emotional and mental health and any behavioural problems that may be presenting?

If we return to our student, Sean, he is bored in your lesson and fails to understand the learning taking place. I say this because I know it happened in my classroom. I also know that there is a colossal range of factors outside school that will determine the mood of a child. This, coupled with the pressure of performance and the high expectations on teachers, makes schooling a pressure cooker for Sean and students like him.

How much of this pressure could you soak up each day, if you were Sean? I know that if I have just one unsavoury interaction, it affects me for the entire day. Sean is experiencing this four or five times a day, naturally becoming increasingly grumpy and frustrated, and quickly reaching tipping point, where one more incident will send him over the edge. It could quite easily be in your lesson that a comment from a peer will be just the thing that does it.

It will be at this stage of the process that anything *any* teacher says is simply white noise. The student fails to see clearly; the bigger picture is a blur; conversations are muffled and behaviour can become challenging. Any further reprimands become background noise. The student turns off.

After several of these instances, Sean's attendance and academic performance deteriorate. A specialist is required, but this is becoming increasingly difficult for schools in England to secure due to reducing budgets.

Interventions and lesson planning

So, as classroom teachers, what can we do when planning lessons to prevent behavioural issues in our classrooms? A teacher should have the flexibility when planning their lesson to choose the interventions that will work with their students. Let's take a look at some guidance from the Teachers' Standards in England. Teachers should:

- 'Know when and how to differentiate appropriately, using approaches which enable pupils to be taught effectively.'

- 'Have a secure understanding of how a range of factors can inhibit pupils' ability to learn, and how best to overcome these.'

- 'Demonstrate an awareness of the physical, social and intellectual development of children, and know how to adapt teaching to support pupils' education at different stages of development.'

- 'Have a clear understanding of the needs of all pupils, including those with special educational needs; those of high ability; those with English as an additional language; those with disabilities; and be able to use and evaluate distinctive teaching approaches to engage and support them.' (DfE, 2011)

I suggest that it is essential for all teachers to take the above guidance into account when they plan lessons. With effective differentiation and an understanding of every child in your class, you will be on your way to keeping your students engaged and therefore help to prevent boredom, frustration and ultimately, disruptive behaviour.

However, when behaviour problems do crop up in class (and they will, despite our best efforts), lesson planning often has to take a backseat. If you find yourself in a situation where you suddenly need to turn your focus to behaviour, try the following seven-step behaviour script:

1. Getting behaviour right is a complex process. Approach any situation calmly.

2. Aim to have a quiet conversation with the student. This avoids the student 'losing face' in front of peers and, on your part, ensures other students cannot intervene with comments or reactions. If the student refuses to come with you – even if it is just to the back of the classroom five to ten metres away – if possible have the conversation later (barring extreme situations).

3. While having the conversation, adopt a non-threatening, neutral body position, where the student's vantage point is restricted. If necessary, ask the student to turn around to face away from peers.

4. You need to communicate WHAT has happened and that the student will have an opportunity to respond at the end of your initial explanation. Identify what specific behaviour you are talking to them about.

5. Provide the student with a reason WHY you have intervened and have a pep-talk with them. At this point refer to two or three keywords (no more) from the school's behaviour policy.

6. Explain HOW the student could make this better. The most effective strategy I have found is to show HOW (through explanation and modelling) the behaviour will be perceived by other students, other teachers, visitors and, most of all, their family.

7. Finish by ending the pep-talk with a question. Ask the student if they would like you to feel proud of them. Every single time I have asked this question to a child, their response has always been a 'yes'. Who wouldn't want admiration? Most importantly, keep your message simple. Focus on the primary behaviour.

I would like to make one final point that we must consider. Devolution of classroom accountability should be the new norm. We should be able to abandon our lesson plans without fear of reprisal, in order to provide on-the-spot support to students like Sean. We should be able to change the task we had planned for the class, in order for students to be able to work independently while we seek a quiet space in the corridor to help Sean deal with any emotional issues and offer counselling until additional support arrives. Wouldn't that be a climate all teachers would like to work in? It would certainly work for me and it would have an impact for Sean, too.

EVIDENCE

There is an increased call for evidence in teaching and a demand for teachers to be informed more reliably than ever before. Advances in neuroscience have resulted in the investigation of the mind (the software) being combined with the investigation of the brain (the hardware). This is a branch of psychology known as cognitive neuroscience.

I am no expert here, but I do wonder if teachers have always been interested in how the mind works. With a vested interest in learning, surely teachers have always wondered how we learn. I would be very curious to go back in time and discuss these questions with the teachers who taught me thirty years ago. At that time, there would have been far less material available to help the everyday classroom teacher work smarter and implement ideas similar to the evidence-informed strategies I have been suggesting in this book.

CONTINUES OVER PAGE

Cognitivism is a rejection of psychoanalytic approaches, which try to understand the mind in terms of myth, and of behaviourist approaches, which try to understand the mind in terms of behaviour only. Cognitive strategies are one type of approach that students can use in order to learn more successfully. For example, successful problem solving strategies require us to go beyond the information provided and engage in abstract thinking. This could also include organising new language, summarising meaning and using memory.

This demand for evidence never existed in my formative years as a teacher (roughly twenty years ago), nor did the notion of evidence ever cross my lips during that time. However, this is not to say that teachers should not now want to use or access research to improve teaching. They should. But I hope there is not a danger of research-hungry educators accepting claims of what works in the classroom only if there is hard evidence to support them. And I also hope that we can still consider that a teacher knows best and what works in their classroom is a valid evidence base on which they can build effective teaching strategies and develop their practice.

I'd like to argue that teachers should still continue to do what works for them without the need for evidence. But this will come at a price. If teachers are told to do X, Y and Z by senior leadership teams because external agencies have suggested that this is what 'good teaching' looks like with no evidence to back them up, we will continue to find various classroom gimmicks being peddled at conferences and on the Internet. Teachers will continue to do all sorts of tricks and one-off performances to please observers, even though there is no evidence to suggest they actually have an impact on learning.

Nevertheless, something has to change. We must be able to trust our teachers to get on with the job they do best. And sometimes, just sometimes, this can be done without any evidence to inform best practice. Do we really need league tables? Do teachers really need lesson plans that run to several pages? If we do, I fear for the mental health of our next generation of teachers. If we are to create a system where teachers can continue to have autonomy in their classrooms, the current climate of testing, measuring and evidencing needs to be eradicated or at least reformed. We must avoid ideological templates at all costs because the students I've taught will have entirely different needs and a very different context when compared to students in other parts of London, England or the world. It is vital we allow our teachers to plan, mark and teach with freedom and flexibility.

Psychology and...
behaviour that is challenging

When I refer to 'challenging behaviour', I mean behaviour that provides a challenge to the teacher, the school ethos, to other students or to the student who is presenting the behaviour. Behaviour defined as challenging should lead teachers to find solutions that make a positive difference rather than become stuck in the psychological cul-de-sac of problematising 'negative' behaviours.

All behaviour is communication and behaviour that is challenging can communicate needs that are unresolved or unmet. Causation may be related to, for example, emotional distress or trauma. It is the function I shall focus on, as establishing the function can provide solution-focused responses. Let's consider four overarching reasons why people behave in a challenging way. The function of the behaviour might relate to one of these reasons or could lie in varying combinations of the four.

1. **Give me some attention:** People may behave in a challenging way to communicate a need for attention – whatever that attention may look like. For some, it does not matter if the attention they receive is positive or negative, as long as they are gaining attention of some description.

2. **Get me out of here:** Challenging behaviour might communicate a need to escape from a situation that a person does not want to be in. Whatever the reason, the desire to escape is communicated through behaviour.

3. **It feels good:** Challenging behaviour may have a sensory function. Some young people behave in a challenging way because, for them, it just feels good to do so at the time. This is especially relevant for those who feel an unrelenting sense of powerlessness as individuals within the systems that they exist in – in education and beyond.

4. **I want a reward:** Challenging behaviour may relate to the desire for a tangible reward. For example, a young child screaming in the back of a car may not want the attention of their parents. They may have learned that if they persistently scream, they will eventually get their favourite sweets to eat because their parents cannot bear the noise and need it to stop.

All schools should be clear about behaviour that is deemed to be challenging in their context and how they seek to find solutions. As well as offering support to students who are presenting with challenging behaviour, schools must also offer support to teachers who are searching for solutions to challenges. Teachers have needs too.

– Professor Tim O'Brien

IDEA 10

Reality check

IDEA SNAPSHOT

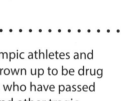

In this final idea of the section, I raise some important issues about the education system. Teaching is a complex business and with the reality that all teachers face in classrooms across the world, a good lesson plan is sometimes not enough.

In my time as a teacher, I have taught future footballers, Olympic athletes and popstars. I've also taught a number of students who have grown up to be drug dealers and thieves, and very sadly intelligent young minds who have passed away from natural causes or in road accidents, house fires and other tragic incidents. When working with children, things will always go wrong, yet much of what we do in the classroom can alter their journey through life. Although the home environment plays a significant role, the teacher also has an important influence and can be the difference for some vulnerable young people.

Over the last few years, there has been much discussion about teaching children resilience and character education, but I'm frustrated with these new terms and definitions. As we grow up, we each need to learn how to be resilient about the world around us, and we should also develop a well-rounded character, contributing to society as global citizens. Although these are distinct traits, schools are already going some way to teaching young people the prerequisites to achieving them. Some are taught through distinct curriculum teaching, and others are what we all learn in the wider world from the people around us, including in the playground. One day, we will call this simply an education.

To achieve all the above, we must enable teachers to collaborate, research and have the time they need to complete their tasks. Teachers must develop the confidence to deal with mistakes and external circumstances that are out of their control. In the book *Be More Toddler*, Emma Turner (2019) sets out the journey she faced being a mum of three and a co-headteacher:

> 'When you build a culture of trust you also build resilience for when the journey takes a sudden turn for the worse. Sadly, too many leaders focus on the managerial aspects of "checking up" and not the leadership aspects of "checking in".'

Building on what Emma has written, we should also take this advice for ourselves as teachers:

1. How often do we set ourselves up to fail?

2. How often do we over-plan curriculum maps, lesson plans or classroom resources?

Of course, as we build a culture of trust in our classrooms, we are also building resilience in our young people and, when things do go wrong, we are prepared for any 'sudden turn for the worse'. Despite our best efforts to improve our practice and plan lessons that will have an impact on students, there are a variety of internal pressures that can stop even the best teacher in their tracks. These are often the result of pinch points in the academic year, which have a direct impact on the time available to create, modify and carry out effective lesson plans.

And in some very extreme cases, the lesson plan will be the last thing on the agenda – especially when student safety is paramount. When I started teaching in Tottenham, I would consider a lesson to have been a success if a chair hadn't been flung across the room! Learning was right at the bottom of my to-do list, and this is still the case for most newly qualified teachers today. Although I would argue we do not have a behaviour crisis, teachers have to deal with challenging behaviour on a daily basis and we must do more to support them with this. We have all had those lessons we dread and these situations, sadly, make teachers fearful. That's the reality.

Teaching is a lifelong journey with no perfect solution, yet our schools and our school systems place unwieldy demands on teachers to perform. In an increasingly high-stakes profession, teachers are destined to fail, especially if we force them to use other teachers' lesson plan templates, PowerPoint slides or marking methods simply because they're easier for observers to track. It is important to remind ourselves that teachers are qualified professionals. Not everyone can keep a roomful of thirty students silent for an hour or control an assembly and make every student in the room feel empowered. Teachers are incredible professionals and the sooner we respect one another, the greater our teaching profession will be.

Teacher wellbeing and mental health

Here's a question for you. Throughout the academic year, which term do you think would be the busiest for a classroom teacher? In some fascinating research, Allen et al. (2020) analysed teachers' working hours over the academic year. Their conclusion? There

is no such thing as a quieter term or a summer-term lull. Teachers are, on average, working at the same level throughout the academic year.

Teaching, at least in England, is not conducive to having a weekend or logging off the computer at five o'clock each evening. Why is teaching a career that is so complex and time-consuming and why does it cause people to burn out far too quickly? And why do we continue to find it acceptable that so many teachers leave the profession after just one year? Did you know, the average teaching career in England lasts a mere 13 years?

The 'Teacher Workload Survey' (DfE, 2019b) acts as a national barometer for teachers' working conditions. Here are the key findings:

1. Teachers and middle leaders report working fewer hours in total in 2019 than they did in 2016, and working fewer hours out of school. (I still find this hard to believe; when I share this statistic with teachers, it always raises a laugh.)

2. Senior leaders also reported working fewer hours in total in 2019 than they did in 2016. However, the crux of the issue for me is still insufficient funding to reduce contact time for school leaders during the working day.

3. Most were positive about the professional development time and support they receive.

4. Most reported that their schools had made efforts to change their policies and approaches to reduce workload, but these had met with mixed success to date.

From this, you'll see that some progress has been made since the previous report in 2016. However, most respondents still reported that they could not complete their workload within their contracted hours, that they did not have an acceptable workload, and that they did not achieve a good work–life balance. So, it's clear we still have some way to go.

Even more worryingly, in some schools where leaders have attempted to reform policies and approaches in a specific attempt to reduce workload, they have actually added to teachers' workloads. Take behaviour, for example. 69% of respondents said their school leaders had made reforms in order to reduce workload. However, only 10% said these reforms had actually reduced their workload, while 26% said they'd made no difference to workload and 33% said they had actually added to workload.

What on earth has gone wrong? Why are we putting so much strain on classroom teachers with policy changes that actually make things worse for them rather than better? It would be foolish for any headteacher not to reshape their policies on a frequent basis, but why would you want to introduce changes that make teachers' lives even harder?

As a country, we must do better to appreciate and take care of our teachers. As a profession, school leaders must do more to support their teachers. Of course, money will help, but there are many things that cost nothing at all and are driven simply by the decisions and choices that school leaders make.

What about the students?

Accountability is also certainly impacting on our students in terms of expectations and the pressures facing our young people today. According to the mental health charity YoungMinds (2019), 1.2 million young people are living with a diagnosable mental health condition in the UK and three-quarters of five- to 19-year-olds with a diagnosable mental health problem have had no contact with the mental health services, let alone received the support they need. The charity also states that 47% of 17- to 19-year-olds who are experiencing emotional disorders such as anxiety and depression have self-harmed or attempted suicide.

I can recall at least two students in each of the schools I have worked in as a senior teacher who have self-harmed in my presence. Once, I was covered in blood after pulling the student back as he repeatedly head-butted a wall. Another student showed me the razor blade he had just used to slash his abdomen. We know our hospitals are stretched, our schools and teachers are stretched, and we do not have the skills or resources to be able to offer the support our young people need.

My childhood background with the social services, with having to deal with physical, sexual and drug abuse, death and self-harm have given me sufficient experience to be able to deal with these situations as an adult and as a teacher. Yet, I have never felt confident enough to offer expertise. The job of teachers first and foremost is to teach. Teachers are not experts, nor should they be expected to deal with mental illness. But no matter how well we plan a lesson or tell a student how to behave, sometimes it just isn't enough. Every adult working with children must have the highest regard for safeguarding and, in whatever form, we must do what we can.

As a nation, we need a reality check. For most people working on the frontline, not only in our schools, but also in our hospitals and our emergency services, every day is a struggle. Three years after this book's first publication, we have not seen any significant investment in our national services, despite promises and despite everything they have had to face from terrorist attacks to a global pandemic. In the Queen's Speech of December 2019, after ten years of austerity under a Conservative government, Her Majesty Queen Elizabeth II said: 'Mental health spending is at a record high, reaching £12.5 billion in 2018-19' and 'To ensure every child has access to a high-quality education my ministers will increase levels of funding per pupil in every school.' But will this be enough, especially given the potential long-term impact of the COVID-19 crisis on children's wellbeing?

Given the many challenges our teachers face as they deal with the complexities of school life and do their best to help vulnerable children, I wonder why some school leaders go around bullying staff, enforcing endless data consumption and detailed, written lesson plans, pushing them further away from actually doing what's best for the children they teach. We must support one another and realise that teaching is more than just a great set of examination results. Success is not just about going to university. For some children, just turning up to school is an achievement.

It is essential we do not lose sight of what is important. We must move away from teaching to the test and instead nurture a love of learning. We need better partnerships between home and school, and schools that are more of a community hub rather than somewhere we all once went as children.

Self-harm

Natasha Devon MBE is a writer and a social critic, who founded the Body Gossip education programme and Self-Esteem Team, designed to educate teenagers, teachers and parents about mental health and body image. On 30th August 2015, the DfE appointed Natasha as its first ever mental health champion for schools. One year later, her role was axed after she criticised the government's testing regime in schools. Below, Natasha offers an exclusive opinion on self-harm for readers of *Mark. Plan. Teach.*

'I've heard many people who have self-harmed speak about why it served a critical purpose for them, during a difficult period in their lives. For some, it provides a distraction from emotional pain. For others, it is a way of expressing difficult feelings physically, in a way others can understand. Many talk about self-harm in language traditionally associated with addiction, describing the rush they get in the immediate aftermath and the way they have to increase the severity of their behaviour over time in order to get the same 'high'. There's also a sub-set of young people who don't see self-harm as radically different from a piercing or a tattoo, using it to self-identify into a group they feel an affinity with.

Self-harm marks the intersection at which mental health, first aid and safeguarding become indistinguishable, making how teachers handle it crucial.

Whilst every case is different, my advice would be not to show disapproval or shock, but instead demonstrate a genuine desire to help, initially by providing physical first aid and then emotional support. Bear in mind that self-harm, like eating disorders, is shrouded in a bizarre pairing of secrecy and competitiveness, so you are likely to encounter a mixture of reticence and perverse pride. Try to replace the phrase 'attention seeking' with 'attention needing' in your mind.

Remember at all times that self-harm is in most cases a coping mechanism, so the ultimate aim is not to make the behaviour stop and nothing more. In fact, to do so might put the young person at increased risk of suicide since they no longer have an outlet for the difficult emotions they may be grappling with. By all means, suggest alternatives for distraction, self-expression and endorphin production, such as sport, creative writing, music, or even screaming or punching a pillow.

If you do recommend a student goes online for more information, make sure it's a forum that monitors its content, so they won't find themselves in a so-called 'pro-self-harm' environment (where techniques and triggering photos are shared between users). The Self-Harm Network is a good example of a safe website.

Finally, remember that no matter what your leadership team or parents might imply, it isn't your job to 'fix' the young person. You can be a sympathetic ear and a signpost towards further sources of support and information, but you are not a mental health professional and it is unreasonable to expect you to be.'

Psychology and...
teacher wellbeing

Ross highlights that there is no one-size-fits-all, perfect solution available for teaching. This may be one of the reasons why the teaching profession has been so susceptible to gimmicks and fads. In the search for a universal solution, one approach after another competes to become the only approach in town. Teachers do all that they can to make that approach work in their context. Then the approach falls into disrepute or fades into the mist. When this happens, the teaching profession cannot be seen to be in a state of not knowing – which is, by the way, a stimulating psychological state to be in – and the void must be filled. And so the process continues. Fortunately, becoming a more evidence-informed profession enables teachers to adopt an increasingly critical gaze and challenge taken-for-granted practices that, in the past, have been presented to them as indisputable common sense.

For decades, teachers have committed to government initiatives regularly imposed upon them without consultation. Then there is the accountability agenda. I recently conducted research for The Chartered College of Teaching, and it was evident that teachers in that research study had no problem at all with being accountable. Their concern was the way that accountability has been applied, creating a culture of fear. My view is that the current system of hyperaccountability places teachers in a state of manic vigilance that generates anxiety, guilt and stress.

All that I have described so far inevitably impacts upon teacher wellbeing. The situation has to change. The wellbeing needs of teachers have been overlooked for too long. However, identifying teacher wellbeing needs is not straightforward because wellbeing itself is a contested construct. Wellbeing can be understood from many perspectives, including mental health, physical, psychological and spiritual. Wellbeing can be seen as having dimensions that are measurable, yet it can also be seen as culturally constructed and therefore shifting in meaning and interpretations. We also have to consider whether teacher wellbeing actually exists as a separate domain of wellbeing and, if so, whether it is qualitatively different to wellbeing in any other profession and why.

I propose that one way of understanding wellbeing is to think about unwellbeing; what would be missing that would have a negative impact on wellbeing. What would that be for you? Perhaps professional autonomy? Enjoyment? Being valued for what you do? Collaboration? Or a sense of meaning and purpose?

– Professor Tim O'Brien

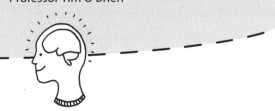

Section 2: Summary

Planning is deliberately positioned right in the middle of the **Mark. Plan. Teach.** cycle because I believe it is the pinnacle of everything a good teacher must be able to do. Providing feedback to your students through assessment will enable you to check your students' understanding of their work. If you do this regularly, assessment will inform all aspects of your short-, medium- and long-term planning. It will allow you to adapt your lessons (either by careful design or on the spot) to the needs of your students and help them become more engaged in their learning. As you interact with students, you will be able to see their progress (or lack of) and this will inform future teaching and possibly even help shape future schemes of work, differentiation needs and opportunities for intervention.

No matter how you look at it, planning is a pillar in the **Mark. Plan. Teach.** cycle and it supports marking, feedback and teaching.

As a reminder, here are the headlines of this section of the book: ten ideas to help your lesson planning inform your marking and teaching and ultimately enable you to have a greater impact on your students' learning:

1. Be clear and precise about the knowledge and skills you want students to *learn*, not what you want them to do. It is important to shift the focus away from activities to what we are *learning* and why. Only then will the teaching and learning have any substance and you can ensure that students will have a chance of learning and making progress.

2. Apply the 'why?' test to all learning activities, including homework, so your planning is designed to facilitate learning and not to keep students busy. Make sure you can explain to students clearly and succinctly why they are learning things to deepen understanding and increase engagement.

3. Integrate imaginative teaching strategies, such as storytelling, into your lessons to keep your students engaged but plan how and when to use them carefully to ensure they impact on learning. Remember, telling stories brings the curriculum to life and can support long-term memory.

4. Embed stickability into your lesson planning. Think about what learning should stick in the minds of your students and the key points you want your students to remember and bring back to the next lesson. Teach students study strategies that involve retrieval practice, spaced practice and interleaving to help them make their learning stick.

5. Plan to keep students in the struggle zone to ensure they feel sufficiently challenged but not stressed or anxious. Embed assessment methods, such as questioning, into your lesson plans to help you achieve this.

6. In lessons that get off to a flying start, students learn more purposefully from the beginning. Simple flying starts – that don't require hours of planning – often have the greatest impact and are the perfect opportunity to embed literacy and retention of knowledge into lesson plans.

7. Differentiation should be planned over time to ensure a quality first teaching approach that meets the needs of all students. Use seating plans based on your knowledge of each student to support this. Planning should also maximise the use of any additional adults in the room and don't forget to have conversations with TAs outside of lesson time.

8. Make sure you have time to focus on your professional development. Work collaboratively with other teachers in your department or school to keep up to date with research and create a bank of ideas you can rely on in lessons.

9. Be aware that when dealing with challenging behaviour, you may need to change your lesson plan on the spot. Knowing your individual students, their specific contexts and motivations for an outburst in class will help you provide the right intervention at the right time, and it is important that your school grants you the flexibility to do this. If you find yourself in a situation where you suddenly need to turn your focus to behaviour, try the seven-step behaviour script.

10. Finally, when it comes to lesson planning, we all need a reality check once in a while, especially those involved in decisions about our national education system. External accountability is impacting the mental health and wellbeing of our teachers and our students. Teaching is about more than examination results and just sometimes, a great lesson plan is simply not enough.

Section 3:
TEACH.

There is no such thing as a quintessential teaching style. Our own unique teaching style develops over time. Those who have mentored us – or at least those who mentored us *well* – will want every teacher to find out what works best for them and their students, rather than adopt a specific style or approach.

We've all encountered good teachers and those who have lost their mojo in our own school experiences, and we all have ideas about what makes one teacher better than another, but all teachers will, of course, teach differently in different settings. If you are reading this book as a teacher – and there is a high chance that you are – then I know I am preaching to the converted. You will be able to think of some amazing teachers you have worked with and be able to jot down on paper what it is that makes them so great. Equally, you will be aware of some teachers who have needed extra support and you will know that the real issue is how that support has been provided and why.

Teaching is a team sport. No individual can resolve complex classroom problems on their own. However, this needs to be balanced with ensuring teachers have the autonomy to develop professionally, think creatively about their classroom practice and teach freely, without pressure from external influences. It's important that school leaders create the conditions for this through careful support and sufficient challenge.

It's always tricky to strike the balance between teamwork and individualism. The footballer Eric Cantona is a classic example of this due to his maverick reputation. He was football heaven and hell. A talented player, famous for being larger than life, physically strong, hard working and a tenacious forward, he combined technical skill with creativity, power and goal scoring ability. Despite his incredible footwork and vision, however, his notoriety came from an off-the-ball incident many thought far outweighed the greater good he brought to the team and was in fact detrimental to his (and the team's) overall success.

However we choose to define a maverick, whether risk taking, creative or unorthodox, I am certain we can all remember someone in our school who has broken the mould. Some readers may also consider themselves to be somewhat maverick.

As for myself, I was promoted in my third year of teaching. I was 26 and had barely mastered the classroom. In my heyday as a middle leader, some six or seven years later, I was becoming more creative and would have considered myself to be a maverick. I was confident, experimental and had overcome the difficulties we all face in our first year of teaching, but I was also a world apart from the policies of senior leadership. Despite leading a team of 13 staff and being on the cusp of school leadership myself, I was still a huge step away from having any whole-school perspective. I rarely observed colleagues outside my own department in a climate where all schools were grading lessons but colleagues were only observed for three hours per academic year. This was nearly 20 years ago but it is still happening in many schools today.

Observing other teachers was often voluntary and something you did in the little free or non-contact time you had available. Whole-school systems for using observations to develop and help coach colleagues (Section 3, Idea 10, p. 164) were few and far between. I had also not yet been faced with having to support or challenge experienced teachers who were reliable and all-round solid but whose personal confidence sometimes undermined the collective school vision because they would ignore policies and procedures. I had not yet understood, or been encouraged to recognise, that these behaviours may not be helpful to the overall success of a school.

Today, my experience of lesson observations has grown significantly. I would say I have observed tens of thousands of lessons, from foreign language lessons where I couldn't understand a word of what was being taught to Early Years lessons where teachers had carefully designed learning in sandpits or with water, earth, wood and clay. As a senior teacher, I was placed in a privileged position where I could observe, support and challenge colleagues who might have been undermining each other – never because they took risks or used a particular teaching style but because they ignored procedures or (more likely) were inundated with requests to 'do this', 'fill this in', 'complete that' or 'go there at this time'.

Of course, school leaders, using their wisdom and expertise, should steer teaching and learning, but for me, the real power comes from staff sharing their difficulties as well as their successes and finding solutions together. As I've said previously, not one school I have visited has achieved consistency, regardless of whether they're a primary school rated 'outstanding', a secondary school in 'special measures' or an international school charging up to £100,000 in fees. This isn't to say that we should not seek some degree of consistency, but I think it's the wrong choice of language. Consistency sets us up to fail. It doesn't encourage maverick teachers. It puts off those teachers who have lost their edge, as well as inexperienced teachers or those with great experience and approaching retirement, who may have slowed down for one reason or another. Instead, school leaders must seek clarity and coherence. They should strive to be in a position where all teachers are clear and precise about the school's vision and teaching and learning policies and where teaching culture is built from the ground up and sustained on a weekly basis through simple conversations.

With this vast array of experience in lesson observations, I can say with confidence that one size does not fit all. One size fits one person. School leaders must work hard to adopt methods to enable reliable evaluation that supports teacher development. Teaching is adaptive and this is what makes it an incredibly complex and difficult area to get right. Although the Grim Reaper is clear that we must not champion one particular style of teaching over another (and school leaders should be too), you can see the government in England working very hard to drive a particular pedagogical approach. This is only destined to fail.

So, with all this in mind, let's go back to my opening paragraphs about what you think makes a good or 'not yet' good teacher. Make a note of a few characteristics that spring to mind for each and even better discuss this with a colleague. Now, take a look at your list. Who did you have in mind when you wrote the list of good qualities? What makes them special? How long have they been teaching? Are they a maverick? Do you find yourself learning from them to this day? Does this person still have a learning mindset? What makes them vary wildly to the person (or set of characteristics) you have described for a 'not yet' good teacher? Which teacher is most likely to understand your school's policies and procedures?

Teaching in line with school policy

Teaching in line with school policy, beyond my formative (and occasionally painful) years as a newly qualified teacher, was a steep learning curve when I became a middle leader. Mastering the art of teaching, as well as learning the trade of middle leadership, was a tough journey. However, as my confidence in experimenting with teaching evolved, my willingness to take risks and my subject confidence both soared. Middle leadership was the happiest time of my teaching career. Growing into the role of middle leader exposed me to a wider world beyond the classroom. I soon realised the need for every teacher, including myself and my colleagues in other departments, to be working in line with school policy and, at senior leadership level, with parent unions and governors.

This would ensure that colleagues did not undermine each other and, more importantly, students would know that there would be no slippage, no gaps in the system that would be exposed between classrooms. We could be confident that what one colleague was saying or doing in one classroom would be more or less the same as what another was saying or doing in the classroom next door or even on the other side of the school building. How often have your students quoted the school rules back to you? If this happens regularly, the students clearly understand the rules and they must be working! They're quoting them because the teacher has gone off piste. Understanding the bigger picture and collective purpose of the school, and therefore why teaching in line with school policy is so important, is something that is difficult to communicate to classroom teachers who don't have the opportunity to observe each other. I, for one, only grasped the importance of school policy when I observed colleagues as a young middle leader.

I believe that a good teacher is one who is given the freedom to teach in a way that suits them and their students. A good teacher takes risks, is creative, enjoys their subject and develops their students' love of learning, but also understands the importance of remaining within a defined set of boundaries and expectations for the greater good of the school. Only then can a teacher achieve the perfect balance and reach autonomy, as shown in the grid below.

Accountability	Autonomy	Absence
Compliance	Efficacy	No dialogue
Frequency	Regular CPD	No interest
Leadership driven	Research-informed	Discouraged
External pressures	Open doors	Closed doors

How can we improve teaching and learning?

In this section, I offer a range of teaching ideas that will help you to put Sections 1 and 2 into practice. With clear explanations, teachers can make learning stick (Section 3, Idea 1, p. 122 and Idea 2, p. 127), and with an established culture, high expectations, routines and conditions, teachers can go with the flow of learning, confidently adapting their lessons to meet the needs of students (Section 3, Idea 3, p. 131), all the while using questioning to check learning has stuck (Section 3, Idea 5, p. 140).

Encouraging teachers to take risks and 'go with the flow' in classrooms is all fine and dandy, but teachers need a safe and rewarding climate in which they feel comfortable to do this. We know that this is rare in our current school system, but as David Weston says, 'if we want the best for our children... [we need to] do the best for our teachers' (Weston, 2015). This section will, therefore, also look at what school leaders can do to introduce and embed a simple teaching and learning policy, underpinned by high expectations and a simple and robust behaviour policy, that enables teachers to teach without fear of tick-box templates, stringent lesson plans or choking schemes of work (Section 3, Idea 4, p. 134). It will also consider how a culture of continued professional development (CPD) can be built by using lesson observation to develop teachers, not judge them. Staff should be given time to observe each other's lessons, to learn from one another and to reflect on their own teaching (Section 3, Idea 8, p. 157). A system of coaching can also work wonders to encourage staff to develop their practice and, ultimately, believe in what they are doing to improve the lives of the students they teach.

Direct instruction

IDEA SNAPSHOT

In Section 2, Idea 2, p. 70, I discussed the importance of students understanding *why* they are learning what they are learning and I explored how you can embed this into your lesson planning to deepen understanding and increase engagement. When you are teaching, it's essential that you are explicit about the learning outcomes, success criteria and the keywords that form the foundations of your lesson; students must understand the knowledge and skills you want them to learn and the language they are expected to understand and apply. This idea looks at how this can be achieved through a combination of direct instruction, self-regulated feedback and 'nudge theory'.

Direct instruction is an approach developed by Siegfried Engelmann and Carl Bereiter in the late 1960s, supported by a great deal of research in developing literacy and numeracy. It has a strong evidence base, with John Hattie (2009) giving the effect size as d=0.59. Direct instruction is essentially explicit teaching. In other words, teaching that is structured, sequenced and led by the teacher. All coherent schemes of work already have episodes of direct instruction included, so the job of the teacher is bringing these curriculum plans to life through effective teaching methodologies. Put simply, the teacher must establish learning objectives and make sure students have gained the requisite knowledge. This is then supported through a series of lessons where students move towards a stronger understanding of the knowledge, with the teacher reviewing instructions for each activity by modelling, thinking out loud and providing worked examples. It's essential to give students clear explanations and ask them a number of questions to check understanding. Direct instruction stands in contrast to teaching methods where students construct their own understanding and knowledge of the world.

A key part of direct instruction is being explicit about the learning outcomes. The standard method of doing this is to share them, along with keywords, on the board at the beginning of the lesson. However, it isn't necessary for this to be a routine to open every lesson. There are more sophisticated variations available and you can even use them to support students' long-term memory. Simple retrieval practice exercises throughout a lesson are critical, so here are three suggestions for using learning objectives in this way:

- Ask students to remind you of the learning outcomes and keywords from the previous lesson and give them time to speculate on what they might be for this lesson.

- Complete the first activity you have planned (it could be a flying start) and then ask the class what they think the learning outcomes and keywords might be.

- Teach the entire lesson and then ask students what they think the learning outcomes and keywords might have been.

When it comes to keywords, it is essential to embed them into the lesson and into the language you use with your students. Keywords mentioned at the beginning of class and then never again serve no purpose. If your high expectations are represented in your language, at least some of the keywords you are using will not be commonly understood by the class and the process of explaining them (and enabling students to use them) will be a very significant part of your lesson. By definition, the number of keywords you introduce should take into account cognitive load theory and how this translates in the context of the students you teach, in order to avoid overloading their working memory. It is a high-level teaching skill to be able to build your lesson around a couple of keywords, so see Section 2, Idea 6, p. 89 for some more guidance.

'Teacher clarity'

Professor John Hattie says that 'teacher clarity' has a positive influence on student achievement. Hattie defines 'teacher clarity' as 'organization, explanation, examples and guided practice […] of student learning' and he believes that 'clarity of speech [is] a prerequisite of teacher clarity' (Hattie, 2009). I see 'teacher clarity' as the importance of clearly communicating the intentions of a lesson and the success criteria, namely the learning outcomes and keywords and, in fact, clearly communicating all direct instruction or teacher-led learning. Whenever your lesson involves direct teaching, you should ensure all instructions are delivered clearly so students know what they are doing at any given point in the lesson. The MINT strategy is one way of doing this successfully.

The MINT strategy

For a long time, I have applied the MINT strategy to everything I do in the classroom, and I also now use it in teacher training sessions and other aspects of life outside school. It's a perfect example of how to use 'teacher clarity' in the direct instruction elements of your lesson because it helps you ensure that all instructions are delivered with clarity and in bite-sized chunks. Let's look at how it works.

Firstly, the acronym MINT stands for:

M = Materials

I = In or out of seats

N = Noise level

T = Time

To explain further, here's how I would go about using MINT when teaching a lesson:

Materials: simply means resources to be used; do not overcomplicate things – if there are five objects in a box, state the box and not the five individual objects.

In or out of seats: even in a practical subject, not every lesson will involve activities out of seats and in more theoretical subjects, such as maths, students may need to work around the classroom, solving problems with peers.

Noise level*: be clear about the accepted volume.

- Volume 1 = No talking; individual, silent work
- Volume 2 = Paired discussions
- Volume 3 = Whole-class discussion

Time: specify clearly the time needed to complete the activity, including final warning.

*As much as I detest noise-o-meters when used to monitor whether classroom noise levels are acceptable or not, they can work wonders in primary settings and with 11- to 14-year-olds to help students learn how to manage their own classroom discussions.

Here's an example showing exactly how I might apply the MINT strategy in any part of a lesson, using it as a framework for direct instruction:

M: 'You will need a piece of A3 paper, a pencil, a ruler and this pink A5 worksheet.'

I: 'You will be working out of your seat, moving slowly around the classroom, visiting various sources on display.'

N: 'The noise I would like you to maintain is a quiet conversation in your groups.'

T: 'The time you have to do this is seven minutes. I will also give you a final one minute warning before we stop.'

Self-regulated learning

One of our key missions as teachers is to help students take control of their own behaviour and learning, in other words to become self-regulated learners. Key to this is using principles of direct instruction and feedback in order to create a feedback loop that enables students to monitor and regulate their own learning and performance. Based on the seven principles of good feedback from Nicol and Macfarlane-Dick, as highlighted in Section 1, Idea 9, p. 47, and also a model by Butler and Winne (1995), I have devised a seven-step feedback plan to support this:

Step 1: The teacher uses direct instruction to set the task, clarifying the success criteria and modelling the exercise using 'I do, we do, you do' (see Section 3, Idea 2, p. 127). Based on their existing knowledge, the strategies they can adopt and their motivation levels, the student internally sets their own goal for the task.

Step 2: The teacher sets the students off on the task and facilitates a range of self- and peer-assessment strategies to determine how they are progressing.

Step 3: As the students progress, the teacher provides micro, high-quality feedback in conversations around the classroom. This is supported with simple questions: 'What if…?', 'How might you…?' and 'Describe to me why you have…'.

Step 4: As the feedback is offered, the teacher encourages peer-to-peer dialogue. Try C3B4ME.

Step 5: The students will experience a range of successes and failures throughout the task. The teacher should encourage positive motivation and self-esteem by asking the students to explain what they've learnt and evaluate what they need to do next. A wide range of metacognitive strategies are advocated here.

Step 6: Provide opportunities to close any gaps students might have in the knowledge or skills required to meet the success criteria. This is the most difficult part for the teacher. You need to consider what intervention is needed – and when and where to administer it – based on your knowledge of each student's needs, and plan to evaluate its impact.

Step 7: The teacher should now evaluate next steps for themselves and the learner.

As part of this feedback loop, using unconditional positive regard and nudge theory alongside direct instruction is strongly recommended. Context is key, so think carefully about what will be most suitable for your learners.

Unconditional positive regard and 'nudge theory'

Relating to 'teacher clarity' and direct instruction, 'unconditional positive regard' (UPR) is a concept first brought to my attention by Hywel Roberts in his book *Oops! Helping Children Learn Accidentally* (Roberts, 2012). The term was first devised by the psychologist Carl Rogers and it describes how children should be accepted and supported, irrespective of their actions. Even the most challenging and humble of students need UPR offered through 'teacher clarity' and direct instruction. Those not exposed to UPR may come to see themselves in negative ways. Clear and direct UPR helps children accept responsibility for themselves, aids their personal growth and allows them to be spontaneous without fearing that others might lose respect for them.

However, 'nudge theory' argues that using positive reinforcement or indirect suggestion is far more effective than direct instruction or enforcement when trying to persuade people to do something. As first proposed by Richard Thaler and Cass Sunstein in their book *Nudge*, 'nudge theory' suggests that spending lots of time *telling* students to do something or making rules is not very effective and becomes even less effective over time (Thaler and Sunstein, 2009).

There are lots of examples of good behaviour management where 'nudge theory' is used. Rather than reprimanding children, for example, we may praise other children near them for doing the right thing. I have used this in countless behaviour scenarios to deflect positive behaviours onto nearby students who are either misbehaving or are disrupting the teaching and learning. It takes practice, but it does work.

Other examples of 'nudge theory' include arranging the chairs and tables in our classrooms to facilitate certain behaviours that we require in that lesson. Teachers can also reward students for doing the right thing, such as arriving in the classroom with their ties done up or having their planners out on their desks to start the lesson.

Teachers then allocate rewards throughout the lesson, referencing 'correct' behaviours identified earlier, to embed actions they want to see in their students.

In my opinion, both direct instruction and 'nudge theory' have a place in every classroom, so teachers offer students clarity but do not constantly *tell* them to do things or make rules. You should share learning objectives and keywords in your lessons but this could be done through direct instruction and 'teacher clarity' one week, then the next you could 'nudge' students to decode the objectives and keywords independently. Combining these two techniques will help deepen your students' understanding of what you want them to learn in your lessons and why.

EVIDENCE

Direct instruction is by no means the only effective approach to teaching, but it does work better than many other teaching techniques. Direct instruction is teacher centred but it does not require teachers to entertain their students and it is not the same as rote learning; like most other teaching approaches, it asks students to be persistent and reap the rewards of hard work.

Research from the Education Development Trust and the University of Oxford (Ko et al., 2014) demonstrates the value of direct instruction. In a review of the literature, the research found a number of studies provided evidence that teacher-directed approaches have a strong positive effect on attainment, especially among younger students and those from a more disadvantaged background. The research goes on to claim that although direct instruction is important in group and paired work:

> 'organising students as a whole class for a significant proportion of a lesson helps to maximise their contact with the teacher so every student benefits from the teaching and interaction for sustained periods of time.'

This suggests that direct instruction might be the most efficient way of teaching large classes of students effectively.

Most importantly, however, the report found evidence that 'learning can be greatly accelerated if instructional presentations are clear, minimise misinterpretations and facilitate generalisations'. This just shows how essential 'teacher clarity' is in all elements of direct instruction and is backed up by John Hattie's 'ranking of effect sizes'. According to Hattie, direct instruction has an impact of d=0.59 on student learning and achievement, while 'teacher clarity' has an even greater impact of d=0.75 (Hattie, 2009).

It's clear that direct instruction, when conducted with 'teacher clarity', can have a significant impact on progress and achievement, but it would be interesting to understand *why* direct instruction works. I personally suspect that a confident, consistent teacher, secure with subject knowledge and clear expectations of behaviour for learning in the classroom, may be the answer.

Modelling

IDEA SNAPSHOT

Modelling is an important method of direct instruction (see Section 3, Idea 1, p. 122). There are a number of modelling strategies that can be applied to help students develop key skills in literacy and numeracy in all settings and subject areas. This idea will explore some of the best.

We are all teachers of literacy and numeracy, regardless of the age group and the subject we teach. The quality of a student's written and oral language, namely whether it contains sharp, accurate and well-developed descriptions, explanations and vocabulary, is a significant determinant of progress. A strong mathematical grounding is also beneficial in a wide variety of subjects, including the STEM subjects (science, technology, engineering and maths), but also geography, computing, art, PE, economics and so on.

When it comes to teaching literacy and numeracy, modelling strategies are essential. By explaining or demonstrating to students exactly what is expected of them (while also keeping expectations high), students will be able to respond more effectively to the tasks you set them. Let's take a look at some modelling strategies that you could implement quickly and easily in your classroom to have an impact on your students' literacy and numeracy skills.

Reading

When tackling longer or more challenging texts, **reciprocal teaching** will enable students to support one another to fully digest what they are reading. Reciprocal teaching is an instructional activity in which students become the teacher in small group reading sessions, equipped with a straightforward set of reading comprehension strategies:

1. Summarising – highlighting the key ideas in the text.

2. Questioning – asking questions about the text (such as whether anything is unclear or puzzling and how the text relates to previous learning).

3. Clarifying – addressing confusing parts of the text and attempting to answer the questions posed in Stage 2.

4. Predicting – thinking about what might happen later in the story or what the author might say in the next section of the text.

Teachers model to students how to guide group discussions using these four strategies. Students are then split into groups and guide their own discussions about the text. One student could lead the entire discussion or the students could divide the four techniques between them and lead on each in turn. The teacher provides assistance as and when necessary.

Writing

Oral rehearsal in preparation for an upcoming writing task is essential. Particularly for students with English as an additional language, the opportunity to rehearse writing by discussing ideas with a partner or in small groups in standard English not only improves content but also helps develop literacy.

Think–pair–share

There are a number of strategies you could use here, including group discussions and presentations, but one approach that is especially effective is **think-pair-share**. In this technique, students first work independently, *thinking* about how they might approach the task, what they might like to write about and how they could put their ideas into words. The students then *pair* up to discuss their ideas and develop them further. Finally, the teacher facilitates a whole-class discussion, asking the pairs to *share* what they have come up with. This builds a model of how the students might approach the writing task and gives them the confidence to put their ideas down on paper.

Note that there is one key problem with the first step of this simple teaching technique. You need to ensure students are actually thinking about your question. One way to do this is to pose a question, give students thinking time and then ask them to write a few words down and show them to you. This also ensures you gather more responses, which will allow you to determine what you need to re-teach, if necessary.

I do, we do, you do

Another simple, yet sophisticated, classroom technique that can build writing skills in all settings is **I do, we do, you do**. This is an important strategy that can be used whenever you expect students to complete any form of extended writing. **I do, we do, you do** is a form of scaffolding that involves:

- Direct instruction: the teacher models the learning activity.

- Guided instruction: the teacher and student complete the learning activity simultaneously; the teacher continues to model but also checks what the students are doing and provides prompts where necessary.

- Independent practice: the student completes the learning activity alone (or in pairs or small groups) without guidance from the teacher; the teacher can provide feedback on the students' work once complete. (See more on this in Section 3, Idea 7, p. 152.)

Numeracy

Students often don't appreciate the value of numeracy but as teachers, it is our job to help them understand just how important it is. Numeracy includes not only significant aspects of what is taught in mathematics, but also the ability to use numbers and solve problems in real life and across the curriculum.

In fact, numeracy is relevant to all subjects and includes:

- Reasoning

- Problem solving

- Decision-making

- Shapes

- Use of space

- Measures

- Calculations

- Data handling…

- …as well as anything taught within the mathematics curriculum.

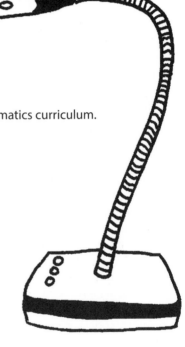

When you are teaching anything that is numeracy related, you should **make it explicit** that you are doing so (to use conscious long-term and working memory). You could use a **visualiser**, a **screencast** or your **interactive whiteboard** to model a problem relating to your lesson content and show mathematical working, so students can visually relate the problem to concepts they may have learnt in maths lessons. This will help students see the relationships between subjects and instil in them the importance of maths across the curriculum and in everyday life.

The process of modelling an activity, then asking students to complete it independently or in small groups will enable students to put their learning into practice, helping them to retain information learnt and skills gained. Of course, context matters, so think about the age of your students, what subject you're teaching, what stage you're at in the academic year and so on. Practical application will also help students to appreciate the value of the information and skills they are learning, not only in the subject being taught but also across the curriculum and in real-life situations, enhancing their engagement and therefore impacting on progress. As always, memory (and forgetting – see Section 1, Idea 6, p. 35) has a significant role to play in learning, be it subject-specific or cross-curricular content. Read on to find out more about memory from Professor Tim O'Brien…

Psychology and...
memory

Memory is complex and multifaceted: autobiographical memory, episodic memory, semantic memory, short-term memory, long-term memory, declarative memory, non-declarative memory, context-dependent memory…

Let's start with autobiographical memory and move on to memory and its association with learning. When we describe incidents that have happened to us years ago, we often say, 'I remember as if it were yesterday'. The problem is, we don't. We like to think that our memory consists of events and experiences that we recollect and reliably reproduce. The problem is, it doesn't. Your memory is not an infallible archive of your life experiences. Remembering is a process that involves different parts of your brain communicating with each other. When you remember something, your memory is prone to errors. Memory is malleable and changeable and our memories can be notoriously unreliable. They can be so unreliable that they can even be false. We construct and reconstruct what we think happened to us in the past rather than retrieve and recall exactly what did happen. The proposition here is that your memory is a series of narratives.

Learning requires memory; remembering and forgetting are components of learning. Earlier in this book, when talking about making and embracing mistakes, I referred to a specific cognitive four-stage model of learning processes (p. 34). Cognitive models often raise interesting issues about learning and memory, especially short-term and long-term memory. They help us to remain conscious that short-term memory is inevitably susceptible to cognitive overload and remind us that overload will have a negative impact on a person's learning capability. In relation to long-term memory, cognitive models remind us that what we have learned can become increasingly unrequired and may appear to be ultimately redundant and hence forgotten. However, what had previously been learned can be brought from unconscious to conscious awareness through the process of cognition – by thinking about what has been forgotten. In relation to the process of learning, long-term memory is central to making the unfamiliar become familiar again; offering a range of memory cues can help this happen.

Conceptualising memory as being malleable reminds teachers and students to accept not only that forgetting is part of learning but also that forgetting can enable learning. It encourages teachers to plan optimistic teaching and learning interactions to allow students to engage in the cognitive (and emotional) rigour involved in making meaning so that they increase their potential to retain and remember what they have learned over time.

– Professor Tim O'Brien

The flow

IDEA SNAPSHOT

Every teacher should have the confidence to 'go with the learning' when they teach a lesson. This means ensuring flow in the delivery of teaching content to enable greater progress. This freedom is far more important than following a lesson plan but it must be encouraged and supported by a whole-school culture that rejects checklists and gradings, and allows teachers to make mistakes and learn from them. Just think about what happens when a flowing stream meets a large rock or a dam. It eventually works out a new path and moves on. This is exactly what you should be doing in your lessons.

Teachers are fearful of taking risks in schools where a growing climate of accountability is endemic (Schleicher, 2018), but often, allowing teachers to take risks and learn from mistakes is the best way of improving teaching and learning.

John Hattie ranked 'collective teacher efficacy' the second most influential factor on student achievement in 2015, meaning that if any classroom strategy is to be effective, it must be underpinned by good teaching across the board. Hattie defines collective teacher efficacy as 'the shared belief by a group of teachers in a particular educational environment that they have the skills to positively impact student outcomes'. If schools wish to roll out a one-size-fits-all approach to teaching and learning, then it will only ever be as good as every teacher in every classroom. Personally, I believe this model is unobtainable. Good teaching will thrive only if there is a culture in the school that is devoid of checklists, evaluations and gradings and allows every teacher to make mistakes and learn from them.

But is this achievable or is this an impossible ask? Can teachers really allow lessons to be loose and should they take risks? Well, I've only ever worked in challenging schools where the pressure is so immense that a one-size-fits-all approach appears to be the best solution, but behind the scenes, this is very far away from the reality, despite what we want to believe. However, I know that if schools and classrooms are to be successful, we must allow teachers and students to go with the flow.

For me, going with the flow means 'going with the learning' to enable greater progress. 'Going with the learning' allows teachers to deviate from their lesson plans as and when necessary to ensure learning is taking place. It is about valuing teachers who intuitively recognise whether students have learnt what they have been taught and who can adjust the lesson accordingly. This freedom is far more important than following an overly detailed lesson plan, enforcing a tick box culture or pleasing an imaginary (or even real) inspector. Lesson planning does still need to be thorough, at least as a coherent thought process, however, otherwise there is nothing for teachers to deviate from. 'Winging it' might be possible in experienced hands, but it is not desirable in the long term and definitely not professional.

Here are my top tips for 'going with the flow':

- Before you can 'go with the learning', you must first be clear about the knowledge and skills you want students to learn and take away from the lesson. In your lesson planning, make sure you shift your focus away from the activities you want students to complete and instead think about what you want students to learn and why. For more on this, see Section 2, Idea 1, p. 64.

- Ensure you have a secure overview of the starting points, progress and context of every student you are teaching (see Section 1, Idea 1, p. 7). This will help you adapt your lesson plans on the spot to meet the specific needs of the students in your class.

- When students are completing a task, keep moving around and sit at each student's desk in turn, working with them closely. Listen, rather than talk. That way, you will be able to spot the students who are progressing and those who may need a helping hand, so you can decide where your lesson needs to go next to maximise learning. Rosenshine (2012) suggests that the optimal time to spend with each student is 30 seconds or less.

- Assess work 'live' in lesson time, with the students by your side, so you can see immediately how your students are progressing and which specific areas they need to improve (see Section 1, Idea 3, p. 18). You will then know whether you can move on to the next phase of learning or whether there are any particular aspects you need to re-teach.

- Use questioning regularly in your lessons to check whether learning has stuck and if not, adjust your lesson plan accordingly. The greater number of questions you ask, the more data you can collect to inform what to teach next (see Section 3, Idea 5, p. 140).

- With colleagues, gather a set of research-informed strategies that will help you to recap on and reinforce the key learning if you sense that something just hasn't stuck (see Section 2, Idea 8, p. 100).

Many lessons do not work out the way they were intended. Sometimes, knowledge and skills do not stick and need to be re-taught. Understanding memory and techniques such as retrieval practice and dual coding will help with this. An unexpected disruption might mean that activities need to be shortened or lengthened or done in a different order. The point of a lesson is to maximise learning, not deliver a plan. It is more important that your students grasp the key learning, rather than complete all the activities you had planned for the lesson, and the only way to do this is to 'go with the learning' and ensure flow in your delivery of teaching content.

Psychology and... flow

Ross refers to a concept of 'flow' occurring in various teaching contexts. Flow is also a well-researched psychological concept. One psychologist in particular, Mihaly Csikszentmihalyi, is well known for conceptualising and researching the psychological architecture of flow.

Csikszentmihalyi (2008) describes flow in terms of it being a state of consciousness where attention becomes a form of energy that promotes a merging of action and awareness, and produces deep levels of enjoyment. Being in a psychological state of flow involves an awareness of, and immersion in, the integrated harmony of what we are experiencing. Not only can a person lose track of time when in flow, they can also lose track of self. Flow creates an experience where there is a complete absence of worry about our own inadequacies because we are concentrated fully on the activity that we are engaged in. When we experience flow, there is no room left for our attention to be distracted towards self-scrutiny as that shifts attention and will naturally break the flow state. Attention is seen as the essential tool for optimising our experience and thus creating flow.

Csikszentmihalyi's research proposes that there are specific external conditions that promote the achievement of flow. Flow can occur when we feel challenged by an activity but are consciously aware that our skills are well matched to the challenges that the activity involves. You will have observed that if skills are not well matched to an activity, the level of challenge will generate anxiety and stress. If an activity is not well matched to skills, lack of challenge will generate boredom and disengagement.

My intention here has been to describe flow in a way that might allow you to connect it to your teaching context in a practical manner. I would also like to raise some broad questions about flow that teachers interested in reflection and action research might want to explore further. Questions like:

- Is it possible to create flow in educational settings?

- Is it easier to intentionally create flow in subjects such as music and PE than it is in subjects such as physics and Spanish?

- Is the experience of flow qualitatively different in early years, primary, secondary and specialist provision?

- Does pedagogic orientation influence the conditions and experience of flow?

- Can a teacher's understanding of flow help to remove barriers to learning for students who experience social, emotional and mental health difficulties?

– Professor Tim O'Brien

What every teacher should know

IDEA SNAPSHOT

I've been reading up on memory for a number of years now, and it is my belief that, besides mastering the classroom in terms of subject knowledge and behaviour management, memory is the number one thing all teachers need to know about. Imagine if all teachers were taught 'how to learn', rather than regurgitating the same techniques they once used at school.

The 'wardrobe metaphor' is a key analogy used to explain how memory works. Jeffrey Karpicke, Tricia Taylor and Henry Roediger use this metaphor, with Roediger (1980) explaining that 'memories are stored objects in that space; and retrieving a memory is akin to searching for and finding an object in a physical space'. I like to take this analogy one step further and think specifically of a sock drawer. Inside, you have a series of thick and thin socks made from different materials. Some will be paired together, others will have holes, some will be loose and others will have lost their partner. No matter what the condition of your sock drawer, you will need to do some rummaging around in it to retrieve the socks you want – in the exact same way that you need to rummage around in your long-term memory to find information that is stored there.

The sock drawer is also a useful metaphor for understanding schemas. Schemas are the connections we make between concepts, rules and facts. They help us to make sense of the world around us and categorise and interpret information. When we pair up our socks, whether it's by stripes, spots, size, material or colour, we are in fact organising them physically through a pattern of thought, just as we do with information. The physical organisation of our sock drawer is like our mental structure: a system of organising and absorbing knowledge. It takes cognitive load to create schemas. I'm reminded of my niece who has worn odd socks her entire teenage and adult life. One day, when I asked her why she wore odd socks, she responded, 'I have enough to think about during the day! Why waste time worrying about whether my socks match up?' Although I would struggle to adopt this particular approach, I understand why she's done it: to reduce unnecessary cognitive load and make her life much easier first thing in the morning!

Understanding memory

Teachers who understand how memory works should become better teachers. The three key areas of memory are divided into short-term memory, working memory and long-term memory.

Long–term memory

Long-term memory consists of explicit (conscious) knowledge and implicit (subconscious) knowledge. It is this information we retrieve from our long-term memory when remembering how to use concepts, rules and facts, as well as produce action, for example riding a bike. However, riding a bike may exist in our implicit memory, which essentially means that it is subconscious knowledge. We can ride a bicycle 'without thinking'. If, for a moment, we think about how we ride a bike and then I ask you to consider teaching this to someone else, the knowledge switches from declarative knowledge (what we know), and is directed to produce action (to know how).

Working memory

As knowledge is used, it exists within our working memory, but our working memory is limited. As the information increases, we increase our cognitive load. This is also known as cognitive load theory. Put simply, think of your memory as a bucket and, when you find learning something new quite stressful, your bucket is simply becoming overfull. This is our working memory. It is emotional, it can become stressful and it is limited in its capacity.

Note, learning is usually identified with the encoding of new knowledge in memory. No matter how good your quizzing techniques are in the classroom, these are themselves not thought to produce learning. However, as Karpicke (2016) writes, 'practising retrieval has been shown to produce more learning than engaging in other effective encoding techniques'. Therefore, teachers must build into their curriculum planning and schematic maps 'opportunities to retrieve' in a crowded curriculum, which is increasingly pushing teachers and pupils towards testing.

Short–term memory

Short-term memory is predominantly when we access new information, or if we draw upon information that is subconscious in our long-term memory and that we have to recall over a longer period of time. One example could be when you first learnt your times tables. I suspect you knew your seven times table when you were at primary school but if you were quizzed today to recall it in order from 1 to 12, you may struggle. As we are quizzed and questioned, the relevant knowledge operates in our working memory and is retrieved from our long-term memory and transferred to our short-term memory.

The world around plays a part in how well you can retrieve the information. This includes your environment, your sensory memory and your ability to pay attention. As teachers, we know that not all children have a level playing field, which is why it is critical that teachers create a secure and safe learning environment and adapt their teaching expertise to meet the needs of their pupils, to play upon their senses as well as teach them the skills required to be able to pay attention, learn and recall new information.

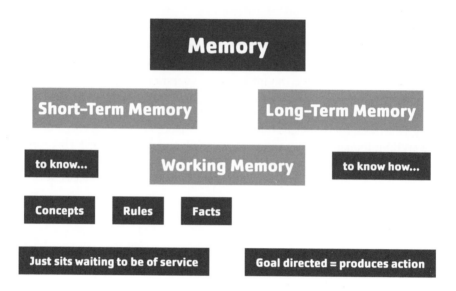

Translating this into practice

It is vital to consider how we can adopt teaching strategies based on what we now know about memory. To have the greatest impact, research-informed techniques should be embedded across an entire setting to enable students to make progress in all their classes. Remember, we know from John Hattie that with 'collective teacher efficacy' across an organisation, overall student progress will be greater (see Section 3, Idea 3, p. 131). So, what do we want our teachers to be able to do to help students make progress? What would you want to see teachers doing consistently in your school to make every teacher's job easier and to impact learning?

The term 'common vernacular' was a poignant phrase I first heard used by principal Alex Thomas. In many ways, my visit to Alex's school formed the beginnings of a common framework that was adapted into a teaching and learning policy that I co-wrote with my headteacher. The phrase 'common vernacular' prompted my research into what common traits could be found in effective teachers and what research-based strategies they use. I wondered how these research-based strategies could be adopted in a script for questioning and for conversations between teachers when they were coaching each other. I also wondered how this could be simplified into a series of coaching prompts, that is to say a common vernacular for teachers to use when developing other teachers in short, focused lesson observations.

Developing this common vernacular then evolved into a short policy that formed the basis of a *Mark. Plan. Teach.* framework that would be used to develop consistency across the entire school. Unbeknownst to me, this would later become the foundations of this book! (See more about that in the Introduction, p. xiii.) We had weekly conversations about this framework and we tinkered with it and debated ideas every month with all staff. Finally, a one-page summary was written and used to communicate expectations and maintain consistency in each and every classroom.

This was delivered in three ways:

- A one-page summary explaining what we would expect from all teachers, in terms of marking, planning and teaching.

- Behind the one-page summary were explicit details, definitions, examples and exemplar material.

- Training, consultation and discussion sessions with all staff.

Depending on how much you've read of this book, you probably already have a sense of what this teaching and learning policy might entail but here it is, simplified into three sentences below. It is what I now call 'the simplest teaching and learning policy in the world'!

The simplest teaching and learning policy in the world!

Mark: Feedback that is regular and diagnostic, so that teachers have a secure overview of where students are going.

Plan: Lesson plans that are clear and consider 'why' students are learning, so that a quality first approach can meet the needs of all students.

Teach: Instructions delivered thoughtfully with explicit use of language, alongside opportunities to act on feedback and embed information into long-term memory through retrieval practice.

There are many different teaching strategies that could be implemented to achieve the above and you will find several that I have used throughout my career in this book. They can, of course, work in isolation but what if I could come up with a shortlist of strategies that could be used by all teachers across my school to really make an impact on student progress? And what if I made using these strategies a minimum requirement for all teachers?

With this in mind, here is my shortlist. They are strategies that I know have worked for me, the students I've taught and the school contexts in which I've worked. They are rooted in what we know about how memory and information retention work. The list is deliberately concise and workable so that all teachers can deploy them successfully as and when they are required. Unless all teachers understand them and use them effectively, then they are as useful as a teacher who has been up all night before a school inspection – useless!

So here you go:

- zonal feedback (see Section 1, Idea 3, p. 18)

- retrieval practice (see Section 1, Idea 9, p. 47)

- think-pair-share (see Section 3, Idea 2, p. 127)

- I do, we do, you do (see Section 3, Idea 2, p. 127)

- pose, pause, pounce, bounce (see Section 3, Idea 5, p. 140).

EVIDENCE

Given what we now know about memory, if there's one thing I absolutely recommend integrating into your teaching and learning policy, it's retrieval practice. In 2011, Jeffrey Karpicke and Althea Bauernschmidt explored why retrieval practice is such a powerful way to improve learning and memory through an experiment involving students learning a list of words in a foreign language. The students saw the words along with their translations on a computer screen and were then shown each word and asked to recall and type its translation. They outlined their findings:

- Merely studying the words once without ever recalling them produced extremely poor performance: the average recall was just 1%!

- Practising until each translation was recalled was much more effective.

- Massed retrieval – repeating the translations three times immediately – produced no additional gain in learning.

- Repeated retrieval enhanced learning only when the repetitions were spaced, and indeed, the effects of repeated spaced retrieval were very large.

- Simple changes that incorporated spaced retrieval practice took performance from nearly total forgetting to extremely good retention (a score of about 80% correct) one week after the initial learning experience.

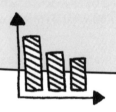

Now, over to you. What key strategies do you use in your classroom and how does this differ from whole-school expectations? Once you have your initial list, what would you say are the minimum strategies that every teacher in your school should be able to use to help achieve consistency and enable student progress across your setting?

If you (or your school leadership team) are able to create a whole-school teaching and learning policy as simple as mine, and can provide a concise list of straightforward strategies to help teachers implement it in every classroom, you will be well on your way to achieving 'collective teacher efficacy', impacting on student learning and making teachers' lives a whole lot easier.

So, the evidence is clear: passive reading produces little or no benefit for learning (all those hours I wasted as a teenager!). In addition, recalling something once doesn't mean you have learnt it. Simple knowledge checks, such as questions in class, or being able to recall something in the short term, do not mean that there has been a shift in long-term memory. Karpicke (2016) says that many students will use a 'one-and-done' strategy: 'If they can recall something once, they believe they have learned it, so they remove it from further practice'.

We cannot have all our pupils repeating the same bland revision strategies you and I used when we were at school. In his 2016 paper, Karpicke highlighted the difference in impact of two different revision strategies: 1) creating concept maps and 2) retrieval practice. The findings report almost a two-fold increase in performance when retrieval practice was used. However, it's worth noting that combining the two techniques – in other words creating a concept map by retrieving rather than reading and copying information – can enhance performance. His research also suggested that closed-book quizzes are more effective than open-book quizzes, which do not require retrieval.

The best news of all is that these techniques are all free! Any teacher can recreate these strategies with no fancy software or theory – just the creativity to design short-term quizzes and techniques in class to help students recall. If you want to improve a pupil's memory and performance, retrieval is the number one technique to build into your teaching repertoire.

Incisive observations

IDEA SNAPSHOT

In every lesson, teachers must check incisively, systematically and effectively that learning has stuck. This enables them to provide their students with feedback and prioritise any particular aspects they may need to explain further or re-teach in the next phase of the lesson. This idea will introduce you to one of the sharpest and most effective ways I have found of doing this: the question matrix.

Far too often, teachers make the assumption that if something has been taught, it will have been learnt. But this is simply not the case. Teachers should not assume something has been learnt and in many respects, it is dangerous to do so. Of course, if a lesson has been planned around the *learning* (see Section 2, Idea 1, p. 64), teachers should be able to gauge whether learning has taken place. But it is not always as easy as that. Learning cannot always be seen. Every teacher has had the experience of writing the same comment in every book or seeing the same mistake in every exam paper because learning was not checked effectively when a specific topic or skill was being taught in the classroom. It is therefore vital that teachers can use teaching techniques confidently and accurately to ascertain whether learning has stuck or not.

You can, of course, ask students directly whether they feel they have grasped the key learning. There are many ways to facilitate this, such as requesting that students indicate their level of understanding with a 'thumbs up' or 'thumbs down', red, amber and green flashcards or hands in the air. Teachers should ask lots of questions, improve their whole-class response rate and support this by regularly thinking out loud to offer cognitive support to students. Good lesson planning is also essential here; if you have planned your lesson carefully, you will be able to move around the room to monitor progress.

However, one of the most effective techniques I can recommend for ascertaining whether or not learning has stuck is the question matrix. When used well, it allows teachers to test confidently, incisively and systematically whether something has been learnt. The question matrix forms a feedback loop, which is absolutely essential to ensuring that teachers are able to decipher what learning is taking place and that students make strong progress over time. It is also useful to reduce a teacher's workload (in terms of thinking) and forms the basis of an excellent scripting tool for teacher feedback and teaching assistants working alongside vulnerable students. Plus, it's great for pupils to use for self- and peer-assessment.

The question matrix

The question matrix is a tool that will help you use questioning more effectively. It is underpinned by the concept of Socratic questioning, which involves a six-step process of asking questions to:

1. Clarify and assess understanding

2. Challenge assumptions

3. Examine evidence to support arguments

4. Gather viewpoints and perspectives

5. Predict implications and consequences

6. Question the question.

The question matrix will enable you to ask the right questions, frame them with the correct choice of language and ensure the level of challenge is appropriate for your students.

I have taught and observed countless lessons, and I've always found that weaker questions aren't necessarily the *wrong* questions but are poorly framed. Often, questions asked in the wrong way lead to students calling out, closed responses, incorrect answers and surface learning. Examples of poorly framed questions include:

- 'Let me ask you all, what is the…?' (Addressing the whole class might lead to students calling out.)

- 'Can anyone tell me…?' (This gives students the option to volunteer or not.)

- 'What does this do *(holds object up)*?' (Most hands go up in the classroom.)

- 'Would this break if I…?' (A leading question that suggests its own answer.)

It's best not to ask questions in this way, so don't waste your breath!

Instead, use the question matrix to ask your students deeper questions – framed correctly from the outset – to elicit deeper responses from your students. It is useful to prepare your key questions for the class during lesson planning, keeping in mind lesson objectives and success criteria. Of course, you will need to have an effective scheme of work in place first (and I am still always surprised to discover how many teachers consider a PowerPoint presentation to be a scheme of work…). Once you do, the question matrix will help you plan questions with low, medium and high challenge that relate directly to the learning. This will allow you to work forwards, rather than plan backwards, meaning you will be planning questions based on what you want your students to *learn*, instead of coming up with a series of questions for students to *do*, in order to fill time in class.

In many ways, I felt liberated once I had the template for this resource in place, as well as having a long list of possible questions linked to specific schemes of work.

So, without further ado, here is the question matrix:

	Is/does? Present	Has/did/was? Past	Can/if? Possibility	Should? Opinion	Would/could? Probability	Will? Prediction	Might? Imagination
What? Event							
Where? Place							
When? Time							
Which? Choice							
Who? Person							
Why? Reason							
How? Meaning							

NOTE: The level of depth and complexity increases in line with the diagonal arrow running across the table.

A few tips for planning questions

When planning questions, every teacher should ask themselves: do I want the students to develop critical thinking skills or deepen their subject knowledge? It can be both. This will determine what type of questions to ask and how to ask them. For example, 'what manufacturing technique are we using here and how does it compare with [another] manufacturing technique?' is a good example of a question that will help develop critical thinking skills. The following question develops knowledge: 'compared to similar techniques used in the cotton industry today, why should this Industrial Revolution technique [tie-dye] be avoided when manufacturing cotton?'

All closed questions, which demand a simple 'yes' or 'no' answer, should be followed up with an additional question. Even simply asking students why they opted for 'yes' or 'no' demands more of a response or an opinion from the student. This could be developed further by asking another student if they agree or disagree with the first student's response and why. You could use the Pose, Pause, Pounce, Bounce technique (see the box on the opposite page), which supports incisive teaching.

During any discussion, posing a single complex question can often reap the wrong results and confuse or panic students. Instead, try using a sequence of questions to build depth and complexity to tease information out of students after you have taught it. This can be done in class discussions with relative ease, but it is much harder to achieve over a long period of time. Try, for example, to provide and model an answer to help a student develop a response to support improvement.

Pose, Pause, Pounce, Bounce

Many years ago, I discovered Pose, Pause, Pounce, Bounce – a brilliant questioning strategy, inspired by a CPD event led by School Improvement Consultant Pam Fearnley. It is a simple, yet sophisticated, way to tease out the learning in class and support differentiation. It also encourages teachers to take risks and vary their questioning techniques.

Here's how it works:

1. **Pose:** Explain to the class the approach you are about to take and insist that students do not raise their hands to answer the question. Pose a question or series of questions, ensuring you ask the students to remain reflective.

2. **Pause:** This is the hard part. Pause for as long as possible before you ask anyone to answer. Ask the class to think and think again. If students are captivated and engaged, push the boundaries and try holding the silence for a little while longer.

3. **Pounce:** Pounce on one student for an answer. Insist the answer comes from Student A, directly and fast! Of course, plan which student you are going to ask before speaking to the class. Ask Student A to respond and don't move. If possible, don't even speak and nip any comments or noises from the class in the bud. It's magic when you can hear, see and feel a captivated learning audience. We've all experienced it. Wait for an answer but provide support (or call on peers to help) if it's clear no answer is on its way. If Student A does manage to answer...

4. **Bounce:** Immediately ask another student for their opinion of Student A's answer and make sure they explain their reasoning. This can be developed by asking a third student their opinion, irrespective of whether the original answer is correct or not.

In class discussions, it is often best to avoid asking more than one question at a time because students may be unsure which question to answer first. But this is not a rule; you are the teacher in charge of your domain and you know what is best for your students, so don't allow this to limit your ability to stretch your students' capacity to learn, retain information, process and then act.

However you choose to use questioning in your classroom, its impact will be determined by the quality of the questions you are asking. If teachers can plan and compose questions more carefully, they will help increase participation and encourage meaningful learning. So why not give the question matrix a go in your next lesson?

EVIDENCE

There is strong evidence linking the quality of teacher instruction – through questioning to assess learning – to student outcomes. I've witnessed teacher instruction in the thousands of classroom observations I've been lucky enough to be part of throughout my career. In the most successful, teacher instruction is straightforward, clear and delivered with command. Any misconceptions are identified and are either re-taught to the whole class or discussed with individual students, allowing others to carry on with the lesson undistracted.

Classroom teachers who review what has been learnt, modelling and revisiting content to ensure it is learnt securely, are able to actively monitor the progress of individual students. If this is not habitual, students soon become accustomed to plodding along in lessons, as there is no expectation that they might be tested on their knowledge at any time.

Keeping students on their toes in every lesson is key to a successful classroom. If a teacher has the skills required to use questioning and lead learning effectively, this will be a powerful tool that will impact student performance. In her book *Enhancing Professional Practice: A Framework for Teaching*, 2nd edition, Charlotte Danielson writes:

> 'Through supportive and deep questioning, teachers become more skilled in analyzing their own practice. Before long, this way of thinking […] becomes a habit of mind.' (Danielson, 2011)

Questioning is an effective strategy for teaching students how to think creatively, for example when solving problems, and can be used as an intervention during the creative process if a student appears to be going off in the wrong direction. Having spent the best part of my life working in creative subjects, first as a student, then as an adult learner and a teacher, I believe questioning to be an essential classroom tool to develop learning, but mastering it requires a great deal of creativity in aspects of the curriculum. However, 'creativity' is often misunderstood. In 2013, Sir Ken Robinson wrote an open letter to former education secretary Michael Gove entitled 'To encourage creativity, Mr Gove, you must first understand what it is' (Robinson, 2013).

So how can teachers make incisive interventions that support the creative process? Well, as research into cognitive psychology has progressed, so too has our understanding of creativity. It is now seen as more of a reciprocal, fluid and adaptive process.

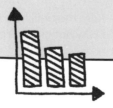

In *Researching Design Learning*, which examines two decades of teaching research and development, Richard Kimbell and Kay Stables look at the approach to designing and making in the Department of Education and Science curriculum of 1987, which acknowledged:

> 'Designing seldom proceeds by way of a series of clearly recognisable stages to a neat solution. There is always the possibility of refinement, of coming at a solution by a better route, or revising the original intention in favour of a simpler or more effective technique.' (DES in: Kimbell and Stables, 2008)

Teachers who teach in creative subjects must reconcile two conflicting possibilities: they could give maximum freedom to students to develop their own ideas and to pursue any approach that seems to them to offer a reasonable outcome, or they could follow a design process that relies on the teacher deciding if the student is ready to move on to the next stage. Ultimately, the teacher must decide what is best for each student, gradually encouraging all students to move towards the first approach, in which every student can develop ideas and solve problems creatively.

So, in a classroom of thirty students, where thirty different outcomes are possible, how does a teacher act incisively so no student moves in the wrong direction? In 'Top 20 Principles from Psychology for PreK-12 Teaching and Learning', the American Psychological Association (APA) identifies twenty principles based on psychological science for effective teaching and learning in primary and secondary settings. The principles include effective use of instruction, assessment and classroom environment, to name a few. According to the APA, asking questions in class not only checks for understanding but 'can help students learn self-regulatory skills [...] to enhance attention, organization, self-control, planning and remembering, all of which can greatly facilitate learning' (APA, 2015).

If I were you, I would start planning right now what questions you need to ask the whole class and individual students in each lesson to pre-empt possible issues and guide learning and creativity.

Übermensch

IDEA SNAPSHOT

An effective teacher can change lives, benefit the local community and contribute towards social mobility in their society. But what is an effective teacher? In this idea, I outline seven traits that I think all effective teachers share. Think about which of these traits you already have and which you could adopt in your day-to-day classroom practice to improve the impact of your teaching.

Man and Superman is a four-act drama written by George Bernard Shaw in 1903. Although *Man and Superman* can be performed as a light comedy of manners, Shaw intended the drama to be something deeper, as suggested by the title, which comes from Friedrich Nietzsche's philosophical ideas about the *Übermensch* – superhuman or, as Shaw translates it, superman – as a goal for humanity to set for itself.

This notorious quote about teaching has become synonymous with the play: 'Those who can, do. Those who can't, teach.' The quote in its original form, taken from 'Maxims for Revolutionists' in *Man and Superman*, is: 'He who can, does. He who cannot, teaches.' There have since been many light-hearted variations of this quote, including one extension: 'Those who can't teach, teach teachers!'

In my opinion, as a 'teacher of teachers', I believe there is a great responsibility placed upon anyone who wishes to upscale other teachers. It's not an easy feat, and you need to be at the top of your game. So, what can we do to make sure we are consistently a *good* teacher, adding value to our students' lives and our local communities? As Geoff Barton says, 'young people appreciate great teachers as much as they ever did, but are more intolerant of mediocre ones' (Barton, 2013).

For years, I have considered the anatomy of what makes a good teacher, or if we think in terms of Nietzsche's *Übermensch*, what is the model that all teachers should aspire to? Former HMI Sir Michael Wilshaw believes:

> 'All good teachers share the same goal: to give children and young people the best chance in life. However, the way in which they reach that goal will depend on what works for them and their students.' (Wilshaw, 2012)

So that's the simple answer: a good teacher is one who aims to improve their students' lives in a way that works in their specific context. We know that teachers can have a great impact on disadvantaged students and can change lives. How many other careers do you know that can do that? But how can we make this a reality for every teacher in every school?

Social mobility

When it comes to social mobility, our current school system is failing. The Social Mobility Commission, a government-sponsored body that promotes social mobility in England, suggests government efforts to improve social mobility over the past two decades have failed to deliver sufficient progress in reducing the gap between those from the most advantaged backgrounds in Britain and those from the most disadvantaged backgrounds (Social Mobility Commission, 2017). Teachers work in challenging circumstances, complex situations and under severe time constraints but they can – and do – have a huge impact on the local community. State schools in this country can deliver social mobility, yet current policy means the school system is fragmented and there is little hope of change on the horizon.

The complicated structure of the school system in this country certainly cannot be helping matters either. Throughout my career, I've come across countless parents, members of the public and even fellow teachers who are confused about the structure of schools in England. We have comprehensive schools, secondary modern, faith schools (voluntary aided), community schools, specialists schools (with a choice of ten specialisms), city technical colleges (CTCs), grant-maintained schools, beacon schools, studio schools, university technical colleges, academies (sponsored or converted), trust schools, free schools, teaching schools, national support schools, state boarding schools, special schools and pupil referral units (PRUs). We even have multi-academy trusts (MATs), virtual schools, hospital schools (for sick children) and Ministry of Defence schools for families in the British Forces, and I'm certain I've missed out others. Is it any wonder we are confused? How can we engage, deliberate and decide on what's best for our education system when it's almost impossible to even understand it? The zigzag nature of policymaking has made it impossible to establish effective solutions and besides, John Hattie's (2009) research suggests that school structure has little impact on achievement for young people. What does? Quality of teaching. It's time we invested our time and our money in the right places.

Unfortunately, this still seems a long way off. As Fiona Millar (2018), British journalist, education campaigner, former policy adviser and author of *The Best for My Child* reflects:

'We appear to be no further forward in encouraging a school system that is epitomised by consistently high quality and equity, so that all children regardless of background have an equal chance of success.'

For the moment, however, the structure of our school system is something that the everyday classroom teacher or school leader has little power to improve. I still dream of a day when this will change but in the meantime we must turn our attention to the exceptional individuals (teachers and school leaders) who provide support day in, day out, often in very challenging situations, and make our schools the best that they can be. What traits do they have that we could all learn from to help improve *our* impact on *our* students' lives? As teachers, what form does our *Übermensch* – our aspirational model – take?

Seven traits of effective teachers

Here are seven traits that I think are common to all effective teachers. Think about which of these traits you already have and which you could develop further to improve the impact of your teaching and benefit the lives of even your most disadvantaged students, your local community and, ultimately, social mobility in this country.

1. Passion

Primarily, teachers love teaching and are passionate about their students, their subject and teaching as a whole. An effective teacher is one who is passionate about education, but that doesn't mean they will be on cloud nine all of the time. They are in tune with the classes they teach and the constraints and pressures they are working under. Sometimes, they wear their hearts on their sleeves!

Effective teachers know that teaching children is meant to be a very enjoyable and rewarding career. They accept that students will want to have fun sometimes and they can see how teaching can be fun too! After all, if the teacher isn't enjoying teaching, the students will probably know it. Rita Pierson once said, 'kids don't learn from people they don't like' (Pierson, 2013). I'm in two minds about this now I understand more about memory and cognitive load theory. However, it's undeniable that relationships enable better behaviour management. Approaching 50 years old, I know I'm a grumpy so-and-so if you've irritated the hell out of me. There's no way I'm open to learning anything! Effective teachers also know that hard work must be the focus in their learning environment. They know teaching is supposed to be tough. In what other profession would you be given the responsibility of shaping the minds of hundreds and hundreds of young lives?

Nevertheless, in good times and in bad, an effective teacher cannot hide their passion for teaching.

2. Planned and organised

Effective teachers are always organised! So much so, they often memorise the schedules of colleagues and students in order to pre-empt potential problems. Their lesson plans – whether lengthy or concise – are well thought out, so they meet the needs of all students; their books are marked smartly, with workload and school policy in mind; and their classrooms are an engine room. Classroom resources are organised in meticulous fashion, laid out carefully in trays, drawers, cups and pots. You name it; this teacher has it covered! Better still, you'll never catch a student abusing any of their well-thought resources; they wouldn't dare.

3. Reflective and open minded

The most effective teachers know that they are constantly being evaluated by their headteachers, colleagues, parents and even their students. And instead of feeling aggrieved at being held to account, they embrace the challenge of teaching and are open minded when receiving feedback about how they can become even better than they are already. Effective teachers know that nobody is perfect and there is always room for improvement, but they also understand that it is a necessity for teachers to reflect on their teaching to develop their practice even further. After every lesson, they think about what went well and what they could do better next time.

4. Comfortable with taking risks and embracing change

In teaching, lessons don't always go according to plan, so there is a huge need to be flexible and 'go with the flow'. Effective teachers know they must adapt to meet the needs of students and the requirements of curriculum and assessment. They know they need to move with the times; what may have worked two or three years ago may not be so effective today. They believe that they are a subject expert and must be at the forefront of their subject knowledge, skills and pedagogy.

5. Collaborative

Effective teachers have a unique way of bringing positive energy into the classroom every single day. We all have personal challenges inside and outside of the school gates, but effective teachers are able to leave all of this behind the moment they step into the classroom. They do, however, share their worldly experiences with students when applicable to the curriculum. Their positive energy is often infectious and can lift the spirits of their colleagues too. Effective teachers never underestimate the expertise that lies within their school. They never forget the importance of sharing ideas with colleagues through a quick discussion or a short observational walk along the corridors.

6. Able to break down barriers

Of course, most teachers break down barriers daily in their classrooms, but an effective teacher knows that literacy, language and social background are not barriers to learning. They accept no excuses from themselves, their colleagues or their students. Effective teachers know that quality first teaching (see Section 2, Idea 7, p. 94) has the greatest impact on their students' learning. Other interventions are offered but they are never a substitute for low standards in the classroom. Effective teachers set themselves – and their students – high standards and expect them to be met.

7. Consistent

Effective teachers are consistent in all that they do. They may be mavericks but they remain in line with whole-school policy and never undermine their colleagues. With an effective teacher, you know what you are getting (even if they do surprise colleagues and students with unusual ideas from time to time!). Their behaviour never raises an eyebrow because their reputation and evidence of prior successes speak for themselves. They always give 100% in everything they do. They are reliable and do what they do because they love teaching, not because they feel obliged to do it.

EVIDENCE

In 2014, the Sutton Trust released a report entitled 'What Makes Great Teaching?' (Coe et al., 2014). The report analysed over two hundred pieces of research to ascertain which elements of teaching have the most significant impact on improving attainment. In this Evidence section, I share the highlights of the report; it may serve as a reminder to us all.

In the report, three key questions are asked:

- 'What makes "great teaching"?
- What kinds of frameworks or tools could help us to capture it?
- How could this promote better learning?'

Let's look at how the report answers each of these questions in turn.

'What makes "great teaching"?'

The report defines 'great teaching' as teaching that 'leads to improved student achievement'. The authors identify six key elements of 'great teaching' based on the research analysed. These six elements include the following and are divided into three categories: elements that have 'strong evidence', 'moderate evidence' and 'some evidence' of impact on student outcomes according to the research:

'Strong evidence'	'(Pedagogical) content knowledge'
	'Quality of instruction'
'Moderate evidence'	'Classroom climate'
	'Classroom management'
'Some evidence'	'Teacher beliefs'
	'Professional behaviours'

'What kinds of frameworks or tools could help us to capture [great teaching]?'

The report advises that teacher quality should be assessed using three key methods:

- 'classroom observations by peers, principals or external evaluators'
- '"value-added" models (assessing gains in student achievement)'
- 'student ratings'.

The report also identifies three further methods to assess teacher quality, although there is currently limited evidence of their efficacy:

- 'principal (or headteacher) judgement'
- 'teacher self-reports'
- 'analysis of classroom artefacts and teacher portfolios'.

'How could this promote better learning?'

The report suggests that a feedback loop to support teachers' own learning and their professional development could have a sizeable impact on student progress. The authors outline six recommendations for providing feedback on teaching (based on the research they analysed) to ensure 'sustained professional learning':

1. Feedback should focus 'on improving student outcomes'.
2. Feedback should provide 'clear, specific and challenging goals' for the teacher.
3. Feedback should concentrate on the learning, not the person, and the teacher should not be compared with others.
4. Teachers should be encouraged to be 'continual independent learners'.
5. Feedback should be 'mediated by a mentor in an environment of trust and support'.
6. School leaders must promote 'an environment of professional learning and support'.

The report mentions one particular approach to professional development that I have experimented with over the past four or five years: lesson study. This approach originated in Japan but has since been used in the UK and the US. It involves teachers collaborating to research, plan and teach lessons, then observing and analysing lessons to see how their ideas work in practice. It is a gradual collaborative process that is very powerful, yet limited by its time-consuming nature and the lack of time and investment available in our schools. The process is very similar to coaching methods, which zoom in on a particular teacher or student need in order to solve a problem through a supportive set of conversations and observations (see Section 3, Idea 10, p. 164). Sadly, lesson study will never take off nationally until schools have the finances to explore this kind of model for lesson planning and teaching. I can't see this happening in state school education any time soon.

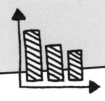

Ten principles of effective instruction

IDEA SNAPSHOT

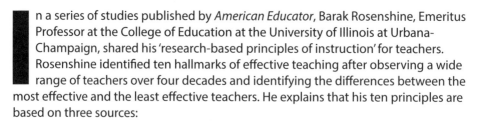

Since I first wrote about Barak Rosenshine's (2012) research on the principles of effective instruction in **Mark. Plan. Teach. 1.0**, a number of teachers have published their own interpretations of the research. It now appears to be reaching schools on the ground and this can only be good news. In this idea, I share my own summary of the research along with guidance for putting it into practice.

I n a series of studies published by *American Educator*, Barak Rosenshine, Emeritus Professor at the College of Education at the University of Illinois at Urbana-Champaign, shared his 'research-based principles of instruction' for teachers. Rosenshine identified ten hallmarks of effective teaching after observing a wide range of teachers over four decades and identifying the differences between the most effective and the least effective teachers. He explains that his ten principles are based on three sources:

1. 'research in cognitive science'

2. 'research on the classroom practices of master teachers'

3. 'research on cognitive support to help students learn complex tasks'.

Over the following pages, I explain each of Rosenshine's ten principles and how they might look in the classroom. It's important to say that it's critical for you to read the original research paper as well in order to adopt your own thinking on these ten principles. Unfortunately, in some schools, the research has been translated poorly and has been turned into an observation checklist. However, in the better examples, schools have translated the research to match their own vision and values and have established their own 'universal offer' within the context of a teaching and learning policy. This is the right methodology to adopt.

1. Review the last lesson

Research findings: The first recommendation from the research is that a daily review is an important component of instruction. A review can help students to strengthen connections between the information they've learnt and this improves recall.

In the classroom: Embed retrieval practice into your teaching, and begin each lesson with a five- to eight-minute review of the last lesson.

2. Present new material

Research findings: We use our working memory to process information but our working memory is quite limited. Presenting too much material at once may confuse students because it swamps their working memory. Therefore, more effective teachers do not overwhelm their students by presenting too much new information at any one time.

In the classroom: Teach new information through a series of short presentations that use many examples and guided practice.

3. Ask a large number of questions

Research findings: Students must practise new material. Asking questions and enabling student discussion are important methods of providing this practice. The most successful teachers in Rosenshine's studies spent more than half of their class time lecturing, demonstrating and asking questions.

In the classroom: Increase the number of factual questions and process questions you ask during guided practice. In the research, test results showed that students achieved higher scores when teachers did this.

4. Provide models

Research findings: In order to learn to solve complex problems, students need cognitive support. For example, the teacher could model and think aloud while demonstrating how to solve a problem.

In the classroom: Offer support by providing prompts, modelling the use of each prompt, and then guiding students as they develop independence. Try giving students words such as 'who', 'where', 'why' and 'how' to help them begin a question.

5. Guide student practice

Research findings: Without sufficient rehearsal, material will be forgotten, so teachers can't simply present new information to students. It's essential that students spend additional time rephrasing, elaborating and summarising new material to move this information into their long-term memory.

In the classroom: Make sure you present only small amounts of material at a time. After each short presentation, allow plenty of time for guiding student practice. The result? Students will be better prepared and achieve higher success rates.

6. Check for student understanding

Research findings: Checks to ensure all students are learning new material provide some of the processing needed to move new learning into long-term memory and let teachers know if students are developing misconceptions. Effective teachers embed frequent checks into their lessons.

In the classroom: Stop regularly to check for student understanding. Ask questions and encourage students to summarise key information. Avoid asking, 'Are there any questions?' If there are no questions, it's easy to assume that all students understand when that might very well not be the case.

7. Obtain a high success rate

Research findings: The optimal success rate for fostering student achievement appears to be about 80%. With this success rate, students are successfully learning the material but are also being sufficiently challenged. This can be judged by the quality of students' oral responses during guided practice and their individual work. This success level can be obtained by teaching in small steps. Practice makes perfect. So, ignore the term 'rote learning' and consider repeating tests and questions as excellent 'practice'.

For me, it's Rosenshine's elaboration on this principle that is the most crucial point for effective teaching: 'providing systematic feedback and corrections'. We must make sure that students are not practising errors! And we know feedback is imperative for students to make progress. Be aware though that this principle is the devil's work if misinterpreted by school inspection frameworks and classroom observers because they are focusing solely on marking in student books and not much else. More importantly, it's completely pointless if a student doesn't actually act on the teacher's feedback – and remember, not all feedback needs to be written, recorded and evidenced! In some cases, it is often not the best, most reliable or quickest method if you require the student to improve the work in the lesson.

In the classroom: Ensure that the pace and level of learning are appropriate for the learners in your classroom to keep them achieving a high success rate while also ensuring they are sufficiently challenged. Teach in small steps, checking understanding, allowing time to practise and giving verbal feedback along the way.

8. Provide scaffolds

Research findings: Effective teachers provide students with temporary supports to assist them in their learning. This could include the teacher modelling and thinking aloud as they solve the problem. As competency increases, the teacher gradually withdraws the scaffolds.

In the classroom: Model aloud as you write a paragraph. Show the thought processes you go through as you determine the topic of the paragraph and then use the topic to generate a summary sentence. You should also anticipate likely mistakes.

9. Require and monitor independent practice

Research findings: Independent practice – where students work alone and practise the new material – generally follows a period of guided practice.

In the classroom: Plan for extensive practice, both in the classroom and as homework tasks. To increase engagement, circulate around the room and supervise students working at their desks. Spend roughly 30 seconds or less with each student.

10. Engage students in a weekly and monthly review

Research findings: Knowledge that is organised into patterns (schemas) in our long-term memory only uses a tiny amount of space in our limited working memory. Effective teachers give students plenty of opportunities for extensive, broad reading and practice in order to develop connections between ideas in their long-term memory. This frees up space in students' working memory.

In the classroom: Try reviewing the previous week's work every week and the previous month's work every fourth week. The research suggests that classes that had weekly quizzes scored better on final exams than classes with only one or two quizzes during the term. Teachers face a difficult problem when they need to cover curriculum material and don't feel they have the time for sufficient review. But the research is clear: material that is not adequately practised and reviewed is easily forgotten. So, go forth and test – and test again!

EVIDENCE

In June 2020, Evidence Based Education published the Great Teaching Toolkit (Coe et al.), an evidence review in partnership with Cambridge Assessment International Education. The Great Teaching Toolkit reviewed existing evidence about what competencies are worth learning in order to improve the impact of teaching. The researchers conducted a systematic review of existing research articles and asked a large number of questions as part of their methodology. In the appendix section of the Toolkit, there is a summary of the countless studies that were reviewed. This in itself is a fantastic reading list for teachers. The summaries also offer teachers first-time access to some key research papers that, in my opinion, all teachers should attempt to know.

Based on the evidence, the authors identify four key priorities for teachers who want to increase their impact on learning:

CONTINUES OVER PAGE

- 'understand the content they are teaching and how it is learnt
- create a supportive environment for learning
- manage the classroom to maximise the opportunity to learn
- present content, activities and interactions that activate their students' thinking'.

In order to achieve these four priorities, Coe et al. list out 17 elements that they consider the 'best bets' for teachers to invest time and effort into developing:

1. deep and fluent knowledge of your subject content
2. knowledge of curriculum sequencing
3. knowledge of curriculum and assessment tasks
4. knowledge of student strategies, misconceptions and sticking points
5. promoting relationships that are based on mutual respect
6. developing a positive climate
7. enhancing learner motivation through competence, autonomy and relatedness
8. creating a climate of high expectations
9. managing time and resources efficiently
10. ensuring that expectations for behaviour are explicit
11. preventing, anticipating and responding to potential incidents
12. giving students an appropriate sequence of learning tasks
13. effective presentation and communication of new ideas
14. using questions to elicit student thinking
15. responding appropriately to feedback from students
16. giving students tasks that embed and reinforce learning
17. helping students to plan, regulate and monitor their own learning.

Take some time to think about which of these competencies you might want to prioritise when it comes to your own professional development.

The third degree

IDEA SNAPSHOT

In schools, everyone's time is precious and if school leaders believe in research-informed practice, they must also be willing to use the research around graded lessons, one-off observations and performance-related pay in order to influence change. The ultimate goal of lesson observations should be to improve teacher performance, not check in on consistency and give one another the third degree. We must equip ourselves to observe one another more reliably.

When I started my doctorate degree, I discovered another version of observation in the classroom, based on academic methods that would elicit more reliable and more valid judgements. I thought I knew everything there was to know about coaching, feedback and observations until I discovered an alternative methodology: observing as a researcher. I have since developed a training process to help teachers better understand lesson observation. As a result of this process, evaluating the quality of teaching and learning will improve, classroom doors will open and teachers will develop. This is a bold claim to make, but I have already lived this methodology in a large number of schools around the world. I will do my best to describe this process on paper.

Do observations have any impact?

I've tried every possible version of observations. I've conducted some horror stories and I've also produced the best spreadsheets and lesson feedback conversations that would be worthy of an Oscar nomination. Yet, I really don't know if any of these learning walks or one-to-one conversations has had a long-term impact on an individual teacher. Of course, I've tried to evaluate methods and processes to determine whether they do have any impact or not, but I suspect each and every teacher will have their own version of events!

I do believe learning walks serve a purpose: monitoring, checking in on habits, such as displays and keywords, to develop a degree of consistency across the school, but surely the ultimate goal for everyone is improving teacher performance? If we get this right, the impact on pupils should be two-fold.

When you ask a room full of teachers, 'Hands up who works in a position of leadership that gives you permission to observe other teachers?', you will see a large number of hands raised. Taking this further, you might ask, 'Keep your hands up if you have received any formal training.' The number of hands up tends to drop dramatically. When you then ask if anyone left has a formal qualification in observational practice, all the hands in any room disappear! I understand why this is the case, but why do we not equip ourselves to observe each other more reliably, particularly when some observations are such high stakes?

I want to change this.

More specifically, I want to improve observation reliability and open-door culture, which are seriously lacking across the teaching profession.

So, what do you need to do?

The following four steps will help you to improve observational skills and reduce observer bias among staff in your school. Run this as an activity in a departmental or whole-school staff training session or with your leadership team. Alternatively, you can simply try it out with a couple of colleagues.

Step 1

Watch a three-minute video of a teacher teaching. Ideally, this should be someone you know, but if you don't have this footage, grab a lesson off the Internet and select a three-minute window. On the first occasion, simply watch the lesson without any context. When the three minutes have ended, take a moment to record your thoughts. If possible, share them with someone else and note your commentary.

Step 2

Now, you are going to watch the exact same video again but you will introduce a semi-structure. This means that, before you watch the same footage, you will know exactly what you are looking at, for example questioning, behaviour management or entry into lesson, and you will know a bit more information about the teacher and students. When watching the video, it is important to record what the teacher is doing and what the students are doing. If possible, choose timestamps in the video, say one every 30 seconds, and make sure you record what is happening at those precise moments.

This semi-structure will allow you to compare your notes against somebody else watching the exact same footage. This will enable you to determine whether you have both come to the same conclusions. What this will do is allow you to compare whether you have both observed the same moments, teaching strategies, pupil responses and so on. You should also compare your observations to those you made in Step 1 when you watched the video for the first time, without context. You have now experienced watching a teacher with an unstructured approach and a semi-structured approach. This is a simple research methodology for ensuring that more reliable conclusions are made.

Step 3

We are now going to introduce a very rigid structure. Watch the exact same video for a third time, but observe what the teacher does and select one student only. Most importantly, imagine the teacher has posed a question and asked you to evaluate their performance against it. For example, 'How might I stop [Student] calling out to my open and closed questions?' Of course, whatever question is asked will be based on you having watched the video beforehand, particularly if you are sharing this in a training session, because part of the process allows the observer to narrow their lens by watching the same lesson footage in a series of three episodes.

To introduce even further structure, select a particular student to observe and introduce several specific timestamps. At these exact points in the video, the observers should record what the teacher is doing and what the students are doing in response to the particular focus.

Step 4

Now think about how you could implement this process in real-life observations not only to improve observational skills but also to reduce observer bias. The result? The teacher is supported to develop. The observer narrows their focus and can target specific methods, strategies used and interventions to help support the teacher, rather than giving broad feedback that ends up with countless suggestions without really giving the teacher anything specific to meet their needs.

EVIDENCE

In July 2016 a study by education and youth development 'think and action tank' LKMco suggested that even middle leaders have very little time to observe lessons and support staff development. Only 3% of the 117 middle leaders surveyed said they spent more than four hours per week observing lessons and only 11% said they spent more than four hours per week on staff development and CPD (Baars et al., 2016).

The study did show, however, that being an organised team leader is key for middle leaders to get the best out of colleagues and students. According to the report, heads of department need to establish efficient systems and processes if their departments are to flourish. They should also take a diplomatic and consultative approach to managing their team, whilst never neglecting the importance of managing up. In this Evidence section, I will look at the methodology and the findings of this research in more detail.

CONTINUES OVER PAGE

In their report, LKMco 'identify the behaviours, characteristics, enabling factors and barriers that contribute to or hinder a middle leader's success'. The research was based on detailed analysis of over 200 English secondary school departments and their performance, as well as a series of interviews and case studies, and was broken down into two stages:

1. GCSE attainment data combined with data on the performance of 209 fellows of Teaching Leaders and a survey of 123 fellows and alumni of Teaching Leaders. (Teaching Leaders is a provider of professional development programmes for primary and secondary middle leaders and they funded this report.)

2. Detailed qualitative analysis of data recorded from interviews with 24 teachers, middle leaders and senior leaders across eight schools. This was supplemented by a review of the literature.

The report found the most effective middle leaders to:

- Be rated highly by their line managers 'in terms of their ability to manage a team'.

- Believe that their success is underpinned by 'team competencies' and other 'team-level factors'.

- Believe 'planning and resource management' to be particularly important.

- Be 'open, consultative and collaborative'.

- Have strong skills in 'communication and diplomacy' and 'knowing, developing and building a team'.

- Be 'professionally informed' and able to '[lead] by example'.

For me, this research indicates that effective middle leadership centres on an ability to build and promote an environment based on teamwork, collaboration and sharing best practice. I would argue that one way of doing just that is by using lesson observations not as an opportunity to give teachers the third degree or beat them over the head with a stick, but as a collaborative approach to improving teaching and learning in every classroom.

My top recommendation for developing school leaders is to create shadow leadership opportunities where less experienced leaders can learn from their more experienced counterparts. I have found that middle leaders in particular want guidance in managing difficult conversations and offering support and challenge to those in their teams. Rather than role plays (which are often false scenarios), allow inexperienced leaders to observe difficult conversations with students, parents or perhaps even governors.

Invisible collaboration

IDEA SNAPSHOT

Collaborative learning increases student engagement, meaning the knowledge and skills you are teaching are more likely to stick. This idea will provide you with an effective strategy to embed collaborative learning in your classroom and will consider how schools can become more collaborative working environments for teachers too.

C ollaborative learning involves students working together in pairs or small groups on a task assigned by the teacher. Students either work together throughout the activity, completing each step collaboratively, or they work individually on different aspects of the task, contributing to a shared overall outcome.

We know collaborative learning is effective because, according to the Education Endowment Foundation (EEF, 2017e), collaborative learning has a 'moderate impact [on student achievement] for a very low cost, based on extensive evidence'. This evidence spans over forty years and includes 'a number of systematic reviews and meta-analyses of research studies'. However, the EEF also finds that in order to have the greatest impact, collaborative learning must involve 'structured approaches with well-designed tasks'.

Back to back

Back to back, or b2b, is a simple and very effective way to engage students in collaborative learning. It is easy to set up activities using b2b in any subject and it can have a positive impact if it is structured in line with the needs and capabilities of your students. You should design your b2b activity with the lesson objectives in mind and you should make sure it is suitable for collaborative learning. For example:

1. Sit students back to back in pairs.

2. Display an image at the front of the classroom.

3. Ask one student from the pair to describe the image on display.

4. The students sitting with their backs facing away from the image attempt to draw what is described to them by the students facing the image.

5. Some form of peer-assessment is conducted based on the outcome.

6. The partners then swap over and another image is displayed or the image is adapted (in line with the learning objectives).

The impact on learning is clear. Engagement increases, active listening is heightened and subject content is more likely to stick. It also gets every student in the class involved and listening to one another, creating a more inclusive learning environment. In fact, it reminds me of an orchestra – the conductor (or the teacher) facilitates but the individual musicians must all listen closely to one other, communicating and collaborating in real time for a shared overall outcome. It may be invisible to the untrained eye, but it is effective.

Collaboration for teachers

In happier schools, leaders create a culture where teaching and learning is discussed weekly, and new teachers are encouraged to take part in CPD and their voices are heard. A culture of research is encouraged and the door is open to others working within the profession. CPD is achieved during the working week. This collaborative approach to CPD is essential to improving teaching and creating a culture in which all teachers can share, grow and thrive. CPD must also go beyond the functional if we wish all of our teachers to renew and sustain their commitment to the broader ethical and moral purposes of teaching.

Researchers Zeng and Day (2019) have explored the context, purpose and practice of collaborative CPD experienced by teachers working in primary and secondary schools in England and Shanghai (a jurisdiction that is high in PISA rankings time and again). The research looked at the levels of 'functional' and 'attitudinal' CPD the teachers received. They described the functional level as lesson plans, resources and evaluation techniques that save time, and the attitudinal level as developing the intellectual and motivational focus of the teacher. Zeng and Day concluded that teachers in Shanghai experienced more attitudinal CPD than their colleagues in England, with rich opportunities for collaboration.

So, does your school create the right conditions for teachers to work collaboratively? What more could your leadership team be doing? Here are a few points to consider:

1. Does your school provide you with the conditions in which to grow professionally?

2. How are you supported and challenged?

3. Does your school leadership team create a climate of trust?

4. How is under-performance tackled?

5. Do new teachers and newly qualified teachers have a voice?

6. Is sharing knowledge promoted?

7. Is the time of teachers valued as the most precious commodity within the school?

8. Are teacher training sessions carefully planned and mapped out to align with teachers' individual needs as well as school priorities?

9. When a member of staff is struggling, do they have a safe space in which to raise the issue without fear of retribution or is having a few bad days viewed as a weakness?

Psychology and... engagement

The mention of an orchestra and the content of what Ross has written about collaboration both prompt me to think about engagement, leadership and inclusion in education.

Engagement is a slippery concept because we cannot assume that engagement always leads to learning. We cannot assume that a quiet classroom means that all students are contemplative and engaged, and that engagement is leading to learning. Likewise, we cannot assume that a classroom buzzing with noise and interaction means that all students are busy and engaged and that engagement is leading to learning. Learning occurs inside someone's head – it is invisible – and knowing if it is occurring or not can be extremely problematic. A student can be engaged in a task but that does not necessarily mean they are learning – especially if they are doing a more-of-the-same activity where no transferred application of what is currently known is required. Interestingly, being engaged in a manner that is clearly directed towards learning can impact upon relevant psychological factors such as persistence and resilience (Kuh, 2008).

The orchestra is a useful working model for leadership. The conductor has to connect with the orchestra so that they can perform at their best; leaders connect emotionally. The conductor places her or his personal interpretation on a piece of music that an orchestra is performing; leaders shape the reality of their followers. Structurally and visually, a conductor appears to be leading from the front. However, having played in an orchestra, you experience a sense that the conductor is actually leading from the centre. So, as a leader, you can lead from the front or you can lead from the centre…but it is likely to be problematic if you try to lead from the back.

An orchestra is also a useful working model for inclusion in education. Inclusion is a process and not a fixed state. In 2001, I wrote that inclusion is about so much more than the inclusive headcount. I expressed concern that our systems can be far more explosive than they are inclusive – especially in relation to those students, teachers and systems that problematise the notion of inclusion. I insisted that if we are to be truly inclusive, we must move from a tolerance of difference to an acceptance of diversity. The orchestra helps us to conceptualise inclusion in education: it is one diverse community coming together, difference is celebrated, collaboration is critical and everyone's contribution is valued.

– Professor Tim O'Brien

What improves teachers?

IDEA SNAPSHOT

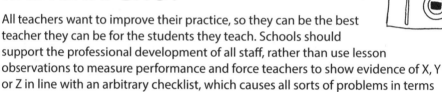

All teachers want to improve their practice, so they can be the best teacher they can be for the students they teach. Schools should support the professional development of all staff, rather than use lesson observations to measure performance and force teachers to show evidence of X, Y or Z in line with an arbitrary checklist, which causes all sorts of problems in terms of teachers' workload and wellbeing. In this idea, I present a strategy that will help schools to develop their teachers, not judge them.

In one of my all-time favourite books, *The Last Lecture*, Randy Pausch (who died from pancreatic cancer in 2008) writes about his last dying wish. 'The Last Lecture' is a tradition held at Carnegie Mellon University in Pittsburgh, Pennsylvania, where Pausch was a Professor of Computer Science and the book captures Pausch's 'Last Lecture' in written form. Professors who are leaving the university are asked to consider their departure and ponder the things that matter most to them. While they speak, the audience is asked to consider these same questions:

1. What wisdom would we impart to the world if we knew it was our last chance?

2. If we had to vanish tomorrow, what would we want as our legacy?

If you have never read the book or watched Pausch share his legacy in his lecture, it is something I would strongly recommend. The full 90-minute lecture will move and inspire you to take some form of action in your life. It certainly did for me when I first read the book in 2008.

So, if I were to see this final idea of *Mark. Plan. Teach.* as my 'Last Lecture', how would I answer these questions in relation to my time in education to date? What advice would I impart to you and what would be my legacy? Well, the second question is tricky. What do you think *your* legacy would be as an educator? What would your colleagues say about you? I think only your colleagues could answer that question – I don't think I could – so I'm not going to attempt it. My colleagues and the students I have worked with will be able to share what my legacy has been only in relation to the connections I've had with them in classrooms, school corridors and offices. I've had so many micro-conversations with so many of you – some who may even be reading this book or training to be a teacher. Maybe *that* would be a great legacy for the profession. Who knows…?

However, I will answer the first question. Former Prime Minister Benjamin Disraeli once said, 'one secret of success in life is for a [person] to be ready for [their] opportunity when it comes'. In my career, this quote has become personal. Through the ups and downs – the promotions, opportunities and setbacks – we all need to use our experiences and our learning to be better than we were before. What drives our desire for constant self-improvement? Well, it comes down to the reason we became teachers in the first place. Why are you a teacher? What gets you out of bed in the morning? My answer for you is this: it's the students.

It's not the data or the number-crunching reports and evaluations. It's not mind-numbing meetings and heaving three sets of class books into the back of your car to mark over the weekend. It's not to be told that your lesson wasn't good enough or to be berated because you are one minute late to your break duty spot. It's the students – and your fellow teachers around you. It's the hope that we may impart a little wisdom on others and help them develop a love for learning. It's also working with people: those who want to help the most vulnerable in society, those who choose to work in challenging schools and be the best they can be for the students to give them and our next generation some hope. We teach because we love learning and we want to inspire our young people to achieve their potential. For me personally, while my focus has been the students for the past 25 years of my life, what gets me out of bed in the morning today are the thousands of teachers I work with across the world.

If I had one regret as a school leader, it would be that I failed to use my wisdom and my position in schools to gather teaching staff together more frequently to talk about teaching, to shape the dialogue and to help them be the best that they can be. I have spent the past three years trying to change this. I have been on a one-man mission visiting schools all around the world, doing my utmost to ensure that school leaders bring their teachers together on a regular basis.

I have unfinished business in education. No matter how many times I've considered quitting and moving on to another job or had to step up to a challenge after a difficult period, I've always remembered that working with students puts us in a very privileged position. It has taken me almost 30 years to learn how best to support other teachers, particularly in my work with lesson observations. We are all in teaching to make a difference and I would encourage schools to allow all of their teachers to get out of their classrooms and observe each other as often as possible so they can learn from each other. This cannot be achieved by only one person or a small group of people observing lessons. We have many, many talented and caring people within our profession, yet observing one another is not feasible or even permitted in some of our schools.

If we do not do something to facilitate a developmental model for school and teacher improvement – one that involves the school and teacher themselves in the process – then I'm afraid I predict that we will never break free from this culture of individual accountability that we have created over the past twenty years in English schools. The retention rate within the sector has been roughly consistent for the past twenty years, but I wonder how many good teachers we are losing to other professions because of accountability and rising mental health issues?

In 2014, the NHS released a report on mental health problems in England. In a survey of 5,000 adults, 26% said they had been diagnosed with at least one mental health issue. The report also found that 'women were more likely than men to report ever having been diagnosed with a mental illness (33% compared with 19%)' (Bridges, 2014). Meanwhile, the DfE reported in 'School Workforce in England: November 2016' that 'almost three out of four school teachers are female and four out of five school employees are female' (DfE, 2017). If we have more female teachers working in our schools, do we not then have a potential problem? The Mindfulness Initiative have published a wealth of research about mental health and wellbeing in the field of education. Only ten years ago, it was very difficult to find, but the good news is that recently we are finding more and more evidence to suggest that high-performing teams are built on a foundation of good mental health. See: www.themindfulnessinitiative.org/educationresearch.

In every school, we must start to address teacher workload and wellbeing. We must move away from the culture of data, teaching to the test and the persistent anxiety of 'Big Brother is watching you' and you will need to show evidence of X, Y and Z. The dialogue is slowly shifting in our schools, yet external accountability is slow to change and must move to a richer and more formative model for assessing the quality of education in our schools. School leaders must challenge external accountability where it is unhelpful or biased.

While we are figuring this out at a national level, there is one strategy that I would like to suggest that will genuinely help schools to develop their teachers, rather than simply measure performance and make staff dance along to a checklist. This strategy is coaching.

Coaching

Coaching is something that will make a difference to all teachers, regardless of the stage you are at in your career and the school context in which you work. Sadly, it has taken me over twenty years to embrace this strategy in all its glory because I have worked in an era of education where we, as teachers, have had little access to educational research and how students learn. Thankfully, there has been a huge shift in access to journals for teachers; with the rise of social media as a professional development tool, teachers can now organise their own 'unconferences', such as TeachMeets. I am connected to a social network of teachers that I have curated myself and that no school has facilitated. It has relied on my own determination to source new ideas, partnerships and techniques for the classroom and for surviving school leadership. But sadly, social media is not the solution for improving teachers' access to research. It is not for everyone, nor should teachers be expected to seek out research online in their free time. Schools must provide some form of access during the working week. The past few years have seen an explosion in the number of organisations publishing research for teachers. On social media and in our schools, there is a huge thirst for access to research. This can only be a good thing and will raise the status of our profession. It will enable teachers to develop, share ideas and knowledge, and define best practice across the sector.

Sharing knowledge and best practice helped me to develop my own ideas of coaching. Coaching has transformed my practice, but my interest in this professional development technique has been heightened even further in the last 18 months. I have been inspired by Doug Lemov's *Teach Like a Champion 2.0*, various coaching programmes and the book *Leverage Leadership* by Paul Bambrick-Santoyo, which have all shifted the focus of classroom observation from assessment to development. I believe this is a mechanism that schools should adopt if they genuinely want to help their teachers be the best that they can be.

This is how I believe coaching could be established in any school setting:

1. Banish lesson gradings once and for all. You should never judge the quality of teaching or the teacher in a single lesson, or over time for that matter. Use a wider range of sources to evaluate the collective quality of teaching in a school.

2. Stop observing teachers once every 12 weeks. I understand why this policy came about with unions wanting to protect their members from losing their jobs because lesson observations and gradings were – despite the evidence – still high stakes in many schools.

3. Instead of all this nonsense, allow every teacher to be coached.

4. Identify a group of teachers who wish to be trained to coach their peers and use them to support colleagues. If your school can find the funding to release teachers from timetabled commitments to do this, then the ideal is for every teacher to be involved, both as a coach and as a recipient of coaching.

5. As a minimum, coach all staff who are new to the school, including every teacher new to the profession, to help develop 'collective teacher efficacy'. In its truest definition, this means working together to have appropriately high-challenging expectations. Remember, a school's teaching and learning policy is only as good as every teacher who must use it.

6. The process should include no paperwork, only a 'common vernacular' (thank you, Alex Thomas) that should be used in all coaching conversations and that must be used as a template for each school adopting their own 'universal offer' (see Section 3, Idea 4, p. 134).

Here is an example of a conversation about lesson observation between coach and teacher:

Coach: How could I best observe you to improve your practice? *(This should be the first question asked in all observation settings. The coach should also agree a date and time to provide feedback before the coaching observation takes place to ensure a commitment is made to discuss the lesson on both sides.)*

Teacher: I think I need to improve… *(The teacher identifies **one** target.)*

Coach: OK. This is all I will look at during the observation. *(The coach specifies they will only look **at**, not for, elements relating to the target identified in the lesson. If the focus is too broad, the coach must work hard to narrow it.)*

After the observation, the feedback session should follow a praise-question-suggestion-action model:

- **Praise:** The teacher should specify which parts of the lesson they were happy with. It would be even better if the teacher could identify a success or assessment criteria and then the coach teases this out through a series of focused questions.

- **Question and suggestion:** A set number of questions would then probe, identify and plan solutions identified by the teacher.

- **Action:** The final stage of the conversation will lock in any agreed actions on the part of the teacher. The coach should ask the teacher, 'how committed are you to achieving this?'. This technique tends to have surprisingly high success rates. A verbal commitment to oneself ensures the teacher holds themselves to account rather than a line manager or a coach who is there to support the development.

Remember, a 'common vernacular' should be used by coaches in all scripted conversations. Here are some suggestions based on the ideas proposed in this book. What would you add or take away in your setting?

Coaching Common Vernacular		
Mark	**Plan**	**Teach**
Secure overview	Clear and precise	Teachers of literacy and numeracy
Primarily formative	Learn, not do	Success criteria
Zonal feedback	'So why?'	Keywords
Proportional to curriculum time	Intent	Go with the learning
	Differentiation over time	Understand memory
	Quality first	Learning has stuck
	Flying start or retrieval practice	

To embed a successful coaching methodology, schools must commit to the following:

- Coaching will replace all formal observations.

- Coaches will be given the time once a week to visit their teacher and every coached observation will last 15 minutes with a focus on one target only. Feedback will take place within 24 hours and be no longer than 30 minutes. The cycle will repeat each week for at least six months of the academic year.

- Every coaching relationship will exist outside of the teacher's subject or age expertise. However, where explicit subject knowledge needs developing, seek a subject expert.

- Appraisals and line management relationships will **never** be a factor when pairing teachers up with coaches.

- At the end of the cycle, the programme will be tweaked and the bank of available coaches in the school will be reviewed in line with staff needs for the year ahead and incoming or departing staff.

- No assessment will be made of the teacher, other than a coaching script used to initiate improvements; any serious concerns will follow normal school procedures; appraisal, capability and safeguarding, for example, all fall outside of the remit of a coach and must follow the necessary formal procedures.

I believe if these commitments can be made, coaching will be a powerful tool to improve teaching and learning in every classroom and school.

EVIDENCE

It is rare for teachers to have an opportunity to observe and learn from each other. And when they do get the chance, they often do not have the structure or language to discuss teaching and learning in any great depth. Why? Because they are seldom asked to observe when 90% of their time is spent actually teaching lessons themselves!

I was delighted when former headteacher Kenny Frederick wanted to conduct research for her doctoral studies at Brunel University London with the school where I first developed the *Mark. Plan. Teach.* methodology. Her research study aimed to examine what happens when 'Teacher Rounds' were introduced as part of a professional learning programme. This was something I was keen to welcome into the school. Teacher Rounds are a collaborative form of peer observation and continuous professional learning, much like the coaching process I have explained in this idea. However, there are some key differences.

Teacher Rounds occur in the classroom, in real time, and aim to help teachers work in a group to develop their own practice and learn from each other's practice too. It is not a process of evaluation. No judgements are made – ever! The rounds involve everybody in the group, and they take it in turns to be the host teacher, identifying the 'problem of practice' that will be the focus of the observation. The process involves a short pre-round meeting prior to the observation, where the host teacher describes the context of the lesson, talks through the 'problem of practice' and shares the lesson plan. Following the observation, there is a post-round meeting to reflect on what happened during the lesson.

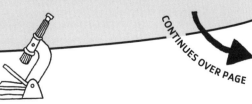

CONTINUES OVER PAGE

The process has its roots in 'doctor rounds', whereby the medical team walk their way around a hospital ward to diagnose patients. If you've ever been unlucky enough to find yourself in hospital, you will have witnessed, possibly unbeknownst to you at the time, this collaborative process taking place among hospital staff. I was in hospital when I was 23 years old, and I mostly saw this happening at 8am after having been woken up every other hour to take medication throughout the night. I remember trying to stay awake to earwig on what the doctors were saying to one another. What is actually happening on these rounds is not only that you (the patient) are being listened to, but also information is being shared between professionals and this is used to inform the decisions being made. It is very much an iterative process, achieved through collaboration.

This is the polar opposite to what most schools across the world have set up, particularly in OECD countries. Teachers largely work in isolation with their students, yet come together to reflect when no students are actually present. How can our diagnoses of the 'problems of practice' be accurate when often our evaluations are made in hindsight, rather than live in the lesson?

Teacher Rounds are a way to bring an extra pair of eyes and ears to the task in hand (something that we, as teachers, often lack) to observe what students are thinking and doing, what is engaging them and what the resulting impact is. Typically, the process involves a minimum of three and a maximum of seven teachers. This ensures that a range of experiences and multiple perspectives are brought to the process. What ensues is intentional reflection, observation, inquiry and collaboration where all members of the group are reflective partners and can take something away from the lesson.

Teachers who make up the group must be volunteers and must agree strict protocols for working together. When the research period ends, the group can then feed back their reflections and what they have learnt so the whole school community can benefit. The teachers involved will also be in a good position to set up another group in their school and make Teacher Rounds a sustainable form of professional learning. I can vouch for the impact it has on individual professionals.

Psychology and...
coaching

When coaching first began, it was a remedial intervention that occurred within a deficit-focused framework. Now, it is seen as a methodology for growth and development. This is particularly highlighted in the prevalence of executive coaching in business. I am an executive coach and have seen first-hand how, in the business world, coaching is framed as being about developing your staff so that you can optimise their performance and potential. In a meta-analysis of research relating to coaching effectiveness, Theeboom et al. (2014) emphasise that coaching adds value. It has a positive impact on self-efficacy, personal wellbeing, goal orientation and performance.

I would like to raise a potential gender-related issue. In organisations, women may encounter gender stereotyping and gender assumptions about ways of being and behaving. 'Executive coaching', as a model, was initially a male-dominated activity. I propose that when coaching women in any organisation, the coach should be sensitive to the particular challenges that women, especially women in leadership positions, may encounter in the workplace that are different to those of their male counterparts. I would also add a vice-versa here.

In terms of psychology, there is a challenge that every coach will encounter: understanding hierarchies of significance. In *Inner Story* (O'Brien, 2015), I describe how we constantly create and recreate hierarchies of significance inside our minds, structuring things in terms of how important they are to us in our world. This is a natural activity, as one way that we make meaning out of our world is by establishing what matters more to us and what matters less. Coaching involves seeing the world from the perspective of another person: being led into their reality in order to help them develop. As a coach, when someone presents you with their 'challenge' or 'problem', it will instantly fit within a hierarchy of significance in your mind. Such hierarchies in your mind have to be flattened because it is how the problem fits into a hierarchy of significance in the other person's mind that really matters.

The relationship between the coach and the coachee is a critical predictor of coaching impact. Therefore, coaching should happen 'alongside'. Coaching is an exploratory and developmental activity and not based on a hierarchical model. Coaching cannot work effectively if a coach is on a status-driven ego trip. As a coach, I can see multiple benefits of coaching at all levels in an education context – from NQT through to headteacher.

– Professor Tim O'Brien

Section 3: Summary

· ·

Teaching *is not* about 'following a lesson plan' to the letter; it is not about 'engaging' students with as many jazzy, practical activities as you can think of; and it is not about keeping students 'under control'. Teaching *is* about helping your students to progress in their learning in a way that works for both you and them, while also ensuring you don't undermine what your colleague is doing next door to you. Teaching is about having a solid lesson plan based on the learning, but being confident enough to deviate from this to help students progress; and teaching is about using marking and assessment to inform where a lesson needs to go next.

In this final section of **Mark. Plan. Teach.**, I have aimed to provide you with a range of teaching strategies that will help you to improve your teaching, so that it can be all of the above – and more! I know for a fact that every teacher in every school wants to be better for their students, but I also know that continuing professional development (CPD) can be a pretty gloomy and frustrating prospect in many schools, where a one-size-fits-all approach is taken and CPD sessions are used to hammer home new national directives or inflexible whole-school policies. Thankfully, this is changing but it's still vitally important for teachers to take back control of their own CPD. With this autonomy, teachers can determine the type of CPD that works for them and that takes into account the context in which they are working, so it has a deeper and more meaningful focus.

Teachers *must* be given time out of their classrooms to reflect on and improve their practice. Training and high-quality development opportunities should be available to all staff, not just those who are newly qualified, and should be part of our established weekly routines. We all have something new to learn. After all, we are teachers – learning is the true nature of our profession. I also think that schools can engage their staff with well-planned CPD sessions that take into account the context of the school and share evidence-based methods (such as those in this book) to develop whole-school consistency, while also motivating teachers to continue developing their practice and encouraging their creativity to know no bounds.

So, with all this in mind, let's reflect on the ten evidence-based teaching ideas I have suggested in this final section:

1. Be explicit about the learning outcomes and keywords that form the foundations of your lesson through a combination of direct instruction, self-regulated feedback and 'nudge theory'.

2. Apply modelling strategies, such as reciprocal teaching, think-pair-share and I do, we do, you do to help students develop their skills in literacy and numeracy.

3. Have the courage to go with the flow of learning instead of following lesson plans to the letter. This must be supported by a whole-school culture that allows teachers to make mistakes and learn from them.

4. Make sure you have a secure grasp of how memory works and how students learn and retain information. Use this to develop a simple, evidence-based teaching and learning policy to achieve 'collective teacher efficacy', reduce workload and maximise student progress across your school.

5. Use the question matrix to plan the questions you want to ask your students and how you will frame them in order to check incisively, systematically and effectively that learning has stuck. This will enable you to provide feedback and pinpoint any knowledge and skills you may need to re-teach.

6. Adopt the seven traits of an effective teacher to help improve the impact of your teaching, so you can change lives, benefit the local community and contribute to social mobility.

7. Think deeply about how you can embed Barak Rosenshine's ten principles of effective instruction in your practice. Take the time to consider priorities for your own professional development and how you could increase your impact in the classroom.

8. Improve lesson observations in your school by training observers using my four-step process. This will improve the reliability of observations, reduce observational bias and develop an open-door culture. The end result is a happy, confident teaching team who feel supported to develop.

9. Prioritise collaboration. Embed collaborative learning strategies, such as back to back (b2b), into your classroom to increase engagement in your lessons and create an inclusive learning environment. As a department or whole school, develop the right conditions for teachers to work collaboratively in order to improve practice and ensure CPD goes beyond the functional.

10. Establish a system of coaching in your school to support the professional development of all staff and improve teaching and learning in every classroom.

And finally

For a generation, teachers have been told how to teach by external watchdogs, politicians and think tanks, by heads of department, senior leaders, and education experts. Teachers have been constantly observed, monitored, judged or graded, and given feedback on what they need to do to improve their practice. Teachers have been made to feel that they are no longer the experts in their own classrooms.

Imagine constantly being told you must be better than you were before. Teachers have come to accept this as their default mode. They have a never-ending to do list and are under relentless pressure for *this* lesson to be better than the last and *this* year's examination results to be stronger than ever before, even if their classes are already meeting or exceeding expectations.

Unfortunately, the guidance teachers receive often comes from those who have little sympathy for teachers. We must trust good teachers to get on with their jobs. Nevertheless, weaker teachers – and yes, there are some, but thankfully they are in the minority – do make a rod for their own backs when support offered by peers and managers is ignored and relationships with students, parents and colleagues grow increasingly fraught.

There is no doubt that teaching can be incredibly demanding, exhausting and, at times, even demoralising, but we choose teaching because we want to make a difference. We don't come into the job to purchase highlighter pens, staplers and glue sticks, or to plough through non-stop piles of marking. Although it's not acceptable, we also come into the job *expecting* a low salary and longer working hours than most. However, what we *do not* opt in for are performance management targets or reams and reams of data collection that leave us feeling that all our enthusiasm for the classroom has been sucked out of our souls.

We all have our own lives to live outside of school and our personal lives can sometimes influence our career decisions. Equally, there may be factors in our national education system, or in the specific schools in which we work, that can shape our 'love for the job'. But why do some of us grow and flourish as teachers, while others fail to take root? Why do some of us see privilege and inspiration in the role of a teacher, while others just can't seem to find the light in the darkness?

There will always be stacks of books to mark, reports to write and leadership meetings to attend. Of course, we would all rather be picking up our own children from school or relaxing with friends, rather than sitting at our classroom desks marking or nodding off in meetings and twilight sessions. Nonetheless, I believe that we have the power to bring about change. If we make a collective stand against the regimes of data collection, lesson grading, detailed lesson planning and the ideology that written feedback is the best form of assessment, we can change teaching for the better – not just for our students, but for ourselves as a profession. Maybe if we remove the external pressures, we might just be able to make schools a happier place for teachers and students alike *and* improve teaching and learning too:

> 'If we want to improve school performance, we also need to start paying attention to teacher wellbeing.' (Briner and Dewberry, 2007)

I am inspired by Richard Gerver when I say that change is a positive thing. In his book, *Change: Learn to Love It, Learn to Lead It*, Gerver writes about the moment he left teaching and 'first stepped out of school':

> 'You have probably experienced a similar moment, when fear threatens to block your progress. Fear of change is so often the result of imagined consequences rather than reality.' (Gerver, 2013)

Gerver says we should never stop changing and I believe this too. Even though we are reluctant to see changes being made to our education system, change can be a positive thing when led from the ground up. Of course, we need structures, systems and policies, but not when political decisions start to interfere with the daily work we are doing in our classrooms. We need to strip back the political hogwash and keep teaching straightforward. Teachers should simply be marking, planning and teaching. They should not be concerned with data collection, performance management and (potential) capability just because their last two observations were deemed to be 'less than satisfactory'.

If we do not simplify what teachers need to do and give them the time and the funding they need to do their jobs well, then it will be forever Groundhog Day; issues of teacher retention and recruitment will remain unresolved. We must invest in our public services. We must also change the viewpoint that it is acceptable for teachers to be working in excess of 60 hours per week just to stay on top of their workload. I don't know about you, but I could not have worked any harder during my time as a teacher, and I suspect I am not alone.

We need to strip back this perception that our teachers and our schools can never be good enough and reverse it. The binary methodology used to evaluate the overall effectiveness of schools – particularly when challenging schools are judged on the same criteria as schools in the most affluent areas of the country – must change. An investigation by *Tes* found that no schools in England had their inspection judgements overturned from 2014 to 2017. That's ZERO (Santry, 2017). *Tes* quotes a response to this from Geoff Barton, General Secretary of the Association of Schools, Colleges and Leaders:

> "'This exposes an ongoing problem with the complaints process. Too many [school leaders] still worry about the inconsistency of inspections and the laborious complexity of the complaints procedure.'"

Having been part of this process almost ten times over, I know that you can complain about the process but not the overall judgement. It's kind of like arguing with a parking attendant when issued with a parking fine. You must ignore the fact that you've been given a ticket and a penalty, and accept that you can only complain about the methodology behind how the ticket was applied. 'Dear Parking Officer, I do not like how you've stuck the sticker on my car window.' Or even better, 'Dear Parking Officer, I know I have parked illegally, but I was not here when you issued the ticket. How do you expect me to explain myself to you when you have made a decision without me even being here?' This is very similar to inspectors having conversations with students without the presence of a teacher. It's not a matter of trust or fear of what is being said; it's a matter of triangulation and consultation.

The same can also be said for many schools that are still assessing individual teachers and their lessons. Imagine a teacher complaining about how they were observed, but not being allowed to comment on the subjective view of an observer. This is an issue that is prevalent in thousands of schools – the appraiser's decision is final, even if they are wrong!

This leaves me with a tarnished view of the schools I have loved working in. Why would any teacher choose to work in a challenging school if it puts their career and personal goals at risk? It makes you feel that no matter how hard you try to better the life chances of the most vulnerable in society, it's never good enough because your successes are still measured by a one-size-fits-all approach. Worse, some teachers are left utterly demoralised by goalposts that are constantly shifting despite school standards improving.

One day, we will all look back and laugh at the current school inspection process in this country and find it unbelievable that it was part and parcel of our education system. It needs rapid reform – and I know it has just had a major reform! I have given my heart and soul to this book and I have tried to distil much of what I have learnt in the schools I have taught in over my career, as well as in the large number of publications I have read. But I ask you, is the book cover an accurate picture of the content? Does the content you have read really give you a comprehensive overview of my lifetime in education? Probably not. I also suspect it may have taken you longer than two days to read this book in its entirety. So, why do we think it is acceptable for school inspectors to assess the quality of education in our schools in less than two days? How do we know that school inspectors are correct in their decisions? There is too much left open to interpretation and this has the potential to damage schools, teachers and our communities. Making valid decisions in school inspections is nigh on impossible. I know I couldn't do it, which is why I refuse to, as would most (if not all) teachers, I suspect…

Professor Robert Coe of Durham University says there is evidence to prove that classroom observation is harder than you think. He shares some startling statistics about the effectiveness and reliability of observers, which further supports the notion that how teachers have been trained to observe one another and make judgements about the quality of teaching is neither reliable nor valid:

> 'A number of research studies have looked at the reliability of classroom observation ratings. For example, the recent Measures of Effective Teaching Project [… suggests] the probability that a second observer would give a different judgement is between 51% and 78%.'

Even more alarmingly, Coe finds evidence that 'if your lesson is judged "Inadequate", there is a 90% chance that a second observer would give a different rating' (Coe, 2014). Sections of our education system, approximately 30%, still choose to ignore what research says and plough on regardless, damaging good teachers and ending careers early. This practice makes it difficult for us to enjoy working within the profession. In my doctoral research at Cambridge University, I'm investigating whether the Grim Reaper grading schools is reliable and whether inspections actually improve standards or make things worse. If the research is clear about one-off lesson observations, we must have a stronger case for school inspections. Can we reliably evaluate complex institutions in 1.5 days?

The statistics speak for themselves. An annual school workforce report by the DfE releases data based on staff working in publicly funded schools in England. The report finds only 74% of those who started teaching in England in 2013 are still in a teaching position three years later. That means over 25% have left even before they've had a chance to master the basics! (DfE, 2017). Interestingly, there was a large spike in teacher applications after the COVID-19 lockdown in spring 2020.

A call to arms

Those who have read this far might be surprised to find out that I too have struggled with teaching as a career, several times. As I write, I am coming to the end of my 27th academic year working in education, having started teacher training at the age of 18 and formally qualifying at 23. It's been great, but I've certainly had my moments.

I accept that every profession has its challenges and that there will always be natural wastage, but it should not be the norm that young teachers enter the profession, work like headless chickens and burn out, only to be replaced by the next bunch of recruits every two or three years. Something isn't right about the system if this is considered acceptable. As educators, we all have a responsibility to use our experiences to help change this landscape and eradicate myths so that teachers do not keep getting forced out of the profession.

However, I have reason to be optimistic. Thankfully, there are still thousands of people who do choose a career in education. They aspire to work with children and want to make a difference to each and every one of them. Classrooms are a fascinating place to work. They are detailed, delicate and delightful, full of character, emotion and sound. Teachers learn to love their students – every single one, even the most challenging. Teachers are able to put their 'empathy hats' on, viewing misdemeanours as learning opportunities and understanding that there is no such thing as a bad person, only an affected person. They know there will be challenges. There will be times when the toughest students make teaching impossible. But this doesn't last forever. Children are more than just a number or an exam result. They are our next generation, our next Prime Ministers, our future.

We will all be able to remember a great teacher – someone who has inspired us and helped shape us into the person that we are today. Because of great teachers, children in England are now receiving the best education this country has ever had to offer. Throughout this book, I have shared the work of some of the great teachers and some of the most brilliant teaching I have witnessed within our fantastic state school system. And thanks to social media and the growth of the Internet, all teachers have the opportunity to share best practice and dispel myths created by policymakers, conference attendees and the inspectorate. Collectively, we can challenge government policy and white papers written by politicians who have not stepped foot in a classroom since they were children. We have a voice and we can shape the education landscape. It is our landscape after all, and in the midst of a battering from the media and a deluge of political claptrap, we must take control of our own destiny. Teachers can make change happen. We just need to believe it and organise ourselves effectively, so let's get started right here, right now.

The first thing we must look at is how we define ourselves in the workplace. We all need to be resilient, but that is *not* the single solution for survival in our classrooms. If we do not fix our work-life balance, we will struggle to recruit and retain teachers. Isn't it about time teachers left the school building at 4:30pm? Isn't it about time we had our Sundays back, free from marking and lesson planning? Isn't it about time we could turn our digital devices off so we aren't tied to our emails 24/7?

We don't have to work this way. Nothing is *that* urgent, surely? And no one can drive teaching and learning stuck behind their desk all day. If I had a bucket list of ways to improve teachers' work-life balance, it would include the following. Admittedly, some will never happen, but it's healthy to dream...

- All teachers to have more allocated time to mark and plan lessons during the school day.

- A one-week sabbatical to be offered, accruing for each year of service.

- Any future Secretary of State for Education to be an ex-classroom practitioner. (Imagine that...policies with a degree of understanding!)

- School inspections to be less high stakes and the Grim Reaper's measurement scale to reduce from 'Outstanding', 'Good', 'Requires Improvement' and 'Special Measures' to simply 'Good' and 'Not Yet Good'; better still, government inspections to be disbanded and to move towards a school-to-school process.

What would be on your bucket list?

Staff wellbeing matters. It is not a peripheral issue; it should be a moral imperative for all senior leadership teams and their governing bodies, and this *is* now gradually reaching the radars of those who impart their advice to schools. Although this is welcome news, the day wellbeing becomes a measurable factor in our schools (and that day will come) marks the day that wellbeing starts to have the exact opposite effect to the one intended. There will be sticky-plaster solutions designed to create the illusion that schools are placing wellbeing at the top of their agenda, but 'Cake Fridays' and 'The Annual Staff Quiz' will simply be papering over the cracks. Imagine a swan calmly gliding across the surface of the lake but with feet paddling at an unbelievable rate beneath the surface. That's sticky-plaster wellbeing. It doesn't cut to the heart of the issue; it simply masks the problem.

For me, the solution is obvious. The crux of the matter is that every teacher must be able to mark, plan and teach with simplicity and passion. We must give our teachers the space to be able to do these things well and be in front of their students but also to reflect and to meet regularly with colleagues to discuss their students, their lessons and their classroom ideas. That's it. Let's not overcomplicate classroom life with shifting goalposts, fads and preferences dictated by external watchdogs and policymakers. Teaching and learning trumps everything we do in schools and the sooner our politicians, experts and school leaders remember this, the better for our students, our teachers and our profession as a whole.

Let's strip back the nonsense, get back to work and focus on what every teacher across the world needs to do: ***Mark. Plan. Teach.***

Bibliography

Agarwal, P. and Bain, P. (2019), *Powerful Teaching*. San Francisco: Jossey Bass.

Allen, R., Benhenda, A., Jerrim, J. and Sims, S. (2020), 'New evidence on teachers' working hours in England: an empirical analysis of four datasets', *Research Papers in Education*.

Allison, S. and Tharby, A. (2015), *Making Every Lesson Count: Six Principles to Support Great Teaching and Learning*. Carmarthen: Crown House Publishing.

American Psychological Association, Coalition for Psychology in Schools and Education (2015), 'Top 20 principles from psychology for preK–12 teaching and learning', available at: www.apa.org/ed/schools/teaching-learning/top-twenty-principles.pdf

Baars, S., Parameshwaran, M., Menzies, L. and Chiong, C. (2016), 'Firing on all cylinders: What makes an effective middle leader?', available at: https://s3.eu-west-2.amazonaws.com/ambition-institute/documents/Firing-on-all-cylinders-What-makes-an-effective-leader_FinFAuz.pdf

Bambrick-Santoyo, P. (2012), *Leverage Leadership: A Practical Guide to Building Exceptional Schools*. San Francisco: Jossey Bass.

Barton, G. (2013), 'What makes a good teacher?', *Tes*, available at: https://www.tes.com/news/tes-archive/tes-publication/what-makes-a-good-teacher-0

Black, P. and Wiliam, D. (2001), 'Inside the black box: raising standards through classroom assessment', available at: https://weaeducation.typepad.co.uk/files/blackbox-1.pdf

Blatchford, R. (2015), 'Thoughts on lesson observations #1: the surgeon and the scalpel', *National Education Trust Blog*, available at: https://nationaleducationtrustblog.wordpress.com/2015/04/19/thoughts-on-lesson-observations-1-the-surgeon-and-the-scalpel/

Bridges, S. (2014), 'Mental health problems', in Health Survey for England 2014. Leeds: Health and Social Care Information Centre, available at: http://healthsurvey.hscic.gov.uk/media/37739/HSE2014-Ch2-Mental-health-problems.pdf

Briner, R. and Dewberry, C. (2007), *Staff Wellbeing is Key to School Success: A Research Study into the Links between Staff Wellbeing and School Performance*. London: Worklife Support.

Brown, P. C., Roediger III, H. L. and McDaniel, M. A. (2014), *Make It Stick: The Science of Successful Learning*. Massachusetts: Harvard University Press.

Butler, D. L. and Winne, P. H. (1995), 'Feedback and self-regulated learning: a theoretical synthesis', *Review of Educational Research*, 65, (3), 245-281.

Carroll, A., Houghton, S., Durkin, K. and Hattie, J. A. (2009), 'Reputation-enhancing goals: the theory of deliberate choice', in: *Adolescent Reputations and Risk*. New York: Springer.

Burgoyne, A. P., Hambrick, D. Z. and Macnamara, B. N. (2020), 'How firm are the foundations of mind-set theory? The claims appear stronger than the evidence', *Psychological Science*, 31, (3), 258-267.

Chiles, M. (2018), *The Craft of Assessment*. Woodbridge: John Catt Educational Ltd.

Coe, R. (2014), 'Classroom observation: it's harder than you think', *CEM Blog*, available at: http://www.cem.org/blog/414/

Coe, R., Aloisi, C., Higgins, S. and Major, L. E. (2014), 'What makes great teaching? Review of the underpinning research', The Sutton Trust, available at: www.suttontrust.com/wp-content/uploads/2014/10/What-Makes-Great-Teaching-REPORT.pdf

Coe, R., Rauch, C. J., Kime, S. and Singleton, D. (2020), 'Great Teaching Toolkit: Evidence review', available at: www.greatteaching.com/

Crehan, L. (2016), *Cleverlands: The Secrets Behind the Success of the World's Education Superpowers*. London: Unbound.

Csikszentmihalyi, M. (2002), *Flow: The Classic Work on How to Achieve Happiness* (revised edn). Rider: London.

Danielson, C. (2011), *Enhancing Professional Practice: A Framework for Teaching* (2nd edn). Alexandria: Association for Supervision and Curriculum Development.

Department for Education (2011), 'Teachers' Standards', available at: https://www.gov.uk/government/publications/teachers-standards

Department for Education (2014), 'SEND code of practice', available at: www.gov.uk/government/publications/send-code-of-practice-0-to-25

Department for Education (2016), 'Eliminating unnecessary workload around marking', available at: www.gov.uk/government/uploads/system/uploads/attachment_data/file/511256/Eliminating-unnecessary-workload-around-marking.pdf

Department for Education (2017), 'School workforce in England: November 2016', available at: www.gov.uk/government/statistics/school-workforce-in-england-november-2016

Department for Education (2018), 'Making data work: teacher workload advisory group report', available at: www.gov.uk/government/publications/teacher-workload-advisory-group-report-and-government-response

Department for Education (2019a), 'Inspecting education quality: lesson observation and workbook scrutiny', available at: www.gov.uk/government/publications/inspecting-education-quality-lesson-observation-and-workbook-scrutiny

Department for Education (2019b), 'Teacher workload survey 2019', available at: www.gov.uk/government/publications/teacher-workload-survey-2019

Department for Education (2020a), 'Statutory policies for schools and academy trusts', available at: www.gov.uk/government/publications/statutory-policies-for-schools-and-academy-trusts

Department for Education (2020b), 'Statistics: school workforce', available at: www.gov.uk/government/collections/statistics-school-workforce

Dunlosky, J., Rawson, K. A., Marsh, E. J., Nathan, M. J. and Willingham, D. T. (2013), 'Improving students' learning with effective learning techniques: promising directions from cognitive and educational psychology', *Psychological Science in the Public Interest*, 14, (1), 4-58.

Dweck, C. (2010), 'Even geniuses work hard', *Educational Leadership*, 68, 16-20.

Dweck, C. (2014), 'The power of believing that you can improve', *TED*, available at: www.ted.com/talks/carol_dweck_the_power_of_believing_that_you_can_improve/transcript?language=en

Ebbinghaus, H. (1885), *Memory: A Contribution to Experimental Psychology*. New York: Teachers College, Columbia University.

Education Endowment Foundation (2017a), 'Research schools', available at: https://educationendowmentfoundation.org.uk/our-work/research-schools/

Education Endowment Foundation (2017b), 'Spaced learning: the design, feasibility and optimisation of SMART spaces', available at: https://educationendowmentfoundation.org.uk/public/files/Projects/Evaluation_Reports/EEF_Project_Report_SpacedLearning.pdf

Education Endowment Foundation (2017c), 'Feedback', in 'Teaching & Learning Toolkit', available at: https://educationendowmentfoundation.org.uk/resources/teaching-learning-toolkit/feedback/

Education Endowment Foundation (2017d), 'Reading comprehension strategies', in 'Teaching & Learning Toolkit', available at: https://educationendowmentfoundation.org.uk/resources/teaching-learning-toolkit/reading-comprehension-strategies/

Education Endowment Foundation (2017e), 'Collaborative learning', in 'Teaching & Learning Toolkit', available at: https://educationendowmentfoundation.org.uk/resources/teaching-learning-toolkit/collaborative-learning/

BIBLIOGRAPHY

Education Support Partnership (2019), 'Teacher wellbeing index 2019', available at: www.educationsupport.org.uk/sites/default/files/teacher_wellbeing_index_2019.pdf

Elliott, V., Baird, J.-A., Hopfenbeck, T. N., Ingram, J., Thompson, I., Usher, N., Zantout, M., Richardson, J. and Coleman, R. (2016), 'A marked improvement? A review of the evidence on written marking'. London: Education Endowment Foundation, available at: https://educationendowmentfoundation.org.uk/public/files/Publications/EEF_Marking_Review_April_2016.pdf

Enright, J. (2013), 'How do you plan your lessons? #DKL, #script or #5minplan', available at: http://think-forty-two.blogspot.co.uk/2013/03/how-do-you-plan-your-lessons-dkl-script.html

Fearnley, P. Contact: pamb566@btinternet.com.

Flavell, J. H. (1979), 'Metacognition and cognitive monitoring', *American Psychologist*, 34, 906-911.

Gerver, R. (2013), *Change: Learn to Love It, Learn to Lead It*. London: Penguin.

Gibbons, A. (2020), 'School funding is down since 2010, DfE finally admits', *Tes*, available at: www.tes.com/news/school-funding-down-2010-dfe-finally-admits

Godin, S. (2012), 'Avoiding the false proxy trap', available at: http://sethgodin.typepad.com/seths_blog/2012/11/avoiding-the-false-proxy-trap.html

Hattie, J. (2009), *Visible Learning: A Synthesis of Over 800 Meta-Analyses Relating to Achievement*. Abingdon; New York: Routledge.

Hattie, J. (2012), *Visible Learning for Teachers: Maximizing Impact on Learning*. Abingdon; New York: Routledge.

Hattie, J. (2015), 'The applicability of visible learning to higher education', *Scholarship of Teaching and Learning in Psychology*, 1, 79-91.

Headteachers' Roundtable (2017), https://headteachersroundtable.wordpress.com

Hattie, J. and Timperley, H. (2007), 'The power of feedback', *Review of Educational Research*, 77, (1), 81-112.

Hogan, S. L. (2019), 'Social filters shaping student responses to teacher feedback in the secondary drama classroom', *NJ*, 43, (1), 4-19.

Holmes, E. (2005), *Teacher Well-being*. Abingdon; New York: Routledge.

Ibarra-Sáiz, M. S., Rodríguez-Gómez, G. and Boud, D. (2020), 'Developing student competence through peer assessment: the role of feedback, self-regulation and evaluative judgement', *Higher Education*, 80, 137-156.

Karpicke, J. (2016), 'A powerful way to improve learning and memory', *Psychological Science Agenda*, 30, (6).

Karpicke, J. and Bauernschmidt, A. (2011), 'Spaced retrieval: absolute spacing enhances learning regardless of relative spacing', *Journal of Experimental Psychology*, 37, (5), 1250-1257.

Kidd, D. (2014), *Teaching: Notes from the Front Line*. Carmarthen: Independent Thinking Press.

Kimbell, R. and Stables, K. (2008), *Researching Design Learning: Issues and Findings from Two Decades of Research and Development*. Dordrecht: Springer.

Kirby, P. and Mclaughlin, C. (2016), 'Teacher agency: an ecological approach', *British Journal of Educational Studies*, 64, (4), 557-559.

Kirschner, P. and Hendrick, C. (2020), *How Learning Happens*. Abingdon: Routledge.

Ko, J., Sammons, P. and Bakkum, L. (2014), 'Effective teaching'. Reading: Education Development Trust.

Kuh, G. D. (2008), *High Impact Educational Practices: What They Are, Who Has Access to Them and Why They Matter*. Washington: American Association for Colleges & Universities.

Lemov, D. (2015), *Teach Like a Champion 2.0: 62 Techniques That Put Students on the Path to College*. San Francisco: Jossey Bass.

Major, L. E. (2019), 'Podcast 59: Does misdirected effort increase teacher workload?', available at: www.teachertoolkit.co.uk/2019/10/06/podcast-59/

Major, L. E. and Higgins, S. (2019), *What Works?* London: Bloomsbury.

Makedon, A. (1990), 'Is teaching a science or an art?' Paper presented at the Annual Conference of the Midwest Philosophy of Education Society (Chicago, IL, 10th November 1990), available at: http://files.eric.ed.gov/fulltext/ED330683.pdf

Marsh, N. (2010), 'How to make work-life balance work', *TED*, available at: www.ted.com/talks/nigel_marsh_how_to_make_work_life_balance_work

Mccrea, P. (2015), *Lean Lesson Planning: A Practical Approach to Doing Less and Achieving More in the Classroom*. CreateSpace Independent Publishing Platform.

McGill, R. M. (2015), *Teacher Toolkit: Helping You Survive Your First Five Years*. London: Bloomsbury.

McGill, R. M. (2019), *Just Great Teaching*. London: Bloomsbury.

McGill, R. M. and Quinn, M. (2019), 'Verbal feedback report', available at: www.ucl.ac.uk/widening-participation/teachers-and-education-professionals/teacher-research-projects/verbal-feedback-project

McHugh, M. L. (2012), 'Interrater reliability: the kappa statistic', *Biochemia Medica*, 22, (3), 276-282.

Millar, F. (2018), *The Best for My Child*. Woodbridge: John Catt Educational Ltd.

Murphy, R. J. L. (1978), 'Reliability of marking in eight GCE examinations', *British Journal of Educational Psychology*, 48, 196-200.

National Literacy Trust (2019), 'Stories in schools: reading engagement report', available at: https://literacytrust.org.uk/research-services/research-reports/stories-schools-reading-engagement-report/

Nicol, D. J. and Macfarlane-Dick, D. (2006), 'Formative assessment and self-regulated learning: a model and seven principles of good feedback practice', *Studies in Higher Education*, 31, 199-218.

Norman, D. (1978), 'Notes towards a theory of complex learning' in A. Lesgold, J. Pellegrino and S. Fokkena (eds), *Cognitive Psychology and Instruction*. New York: Plenum.

O'Brien, T. (2001) *Enabling Inclusion: Blue Skies...Dark Clouds?* London: The Stationery Office.

O'Brien, T. (2015), *Inner Story: Understand Your Mind, Change Your World*. UK: Ideational.

OECD (2014), 'Innovation, governance and reform in education'. Paper presented at the CERI conference (Paris, 3rd November 2014), available at: www.oecd.org/edu/ceri/CERI%20Conference%20Background%20Paper_formatted.pdf

Pausch, R. (2008), *The Last Lecture*. New York: Hyperion Books.

Pierson, R. (2013), 'Every kid needs a champion', *TED*, available at: https://www.ted.com/talks/rita_pierson_every_kid_needs_a_champion

Price, D. (2013), *Open: How We'll Work, Live and Learn in the Future*. UK: Crux Publishing Ltd.

Quigley, A. (2016), *The Confident Teacher: Developing Successful Habits of Mind, Body and Pedagogy*. Abingdon; New York: Routledge.

Roberts, H. (2012), *Oops! Helping Children Learn Accidentally*. Carmarthen: Independent Thinking Press.

Robinson, K. (2013), 'To encourage creativity, Mr Gove, you must first understand what it is', *The Guardian*, available at: www.theguardian.com/commentisfree/2013/may/17/to-encourage-creativity-mr-gove-understand

Roediger, H. L. (1980), 'Memory metaphors in cognitive psychology', *Memory and Cognition*, 8, (3), 231-246.

Rosenshine, B. (2012), 'Principles of instruction: research-based strategies that all teachers should know', *American Educator*, 36, 12-19.

Salles, D. (2016), *The Slightly Awesome Teacher: Using Edu-Research to Get Brilliant Results*. Woodbridge: John Catt Educational Ltd.

Santry, C. (2017), 'Exclusive: the virtually impossible task of overturning an Ofsted verdict', *Tes*, available at: www.tes.com/news/school-news/breaking-news/exclusive-virtually-impossible-task-overturning-ofsted-verdict

Schleicher, A. (2018), 'TALIS 2018: Insights and interpretations', available at: www.oecd.org/education/talis/TALIS2018_insights_and_interpretations.pdf

BIBLIOGRAPHY

Schön, D. (1983), *The Reflective Practitioner: How Professionals Think in Action*. New York: Basic Books.

Sellen, P. (2016), 'Teacher workload and professional development in England's secondary schools: insights from TALIS'. London: Education Policy Institute, available at: http://epi.org.uk/wp-content/uploads/2016/10/TeacherWorkload_EPI.pdf

Sharples, J., Webster, R. and Blatchford, P. (2015), 'Making best use of teaching assistants', London: Education Endowment Foundation, available at: https://educationendowmentfoundation.org.uk/public/files/Publications/Campaigns/TA_Guidance_Report_MakingBestUseOfTeachingAssisstants-Printable.pdf

Sherrington, T. (2017), 'The bell-curve cage: something must break', *Teacherhead*, available at: https://teacherhead.com/2017/03/26/the-bell-curve-cage-something-must-break/

Sims, S. and Fletcher-Wood, H. (2016), 'Characteristics of effective teacher professional development: what we know, what we don't, how we can find out', available at: https://improvingteaching.co.uk/characteristics-cpd/

Smith, J. (2010), *The Lazy Teacher's Handbook: How Your Students Learn More When You Teach Less*, (1st edn). Carmarthen: Crown House Publishing.

Social Mobility Commission (2017), 'Time for change: an assessment of government policies on social mobility 1997-2017', available at: www.gov.uk/government/uploads/system/uploads/attachment_data/file/622214/Time_for_Change_report_-_An_assessement_of_government_policies_on_social_mobility_1997-2017.pdf

Taylor, T. (2019), *Connect the Dots*. Woodbridge: John Catt Educational Ltd.

Thaler, R. H. and Sunstein, C. R. (2009), *Nudge: Improving Decisions About Health, Wealth and Happiness* (2nd edn). London: Penguin Books Ltd.

Theeboom, T., Beersma, B. and Van Vianen, A. E. (2014), 'Does coaching work? A meta-analysis on the effects of coaching on individual level outcomes in an organisational context', *Journal of Positive Psychology*, 9, 1-18.

Tibke, J. (2019), *Why the Brain Matters*. London: Sage.

Turner, E. (2019), *Be More Toddler*. Woodbridge: John Catt Educational Ltd.

Weinstein, Y. and Smith, M. (2016), 'Learn how to study using… spaced practice', *The Learning Scientists*, available at: www.learningscientists.org/blog/2016/7/21-1

Weston, D. (2015), 'Unleashing Greatness in Teachers', *TEDx*, available at: www.youtube.com/watch?v=Ebh7PkuWUe8

Wisniewski, B., Zierer, K. and Hattie, J. (2020), 'The power of feedback revisited: A meta-analysis of educational feedback research', *Frontiers in Psychology*, 10, 3087.

Wiliam, D. (2011), *Embedded Formative Assessment*. Bloomington: Solution Tree Press.

Willingham, D. T. (2010), *Why Don't Students Like School?: A Cognitive Scientist Answers Questions About How the Mind Works and What it Means for the Classroom* (1st edn). San Francisco: Jossey Bass.

Wilshaw, M. (2012), 'What is a good teacher?', available at: www.youtube.com/watch?v=is31rrXubQ0&feature=youtu.be&t=58s

YoungMinds (2019), 'Impact report 2018-2019', available at: https://youngminds.org.uk/media/3236/impact-report-2018-19-low-res-final.pdf

Yue, C. L. (2017), 'Improving learner metacognition and self-regulation', in: R. Obeid, A. M. Schwartz, C. Shane-Simpson and P. J. Brooks (eds.), *How We Teach Now*. Society for the Teaching of Psychology, pp. 95-103.

Zeng, Y. and Day, C. (2019), 'Collaborative teacher professional development in schools in England (UK) and Shanghai (China): Cultures, contexts and tensions', *Teachers and Teaching*, 25, (3), 379-397.

Index